The
Science Fiction and Fantasy Readers' Advisory
THE LIBRARIAN'S GUIDE
To
CYBORGS, ALIENS, AND SORCERERS

ALA READERS' ADVISORY SERIES

The Mystery Readers' Advisory:
The Librarian's Clues to Murder and Mayhem

The Readers' Advisory Guide to Genre Fiction

The Romance Readers' Advisory:
The Librarian's Guide to Love in the Stacks

The Short Story Readers' Advisory:
A Guide to the Best

The Science Fiction and Fantasy Readers' Advisory

THE LIBRARIAN'S GUIDE TO CYBORGS, ALIENS, AND SORCERERS

DEREK M. BUKER

AMERICAN LIBRARY ASSOCIATION
Chicago
2002

The paper used in this publication meets the minimum requirements of American National Standard for Information Sciences—Permanence of Paper for Printed Library Materials, ANSI Z39.48-1992. ∞

Cover design by Angela Gwizdala

Composition by ALA Editions in ITC Clearface and Sabon using QuarkXPress 4.1 on a PC platform

Printed on 50-pound white offset, a pH-neutral stock, and bound in 10-point coated cover stock by Victor Graphics

Library of Congress Cataloging-in-Publication Data

Buker, Derek M.
  Science fiction and fantasy readers' advisory : the librarian's guide to cyborgs, aliens, and sorcerers / by Derek M. Buker.
      p. cm. — (ALA readers' advisory series)
  Includes bibliographical references and index.
  ISBN 0-8389-0831-4 (alk. paper)
      1. Libraries—United States—Special collections—Science fiction.
  2. Libraries—United States—Special collections—Fantasy fiction.
  3. Readers' advisory services—United States. 4. Fiction in libraries—United States. 5. Science fiction—Bibliography. 6. Fantasy fiction—Bibliography. I. Title. II. Series.
  Z688.S32 B85 2002
  026--dc21   2002001494

Printed in the United States of America.

05 04 03 02 01   5 4 3 2 1

CONTENTS

ACKNOWLEDGMENTS   *ix*

PROLOGUE: Science Affliction   *xi*

Book I
SCIENCE FICTION

1 Classic and General Science Fiction   3
    Classic Science Fiction   8
    General Science Fiction   14

2 The Aliens Are Coming! The Aliens Are Coming!   17
    First-Contact Novels   18
    Alien Invasion!   21

3 Celestial Bodies   25
    Mars   26
    The Moon   28
    Other Celestial Bodies   30

4 Androids and Robots and Cyborgs . . . Oh My!   32

5 Attack of the Killer Computers!   36

6 Cyberpunk—Are You Looking at Me?
   Science Fiction with an Attitude   40

7 Virtual Reality   43

8 It's the End of the World: Holocaust Fiction   *46*

9 Alternate History   *49*

10 Time Travel   *52*
    Science-Fiction Time Travel   *53*
    Fantasy Time Travel   *56*

11 Superheroes, Graphic Novels, and Genetic Engineering   *58*
    Superheroes   *58*
    Graphic Novels   *61*
    Genetic Engineering   *63*

12 Thrills and Chills in Zero Gravity: Science-Fiction
Mysteries and Thrillers   *68*
    Mysteries   *68*
    Thrillers   *71*
    Biotech Thrillers   *74*

13 Science-Fiction Humor   *77*

14 Science-Fiction and Fantasy Blenders   *81*

15 Telepathic Mutants and Other Weirdos   *85*

16 Science-Fiction Romance and Religion   *88*
    Romance   *88*
    Religion   *90*

17 Space Operas   *93*
    Star Wars   *96*
    Star Trek   *100*

Book II
FANTASY

18 Fantastic Fantasy   *111*
    Classic Fantasy   *111*
    General Fantasy   *115*

19   The Long and Longer of It: Epic Fantasy   *118*

20   Questing, Questing, Questing   *123*
         Quest Fantasy   *123*
         Dungeons and Dragons   *127*

21   Fairy Tales: Not Just for Kids   *129*

22   Larger than Life   *134*
         Legends and Myths   *134*
         Arthurian Legend   *137*

23   Historical Fantasy   *141*

24   The Dark Side of Fantasy   *145*

25   Ever Since I Died, I Can't Sleep at Night: Vampires,
         Werewolves, Ghosts, and Other Undead   *149*
         Vampires   *149*
         Werewolves   *152*
         Ghosts and Other Undead   *155*

26   Demons Loose in the City: Urban Fantasy   *158*

27   Crossing Over to the Other Side   *162*

28   Sword and Sorcery   *167*

29   The Magic of Music   *171*

30   Talking Cats, Dragons, Elves, and Other
         Mythological Beasties   *175*
         Cats and Other Beasts   *176*
         Heroes: The Breakfast of Champion Dragons   *178*
         Are You Calling Me a Fairy? I'm an Elf!   *182*

31   Humorous Fantasy   *186*

32   You Can't Keep an Elven Sherlock Holmes Down:
         Fantasy Mysteries   *190*

33 Fantasy Romance   *194*

APPENDIX

   Hugo Award Winners   *199*

   Nebula Award Winners   *201*

   Mythopoeic Award Winners   *202*

   World Fantasy Award Winners   *203*

INDEX   *205*

ACKNOWLEDGMENTS

No book can be written without the help and support of many people. First and foremost, thanks to my wife Kris for editing the first drafts, for reminding me to eat regularly, and for the patience and support she has given me for the past eighteen months. To my daughter Sharon, for providing me with the inspiration to write this book and always having a smile for her daddy when he was feeling the most tired and discouraged. To Michael Gannon for passing the buck. To the entire staff of the Charles E. Miller Branch, for putting up with my constant conversations about "the Book" and for keeping me focused on the task at hand; your indulgence for the past year and a half is greatly appreciated. To Steve Wilson for teaching a young writer perseverance and patience. To Ryan Casey for the many discussions of the nature of science fiction. To Blizzard Entertainment, a complaint for making such addicting games as Starcraft, Warcraft, and Diablo 2, but without those games I might have lost my sanity. To the folks at The Calling for putting up with my insanity. To Alan for the endless discussions on the craft of writing and for saying that I'm more than a middle-shelf writer. And finally to my mother for instilling a love of reading in her sons, to my father for buying all those science-fiction and fantasy novels—I bet you thought I would never do anything with them—and to my brothers for sharing their books with their younger brother.

This book is dedicated in loving memory of my mother, Sharon Buker—I wish you had been able to read this book—and to my family for all their love and support.

PROLOGUE

Science Affliction

It always happens like this. You are by yourself on the information desk when a customer approaches and asks the dreaded question: "Can you recommend a good science-fiction book?" Instantly, you feel your face go white even as an anguished scream echoes through your mind. Desperately, you look for an avenue of escape. Perhaps you can hide until your geeky science-fiction-reading coworker comes back from break! Or maybe the customer will go away on his or her own! But neither of these things happens, so you gulp and turn to the computer in order to forestall answering while your mind searches frantically for a clue. Then it hits you! A classic! A classic *has* to be good! Almost delirious with relief, you ask the customer: "Have you read Asimov?"

The preceding is an example of what I call Science Affliction, which is the unfounded fear of science-fiction and fantasy readers' advisory questions. For those of you new to the profession, readers' advisory is exactly what occurred here—a customer asks a librarian to recommend a good book. Even if you do not read in the genres of science fiction and fantasy, you can, by utilizing this book and the reference interview, answer these questions with confidence.

SEND OUT A PROBE, MR. CHEKOV

A large percentage of genre-related readers' advisory queries can be answered with a properly executed reference interview. It is not enough to simply rephrase the customer's request. I say "customer" rather than "patron" because that is the relationship that librarians now have with the public. The library is providing a service to its customers utilizing resources paid for by the community. I will now impart one of the most powerful questions you can use in the reference interview to arrive at the right book for your customer. Are you ready? Repeat after me: "What was the last book you read that you really liked?" You can follow up that question with others, such as: "Did you like [title] because of the writing? The setting? The characters? Do you want a female or male lead character?" With proper probing you can use this book to find an appropriate match for what your customer is interested in reading. Failure to probe could lead to recommending the wrong book and not answering the customer's question. Also, it is important that you listen to what the customer says in response to your questions. I was once on the desk when a customer asked my coworker if she could suggest a good science-fiction book. She asked the all-important question: "What is the last book you read that you really liked?" Good so far. But then she didn't ask anything further after the customer responded "*Mars* by Ben Bova." Immediately my coworker was off to the races and began looking up Mars fiction in the catalog. She made a good suggestion (despite the fact that she wasn't really sure what the customer wanted) with Kim Stanley Robinson's *Red Mars*. But the customer wasn't necessarily interested in fiction about Mars (although he did like *Red Mars*); rather, he liked the way that Bova wrote about technology. I suggested he read some other books by Bova and he was happy with those.

SERIAL READERS

This brings me to another point—science fiction/fantasy readers like to read more books by the same author. I can't emphasize this enough. Sometimes it is so hard to find an author you like that there is a certain level of comfort in knowing there are other titles by the same author. Sometimes it is appropriate to offer another book by the same author, but it is more important to find out if that is, indeed, what the customer is looking for.

BRIDGING THE GAP

On a related topic, occasionally a customer will ask: "I've read everything by so-and-so—what can you suggest?" In this situation it is essential to ask not only "What is the last book you read by so-and-so that you really liked?" but also "What is it about the book that you liked?" In the case of the aforementioned Bova customer, if he had said that he liked reading about Mars (the planet—not the Roman god of war), then the suggestion of *Red Mars* by Kim Stanley Robinson would have been very appropriate; after all, *Red Mars* won the 1993 Nebula Award presented by the Science Fiction and Fantasy Writers of America. I call this *bridging the gap* because it involves finding out what your customer prefers in reading and then making an appropriate choice. Often the customer will read all the books by one author until that option is exhausted, and will then return for another selection, starting the process again. That is where this book comes in handy as it not only covers the two main genres of science fiction and fantasy, but the subgenres as well. For each subgenre, a number of book synopses enable you to assist your customers in finding the right titles for their needs.

Many librarians tend to treat readers' advisory as trivial. It is not. It should be treated as seriously as a law or medical question—except for one vital difference. This is one of the few times you can *give* your opinion! Well, not your complete opinion. Telling a customer that you think science fiction and fantasy are a waste of time wouldn't be the wisest comment and could lead to possible fisticuffs! But you can tell someone whether you personally liked the book (if you have read it) or if it has gotten good reviews. In addition to this book, you can use another important resource for finding good titles for your customers—your coworkers. Most library systems have at least one person on staff who likes to read science fiction or fantasy or both and could recommend a book that he or she liked. This last option is best utilized when the customer doesn't need a book that matches works previously read and enjoyed but just wants a good book.

This brings me back to a topic that I alluded to earlier—the reluctance of librarians to read science fiction or fantasy. Most librarians feel these genres are silly simply because they don't spark their imagination. I've found it is sometimes easier to overcome this reluctance to help customers who read in a different genre by thinking about it from their point of view. Who wouldn't want to stand by Nelson as he sailed into a hail of hot metal against the French and Spanish at Trafalgar? Or track a serial murderer with the help of the Virginia medical examiner? Or find love with a dashing pirate queen or king (depending on your own personal beliefs and interests)? Put in these terms, what somebody else reads isn't an impediment to good service; our own prejudices are. What is most important is that your customer loves books, and it is our job as librarians to help that person find the perfect book.

Another impediment to good customer service is the stereotypical notion that everyone who reads science fiction or fantasy is a geek. Let's do a little exercise. Close your eyes and imagine a skinny guy in a white shirt and black pants. Add a pocket protector to the shirt pocket and make sure to really stock that protector with pens and mechanical pencils! Add to his face eyeglasses that have been broken and repaired with electrical tape and voila! Instant geek! Now imagine a girl standing next to our proto-nerd. Make her kind of short and heavyset with thick, coke-bottle glasses. You can dress her however you want, but you might want to add some acne to her face if you're feeling especially creative today. Do you have the image of our two customers set in your mind? What I want you to do now may seem like a big waste of your time, but stick with me—there is a point to all this. Imagine a huge eraser dropping down and erasing the two stereotypical nerds, because people who look like what I just described to you are no more likely to read science fiction or fantasy than anyone else. What's important to remember when you're helping science-fiction and fantasy customers is that they are *readers,* which are the most important customers a library can have!

WHY NOT A CLASSIC?

At this point you're probably wondering "What if the customer doesn't know what he or she wants other than a science-fiction or fantasy book?" A lot of librarians answer this question by offering a classic or an award winner to the customer. Don't get me wrong—both classics and award winners are universally well written. But they don't always meet the customer's needs, especially if the customer is reluctant to read science fiction or fantasy. Often classics are dated—things that seemed highly improbable in the 1960s may be commonplace in the new millennium. Award winners can be troublesome for those who don't read science fiction or fantasy because such books can be too technical or steeped in a lore that only someone familiar with the genre could understand. So how do you help these customers? Besides using the books recommended for reluctant readers, you can develop your own list of recommended titles. To do this you should be in the habit of reading a science-fiction or fantasy book every year. Not necessarily one of each, but one or the other at the very least. If you like the titles you read, write them in a notebook with a short synopsis. It is better for the synopsis to be in your own words to facilitate "book-talking" the title. And how do you go about developing a list? Talk to those colleagues who do read in the genres, ask them what they would recommend, and be prepared to drop the book if it doesn't work out. It will take time and patience to develop a list of about five to ten recommended titles.

THE READERS' ADVISORY CAR LOT

Developing a list of recommended titles can sometimes lead to offering only one title to customers. Just as a car lot has many models to choose from, readers' advisory has many titles to draw on. I knew a librarian who had read Orson Scott Card's *Ender's Game* and absolutely loved it! He ordinarily did not read science fiction, but felt *Ender's Game* was such an excellent book that he recommended it to every customer who wanted to read science fiction or fantasy. He was selling only one model from a lot that has a wide variety to choose from. This book can help by giving you a great many titles from all the major subgenres. You can use the synopses to acquaint yourself with the leading titles in each subgenre and you can also choose books from the "other recommended titles" lists in each chapter. This will allow you to book-talk the book to your customer. Over time and with exposure to some books from the genres, you will develop a repertoire of titles to book-talk to interested customers.

Book I
Science Fiction

1

Classic and General Science Fiction

If you asked most librarians how much they know about science fiction and fantasy, the responses would range from "as little as possible" to "are you kidding me?" But those same librarians would be surprised to realize they know more than they think. Here's a little quiz to test how much you really know about science fiction and fantasy. You might want to grab a piece of paper and the ubiquitous number-two pencil to compare your answers to those at the end of the chapter.

1. What is Fahrenheit 451?
   (a) The temperature on the surface of the Sun
   (b) The police code for an escaped lunatic
   (c) The temperature at which paper (or a book) burns
   (d) The heat index for a habanero pepper

2. Elves are:
   (a) Tall and extremely beautiful.
   (b) More intelligent and wise than humans.
   (c) Short and jolly.

(d) All of the above depending on the story.

(e) None of the above.

3. What is the name of the little green guy who trains Luke Skywalker in *Star Wars: The Empire Strikes Back*?

(a) Yoda

(b) Worf

(c) Kracken

(d) The Master

4. Who plays Agent Dana Scully on *X-Files*?

(a) Tiffany Amber Thiesen

(b) Vivian Vande Velde

(c) Majel Barrett

(d) Gillian Anderson

5. King Arthur's sword's name is:

(a) Excelsior.

(b) Executor.

(c) Excalibur.

(d) Ernie.

5a. Bonus follow-up question: Is the sword named in question 5 the sword that Arthur pulled from the stone?

(a) Yes

(b) No

(c) I'm riding the fence on this one

6. "Danger! Danger, Will Robinson!" is from:

(a) *Star Wars*.

(b) *Star Trek*.

(c) *Lost in Space*.

(d) *Good Times*.

7. A "hobbit" is:
   (a) One of those new fishing lures.
   (b) Little people who live in the Shire where they tend to get fat in the stomach and do not wear shoes.
   (c) Santa's sidekick.
   (d) None of the above.

8. Superman is faster than:
   (a) A speeding bullet.
   (b) A speeding Yugo.
   (c) A declined credit card.
   (d) A crashing computer.
   (e) All of the above.

9. Who said: "I'm sorry, Dave, I can't do that"?
   (a) Doctor McCoy
   (b) Yoda
   (c) The computer HAL from *2001*
   (d) The guy in the grill section at Wendy's

10. Chewbacca is:
    (a) The short version of the request for "chewin' tobacco."
    (b) A popular dessert that you get from a "wookie jar."
    (c) A Chinese dish.
    (d) Han Solo's sidekick.

11. Harry Potter is a student at:
    (a) Harvard University (where he is studying for an MBA).
    (b) Hogwart's School of Witchcraft and Wizardry (where he is studying to be a wizard).
    (c) The Jedi Academy (where he is studying under Luke Skywalker).
    (d) Lordaeron University (where he is studying warcraft).

12. In the movie *Close Encounters of the Third Kind,* a man built a model of which of the following using mashed potatoes?

    (a) An alien from Roswell

    (b) A spaceship

    (c) A mountain

    (d) A 1967 Corvette

13. The character in H. G. Wells's *Time Machine* encounters which two races in the future?

    (a) Eloi and Morlock

    (b) Eloi and Balrog

    (c) Warlock and Rodian

    (d) Rodian and Balrog

14. Dragons traditionally guard:

    (a) Huge piles of gold and other treasures.

    (b) The gates to hell.

    (c) The White House.

    (d) Sword-wielding barbarians.

15. Who is considered the First Lady of fantasy?

    (a) Nora Roberts

    (b) Danielle Irons

    (c) Mercedes Lackey

    (d) Anne McCaffrey

16. What are the two major science-fiction awards? (No fair peeking at the appendix.)

    (a) The Thurber Prize and the Newbery Medal

    (b) The Hugo and the Nebula

    (c) The Pulitzer Prize and the National Book Award

    (d) The Hugo and the Mythopoeic Fantasy Award

17. Who is generally recognized as the father of science fiction?

    (a) Jules Verne

    (b) Robert A. Heinlein

    (c) Sir Arthur Conan Doyle

    (d) Isaac Asimov

18. Who has won the most Hugo Awards for best novel? (Again, no fair looking in the appendix.)

    (a) Isaac Asimov

    (b) Lois McMaster Bujold

    (c) Robert A. Heinlein

    (d) Arthur C. Clarke

19. Who was the first female writer to win a Hugo or Nebula Award?

    (a) Ursula K. Le Guin

    (b) Mercedes Lackey

    (c) Danielle Irons

    (d) Anne McCaffrey

20. Is *Jurassic Park* science fiction?

    (a) Yes

    (b) No

And . . . pencils down. How do you think you did? Go ahead and check the answers at the end of the chapter—it's all right, I'll wait until you get back. Are you surprised at how well you did? You shouldn't be—science fiction and fantasy have been part of our culture for quite some time. In some cases, for centuries. The last question of the quiz is the curveball. Most people lump *Jurassic Park* with adventure-suspense fiction or thriller fiction. I lump *Jurassic Park* in with science fiction. Science fiction is fiction *based* on science that may or may *not* exist. Robert A. Heinlein said that "science fiction is about *people* responding to a scientific or technological advance" (emphasis added by me). In the case of *Jurassic Park,* Alan Grant, Ian Malcolm, and Ellie Sattler are faced with dinosaurs in the modern world as a result of technology gone awry. It is the *people* who are paramount in the story, not the dinosaurs. But it is a little cool to think about a *T. rex* loose in Manhattan—oh wait, that's *The Lost World*.

John Clute, author of the Hugo Award-winning *Encyclopedia of Fantasy*, said: "Science Fiction has never really aimed to tell us when we might reach other planets, or develop new technologies, or meet aliens. Science Fiction speculates about why we might want to do these things, and how their consequences might affect our lives and our planet."[1] This definition differs significantly from Heinlein's and from my own, and this, more than anything, defines what science fiction is: science fiction is not easily defined. In many cases, the definition is very personal: it can be anything you (or your customers) want it to be. The problem with attempts to define science fiction is that the genre itself is nebulous, blurring on the edges of techno-thriller (*Jurassic Park*), fantasy (see chapter 14, "Science-Fiction and Fantasy Blenders"), and science-thriller along with many others. A simplistic view is that science fiction is about anything science-related (laser guns, spaceships, and so on), and fantasy is about magic. But I wouldn't stick by these definitions—with these two genres, nothing is simple.

CLASSIC SCIENCE FICTION

Nothing is deader than yesterday's science fiction.
—Arthur C. Clarke, 1952

What is a classic? The term used to mean something that had some age to it. A 1957 Chevrolet is considered a classic car today, but age doesn't fully describe what makes it a classic. A great deal of emotional content has to be combined with the age factor to create a classic. Indeed, a further element that must be added to this equation is the sense that the item, whether a car or a book, was from your childhood. Classic rock music for many is rock from the 1950s—Elvis Presley and the like. But for other generations, classic rock is music from the 1960s and the 1970s. I recently overheard a youngster calling the local radio station's *Eighties at Eight* program of music from the 1980s "classic rock." I felt my insides twist as I considered this statement in light of my own age.

For the purposes of this book, I've labeled as "classics" books from before 1980 that have literary merit as well as continued popularity. I suggested in the prologue that a classic shouldn't be recommended to a reader because of the dated material. The comment by Arthur Clarke at the beginning of this section also suggests that a classic isn't a good choice for a reader. Nothing could be farther from the truth. A classic can very often be a great choice for a reader. But keep in mind that the material is dated.

The "Big Three"

The "big three" are names that just about anyone who hasn't been in a cryogenic chamber for the last fifty years should recognize: Isaac Asimov, Robert A. Heinlein, and Arthur C. Clarke. If there were a "holy trinity" in science fiction, these guys would be it. Not that I'm suggesting anything holy about them, except for the reverence in which fans hold them. The following lists are suggested titles by these great writers. Arthur C. Clarke is the only member of this august trio still alive.

ISAAC ASIMOV

The Robot Series   This classic series set the three laws of robotics obeyed by almost every other robot book written. A millennium in the future, humankind has colonized the galaxy and changed the course of all history with the creation of the positronic brain. The positronic brain allows humanoid robots to be capable of independent thinking. Robots are thought to be incapable of hurting a human being until a man is murdered and all evidence points to a robot killer. It's up to Detective Elijah Baley and his robot, R. Daneel Olivaw, to track down the murderer. Titles in series order: *The Caves of Steel, The Naked Sun, The Robots of Dawn, Robots and Empire.* Related book: *The Positronic Man* by Isaac Asimov and Robert Silverberg. Short-story collections: *The Complete Robot, Robot Dreams, Robot Visions.*

The Foundation Series   In the far future, Earth has been all but forgotten by humans who have conquered the galaxy. But the vast empire is being crushed by its own weight. Only psychohistorian Hari Seldon can see the approaching new Dark Age that will throw humankind into chaos and barbarism. Hari has a plan to save the accumulated knowledge of humans in an Encyclopedia Galactica. But will he have time to finish the project? Titles in series order: *Foundation, Foundation and Empire, Second Foundation, Foundation's Edge* (1983 Hugo Award winner), *Prelude to Foundation* (chronologically the first, but written last).

The Gods Themselves   The Sun is on the verge of extinction, and only two humans and an alien from a dying planet know the truth. But can they get anyone to listen? Only this unlikely trio can save all humankind. Winner of the 1972 Nebula and 1973 Hugo Awards.

ARTHUR C. CLARKE

2001: A Space Odyssey   A mysterious monolith has been discovered on the Moon. Scientists determine that the monolith is over three million years old and is beaming a signal to Saturn. A crew, assisted by the self-aware computer HAL 9000, is dispatched to investigate. But something has gone terribly wrong with HAL—it has begun killing the crew. It's a race against time to stop HAL and unravel the secret of the Moon's monolith and maybe humankind's origins. Sequels: *2010: Odyssey Two, 2061: Odyssey Three, 3001: The Final Odyssey.*

Childhood's End   When the giant silver ships descended unexpectedly from space to hover over Earth's greatest cities, many thought human domination had come to an end. But over the course of fifty years, the Overlords have done the exact opposite: They have eliminated ignorance, poverty, and disease, ushering in a new golden age. But having brought humanity this far, the Overlords can do little more than look on as a new generation of human children begins to manifest enormous and incomprehensible spiritual powers as part of a cosmic evolutionary process that is beyond the ken of even the super-intelligent Overlords.

Rendezvous with Rama   An enigmatic ship named *Rama* has entered the solar system, racing toward the Sun at impossible speeds. Earth dispatches a crew to investigate this mystery before the ship disappears. But the crew find more questions than answers in this empty cylinder called *Rama*, along with hints of a superior civilization. *Rendezvous with Rama* won the 1973 Nebula and 1974 Hugo Awards and is considered Clarke's finest work after *2001*. Other titles in the series: *Rama II, Garden of Rama, Rama Revealed.*

ROBERT A. HEINLEIN

The Moon Is a Harsh Mistress   The 1967 Hugo Award winner that launched a political movement, this is the tale of revolution on the Moon in 2076—a revolution led by a one-armed computer technician, a beautiful blonde radical, an academic, and a sentient computer whose slogan is TANSTAAFL (There Ain't No Such Thing As A Free Lunch). It may not be grammatical, but it is catchy.

Starship Troopers   The controversial classic that spawned a terrible film of the same name by Paul Verhoeven (please do not judge Heinlein's work on the basis of that film!), *Starship Troopers* is one of Heinlein's best works. In it, Heinlein postulates how a society based on military service would work. This book is sure to please science-fiction military buffs as well as readers who like to explore new political systems. Winner of the 1960 Hugo Award.

Stranger in a Strange Land   Winner of the 1962 Hugo Award. Valentine Michael Smith is the heir to a vast fortune and empire as well as the owner of the planet Mars. (This was written before the landmark pact signed by President John F. Kennedy that makes the planets the property of no one.) Smith isn't a native of Earth, however. The only survivor of the first manned mission to Mars, Smith was raised by Martians and has returned to Earth as an adult. Turmoil follows Smith as he establishes a church that preaches free love and teaches humans the psychic talents of the Martians. At times *Stranger* rings sour with sexist dialogue, but remember that this book is a product of the sixties and is a cult favorite.

Other Classics

Fahrenheit 451 by **Ray Bradbury**   At 451 degrees Fahrenheit, paper, and specifically a book, begins to burn. In this chilling depiction of the future, firemen don't put out fires, they start them in order to burn books—as trivial information is good and knowledge and ideas are bad. When fireman Guy Montag begins hiding books in his house, his wife turns him in, forcing Montag to go on the run. Montag joins an outlaw band of scholars keeping information alive until people need it again.

***Invasion of the Body Snatchers* by Jack Finney**   Like Helen, whose face launched a thousand ships, *Invasion of the Body Snatchers* launched a thousand films. Well, not really that many. In the quiet town of Mill Valley, California, Dr. Miles Bennell discovers an insidious invasion plot as alien life-forms are taking the place of the residents.

***Dune* by Frank Herbert**   Only the desert planet of Arrakis is the source of the spice Melange, a vital ingredient for interstellar travel. The Atreides family are the stewards of Arrakis, but their deadly enemies, the Harkonnens, have laid a trap that threatens the family's very existence. At the center of this byzantine power struggle is Duke Paul Atreides, who may be a messiah or a superhuman. *Dune* was the winner of the 1965 Nebula and the 1966 Hugo Awards. Other titles in the series: *Dune Messiah, Children of Dune, God Emperor of Dune, Chapterhouse: Dune. Dune: House Atreides, Dune: House Harkonnen* by Kevin J. Anderson and Brian Herbert are prequels to the series.

***Battlefield Earth* by L. Ron Hubbard**   In the year 3000, humans have become an endangered species after a thousand years of occupation by a superior alien race. Jonnie "Goodboy" Tyler is among the few remaining humans in hiding when he is captured by the aliens and learns to turn the aliens' technology against them.

***Ringworld* by Larry Niven**   Two humans and two aliens are traveling in the distant reaches of space in hopes of averting a disaster on Earth when they discover a massive ring-shaped world built by alien hands. The world is many times larger than Earth, and its proximity to a sun means it is capable of sustaining life—it could mean a new start for Earth! Or does it? Winner of the 1970 Nebula and 1971 Hugo Awards.

Other Recommended Titles

The Demolished Man by Alfred Bester (1953 Hugo winner)

Cities in Flight Series by James Blish

A Case of Conscience by James Blish (1959 Hugo winner)

The Illustrated Man by Ray Bradbury

13

The Martian Chronicles by Ray Bradbury

The Einstein Intersection by Samuel R. Delany (1967 Nebula winner)

Do Androids Dream of Electric Sheep? by Philip K. Dick

Martian Time Slip by Philip K. Dick

The Simulacra by Philip K. Dick

We Can Build You by Philip K. Dick

To Your Scattered Bodies Go by Philip Jose Farmer (1972 Hugo winner)

The Forever War by Joe Haldeman (1975 Nebula and 1976 Hugo winner)

Citizen of the Galaxy by Robert A. Heinlein

The Door into Summer by Robert A. Heinlein

Have Spacesuit Will Travel by Robert A. Heinlein

The Number of the Beast by Robert A. Heinlein

Podkayne of Mars by Robert A. Heinlein

The Puppet Masters by Robert A. Heinlein

Red Planet by Robert A. Heinlein

Revolt in 2100 by Robert A. Heinlein

Time Enough for Love by Robert A. Heinlein

Tunnel in the Sky by Robert A. Heinlein

Ole Doc Methuselah by L. Ron Hubbard

Flowers for Algernon by Daniel Keyes (1966 Nebula cowinner)

The Hainish Cycle by Ursula K. Le Guin

Out of the Silent Planet by C. S. Lewis

The Incredible Shrinking Man by Richard Matheson

A Canticle for Liebowitz by Walter Miller Jr.

Gateway by Frederick Pohl (1977 Nebula and 1978 Hugo winner)

Berserkers! by Fred Saberhagen

Telzey Amberdon by James Schmitz

A Time of Changes by Robert Silverberg

The Invisible Man by H. G. Wells

The Island of Doctor Moreau by H. G. Wells

The Time Machine by H. G. Wells

The War of the Worlds by H. G. Wells

DEREK'S PICK

Stranger in a Strange Land by Robert A. Heinlein

BEST PICK FOR THE RELUCTANT READER

The Robot *Series* by Isaac Asimov

GENERAL SCIENCE FICTION

Much of science fiction seems to fall into the various subgenres that make up the bulk of the first part of this book. I don't think anybody sets out to write a book on cyborgs because there is a shortage of books about them. But there are a lot of books that fit into certain categories because of their subject matter. Much of the rest of Book I is about these types of books. But sometimes a book is science fiction (and not a space opera—see chapter 17 for a definition of a space opera) and doesn't fall into any neat categories. I'll be discussing those books here.

The Fountains of Paradise by **Arthur C. Clarke** Two men are linked by their obsessions. One of the men is King Kalidasa, murderous despot of the second century who sought to reach paradise by building his Pleasure Gardens, a Garden of Eden, if you please. The other man is Vannevar Morgan, engineer in the twenty-second century, who seeks to reach the stars through technological innovation, inaugurating a new era in humankind's quest to travel among the stars. Winner of the 1979 Nebula Award and the 1980 Hugo Award.

Midshipman's Hope by **David Feintuch** A series of accidents takes the lives of the senior officers of the UNS *Hibernia* and command devolves to seventeen-year-old Nick Seafort. Seafort must overcome his own inexperience, win the confidence of his crew, and usher his ship and crew safely home. Other books in the series: *Challenger's Hope, Prisoner's Hope, Fisherman's Hope, Voices of Hope,* and *Patriarch's Hope.*

There and Back Again by **Pat Murphy** Ever wondered what *The Hobbit* by J. R. R. Tolkien would have been like if it had been set in space? No? Well, neither have I, but Pat Murphy did. *There and Back Again* is the delightful story of a short norbit named Bailey Beldon who lives a quiet, comfortable existence in a hollowed-out asteroid. Then the Farr family of clones explodes Bailey's quiet existence and, with the enigmatic cyborg Gitana, draw him along on a wild quest that spans centuries and the universe. The book follows *The Hobbit* fairly closely, and fans of the classic by Tolkien will delight in looking for the comparisons.

***Higher Education* by Charles Sheffield and Jerry Pournelle**   Pournelle and Sheffield are part of a new and revolutionary movement to put the science back in science fiction! (Pause for gasps of surprise to die down.) Rick Luban is kicked out of high school after a practical joke misfires. He seems destined for a life in the gutter when a kindly teacher helps him get a job with Vanguard Mining, an asteroid-mining corporation. Once in outer space, Rick is given a crash course not only in asteroid mining, but also in physics, the sciences, and mathematics. Competition is fierce among the miners, and Rick has to bring himself up to speed quickly or wash out.

***Hyperion* by Dan Simmons**   On the brink of galaxy-wide war, seven pilgrims set forth on a journey to Hyperion in the hope of finding answers. They find the Skrike, a mysterious creature who is worshiped by some, feared by others, and hated by those who would destroy it. *Hyperion* was the winner of the 1990 Hugo Award and placed tenth on the list of best science-fiction novels published before 1990 in Locus's 1998 poll.

Other titles in the series: *The Fall of Hyperion, Endymion, The Rise of Endymion.*

Other Recommended Titles

Genesis by Poul Anderson

Harvest of Stars by Poul Anderson

The Stars Are Also Fire by Poul Anderson

A Million Open Doors by John Barnes

Anti-Ice by Stephen Baxter

Peacekeepers by Ben Bova

Privateers by Ben Bova

Earth by David Brin

Glory Season by David Brin

The Dragon's Eye by Joel Champetieur

Merchanter's Luck by C. J. Cherryh

The Light of Other Days by Arthur C. Clarke

Habitus by James Flint

Firestar by Michael F. Flynn

Jumping off the Planet by David Gerrold

Mind, Machines, and Evolution by James P. Hogan

Mission Child by Maureen McHugh

Beowulf's Children by Larry Niven, Jerry Pournelle, and Steven Barnes

Brother to Shadows by Andre Norton

Sewer, Gas and Electric by Matt Ruff

Heart of Gold by Sharon Shinn

Six Moon Dance by Sheri S. Tepper

A Deepness in the Sky by Joan Vinge

Uncharted Territory by Connie Willis

DEREK'S PICK

Hyperion by Dan Simmons

BEST PICK FOR THE RELUCTANT READER

Higher Education by Charles Sheffield

ANSWERS TO TRIVIA QUIZ

1. C	7. B	14. A
2. D	8. A or E	15. D
3. A	9. C	16. B
4. D	10. D	17. A
5. C	11. B	18. C
5a. B	12. C	19. D
6. C	13. A	20. A

NOTE

1. See at: http://cosmics.freeyellow.com/sfquote/clute_j.html.

2

The Aliens Are Coming!
The Aliens Are Coming!

For years humans have pondered the eternal question: "What are we going to have for dinner?" Well, maybe not really, but I'm sure that question is on the top-ten list. I believe that if people ever did invent a time machine and we went back to the time of the cavemen, we would find the following scene:

Caveman: "Ug. What for dinner?"

Cavewoman (sarcastically): "You tell *me,* mighty hunter."

Actually, the question that people have pondered for centuries is: "Are we really alone in this universe?" Depending on who you ask in the scientific community, you'll get varying degrees of answers. Those who subcribe to the pessimist's (the glass is half empty) view say that so many factors had to come into play for life to evolve that it is impossible for life to evolve anywhere else, and for that matter, mathematically speaking, we shouldn't be here either! If you subscribe to René Descartes's philosophy of "I think therefore I am," then if those guys aren't careful they'll think us all out of existence. On the flip side of the outlook coin are the optimists—those who think the glass is half full. The optimists believe that if life evolved here, then it can evolve anywhere, and those beings should come knocking any time. In the middle of the philosophical road are the pragmatists (for lack of a better term). These folks, like yours truly, believe that it is possible for life to have evolved on another planet, but given the age of the universe, such life-forms shouldn't necessarily be more advanced than we are and wouldn't come calling early. I think if there is life in the universe, it isn't necessarily going to be close enough for either of us to pay a visit on the other, not to mention want to take over the neighbor's real estate.

Alien science fiction comes in two flavors—first contact and alien invasion. The two types often blend together, leading to confusion as to which is which. I've combined the two subgenres into one simply because they mingle like desperate single people at a party. First-contact science fiction obviously is about humanity's first experiences with an alien race. Alien-invasion science fiction, however, can be about humankind's first contact with an alien race, but it differs in that the aliens are usually traveling to Earth to conquer it, not to ask to borrow a cup of sugar, plutonium, dilithium crystals, and whatnot. For the purposes of this book, I've limited first-contact science fiction to those occasions where we are meeting aliens for the first time, whether or not the meeting turns ugly. Alien invasion is for purposes of human subjugation, through either peaceful or military means.

FIRST-CONTACT NOVELS

Who knows what will happen when, and if, humans and another race do indeed make first contact? I personally find it hard to believe that aliens would come millions of light-years, expending huge amounts of energy, just to kick a little *Homo sapiens* butt. Even if the energy required were free or easily attainable, it just doesn't make sense to attack any race that has shown the propensity for violence that the human race has. Of course, I don't think that the first contact would run smoothly by any stretch of the imagination—far from it. We can't even get along with our neighbors who at least have the advantage of being from the same planet. What makes us think that we'd get along with our new alien friends? First-contact science fiction is concerned primarily with humankind's initial contact with an alien species from another planet. First contact does not have to take place on Earth or even on a planet where people are living. The contact can take place on the alien's planet, in space between spaceships, or even on a neutral planet.

***Starfarers* by Poul Anderson**   When astrologers discover evidence of an advanced alien civilization, an expedition is formed to make contact. Utilizing newly developed fast-as-light technology, the crew members of the starship *Envoy* plan to make the trip in only a few years whereas eleven thousand years will pass on Earth. The crew is mentally prepared for what they will find when they contact the alien civilization, but are they prepared for the changes that have occurred on Earth in their absence?

***If the Stars Are Gods* by Gregory Benford**   Space travel has caused a great many changes in humankind, not only in terms of the knowledge gained from study of other planets, but also in the way people view the universe. Nowhere is this more true than in the case of Bradley Reynolds, whose one-hundred-year career has seen wondrous sights— from a manned expedition to Mars, to the discovery of life on Saturn, and the arrival of aliens to this solar system who believe that stars are sentient beings. This book was based on the novelette that won the 1974 Nebula Award.

***Foreigner: A Novel of First Contact* by C. J. Cherryh**   Almost five hundred years have passed since the human colony ship *Phoenix* crashed on the planet of the humanoid atevi, where law and order are maintained through the use of registered assassins. Almost immediately war broke out between the atevi and the humans, who through their more advanced weaponry, were able to secure an armistice. In exchange for sharing their technology with the atevi, the humans were allowed to live on a remote island in peace. Only one human, the paidhi, a kind of ambassador, is allowed in atevi society, and he has just become the target of an unregistered assassin. Other titles in the series: *Invader, Inheritor, Precursor, Defender.*

***Probability Moon* by Nancy Kress**   When humans began to explore the solar system, they made an amazing discovery: stargates constructed and left behind by a long-vanished, advanced alien race. These stargates allowed quick transport beyond the solar system. As humans established colonies, they discovered two alien races: one, the hostile Fallers who immediately declared war on the humans, and the other a race called the Worlders who hold a very limited view of reality. A research crew is sent to explore the Worlders' planet and its small moon, believed by the scientists to be a powerful, world-shattering weapon. Can the research team explore and capture the weapon before the Fallers arrive? More important, what will happen when the Worlders realize that the humans plan on taking the weapon for themselves? Other title in the series: *Probability Sun*.

The Bridge by **Janine Ellen Young**   In a distant galaxy, the Kasarans have instituted a program they hope will find other sentient life in the universe. The program launches billions of tiny spacecraft encoded with greetings and other information inside viral packets. Upon reaching Earth, the viral messages set off a pandemic disease that kills more than four billion people. The survivors fall into two categories: those who were untouched by the disease and those, called Pan, who are gripped by strange thoughts evidently originating with the Kasarans. One Pan called Jude has unlocked the secret of the Kasaran messages and has begun the construction of a star bridge to find and meet the Kasarans.

Other Recommended Titles

Camelot 30K by Robert L. Forward

Expendable by James Alan Gardner

Seas of Kilmoyn Series by Roland Green

White Queen by Gwyneth Jones

Pitch Black by Frank Lauria and David Twohy

Decision at Doona by Anne McCaffrey

Independence Day: Silent Zone by Stephen Molstad

Illegal Alien by Robert J. Sawyer

Starplex by Robert J. Sawyer

DEREK'S PICK

Starfarers by Poul Anderson

BEST PICK FOR THE RELUCTANT READER
Probability Moon by Nancy Kress

ALIEN INVASION!

Arthur C. Clarke once said, "A truly intelligent race is not likely to be unfriendly." Anyone who has seen the movie *Mars Attacks!* knows what's coming next. That's right, the aliens pull their laser guns, and good-bye Mr. President! The idea that aliens are out in the universe and that they have every intention of invading and conquering the human race has been discussed (sometimes quite loudly) and written about for a very long time. Even in 1898, people were wondering what would happen if aliens finally came knocking, and in the great-great-great granddaddy of invasion stories, *The War of the Worlds* by H. G. Wells, that question is answered: invasion of the planet Earth and destruction of humankind. Alien-invasion fiction is *always* about the subjugation and possible destruction of Earth and humankind as a race. It, like first-contact fiction, can take place not just on Earth but anywhere in the universe. The invasion doesn't have to be violent in nature, but many times it is extremely violent, especially because the aliens are usually not only technologically superior to the human race but physically superior as well. Invasion fiction also doesn't always cast humankind as the victim of the invasion; humans could be the instigators of the invasion.

The Uplift Series by David Brin In a galaxy where no species can reach sentience without the help of a patron race, the amazing has occurred: Humans reached sentience without assistance. Once a species has been "uplifted," or enabled to reach sentience, it must serve the patron race before in turn uplifting other species. The fact that humans uplifted independently and are now uplifting other races (i.e., apes and dolphins) makes the humans a target for all other patron races. Other titles in the series: the Earth Clan trilogy: *Sundiver, Startide Rising, The Uplift War* (won the 1988 Hugo Award); sequel: the Uplift trilogy: *Brightness Reef, Infinity's Shore, Heaven's Reach.*

***Dawn* by Octavia Butler**   Earth and humanity have been decimated by nuclear war and disease when the alien Oankali arrive to save the planet and the human race. Placing humans in cryogenic sleep, the Oankali repair the shattered Earth as well as cure all diseases, including cancer. They also adapt humans, making them stronger and more disease resistant. Lilith Iyapo is a human who has been awakened from sleep so that she can act as a guide for humans on how they will survive on the new Earth. She will also prepare humankind for the Oankali's terrifying features. But nothing is ever truly free, and the Oankali expect payment for services rendered. They want to blend their genes with humankind's, creating a new, stronger race. Other titles in the series: *Adulthood Rites, Imago.*

***Ender's Game* by Orson Scott Card**   Earth has twice suffered attacks from an alien race and has been only barely able to defeat the invaders. Earth's military has begun an innovative training school to breed and train child geniuses to defend the planet. Ender Wiggin is a brilliant young boy tapped for the program, and his skills quickly make him a leader, both in school and in the battle room, where students fight mock battles in zero gravity. Ender's brilliant sister Valentine and brother Peter, having been passed over for Battle School, launch their own campaign to make Earth a better place. *Ender's Game* won the 1986 Hugo and the 1985 Nebula Awards. Sequels: *Speaker for the Dead* (winner of the 1986 Nebula and 1987 Hugo), *Xenocide.* Companion novels: *Ender's Shadow* (takes place at the same time as *Ender's Game*), *Shadow of the Hegemon.*

***The Puppet Masters* by Robert A. Heinlein**   A spaceship has crashed in a forest in America. Its passengers are the deadly Titans, sluglike creatures that have the ability to control human beings by inserting their tail into a human's spine. The Titans are all connected by a collective consciousness and by their desire to subjugate the entire human race. Unfortunately, very few people know of this insidious invasion save for Intelligence Officer Sam Cavanaugh, who, along with his partner, must stop the greatest threat the human race has ever experienced.

***The War of the Worlds* by H. G. Wells**   Originally published in 1898, this is a tale about an invasion of Earth by Martians, whose one-hundred-foot-tall death machines lay waste to the countryside. It soon becomes clear that the Martians are not only conquering the Earthlings but corralling them for sustenance.

Other Recommended Titles

Brother Termite by Patricia Anthony

God's Fires by Patricia Anthony

Timelike Infinity by Stephen Baxter

The Saga of the Well World Series by Jack L. Chalker

The Faded Sun by C. J. Cherryh

Childhood's End by Arthur C. Clarke

In the Company of Others by Julie Czerneda

Deathday by William C. Dietz

Steelheart by William C. Dietz

Invasion of the Body Snatchers by Jack Finney

Books of the Damned Series by Alan Dean Foster

Nor Crystal Tears by Alan Dean Foster

War against the Chtorr Series by David Gerrold

The Nano Flower by Peter F. Hamilton

The Number of the Beast by Robert A. Heinlein

Starship Troopers by Robert A. Heinlein

Requiem of Stars by Tracy Hickman

Battlefield Earth by L. Ron Hubbard

Virus Clans: A Story of Evolution by Michael Kanaly

Dreamcatcher by Stephen King

Freedom Series by Anne McCaffrey

Independence Day (ID4) by Dionne McNeff et al.

Adiamante by L. E. Modesitt Jr.

The Parafaith War by L. E. Modesitt Jr.

Beowulf's Children by Larry Niven, Jerry Pournelle, and Steven Barnes

Echoes in Time by Andre Norton and Sherwood Smith

Leonard Nimoy's Primortals: Target Earth by Steve Perry

Men in Black by Steve Perry

The Eschaton Sequence (series) by Frederick Pohl

O Pioneer by Frederick Pohl

The Outpost by Michael D. Resnick

THE ALIENS ARE COMING! THE ALIENS ARE COMING!

Gene Roddenberry's Earth the Final Conflict: The Arrival by Fred Saberhagen

Wheelers by Jan Stewart and Jack Cohen

The Fresco by Sheri S. Tepper

World War Series *by Harry Turtledove*

The Apocalypse Troll by David Weber

In Death Ground by David Weber

Conqueror's Pride by Timothy Zahn

DEREK'S PICK

The Uplift Series by David Brin

BEST PICK FOR THE RELUCTANT READER

Ender's Game by Orson Scott Card

3

Celestial Bodies

Don't you understand, this is the first time I've
actually stood on the surface of another planet . . .
a whole alien world! Pity it's such a dump though.

—Arthur Dent in
Douglas Adams's *The Hitch Hiker's Guide to the Galaxy*

Have you ever wondered what it would be like to stand on the surface of another planet? It is an idea that has captivated humankind for years. Indeed, humans have always wondered what lay beyond the next rise of land and, once that had been discovered, what lay beyond the seas. It is this curiosity that drove Lewis and Clark to cross the North American continent and Jacques Cousteau to comb the depths of the oceans, and that someday will drive humankind to explore the depths of space itself.

The books in this chapter revolve primarily around the idea of traveling to a planet with the intention of exploring, researching, or colonizing the planet. For the most part, the books in this chapter are about planets and moons in our solar system. A few involve planets outside our own solar system, but the central theme is of exploration or colonization or both of another planet.

MARS

One planet seems to fascinate science-fiction authors more than any others: Mars. The red planet makes up a good portion of this subgenre possibly because it is the nearest planet to Earth, has the potential to support life, is similar in size to Earth, and at a minimum distance of 35 *million* miles, is close enough to visit regularly. Even in 1912, when Tarzan creator Edgar Rice Burroughs published the novel *A Princess of Mars,* people were wondering what life was like on the red planet. Many of the books in this section are about terraforming Mars into a planet that can accommodate human life. "Terraforming" is the use of advanced technology to alter the environment of a planet to support life. Not all the books in this section are about terraforming, but they do all have one thing in common: they are either about a group living on Mars or about people from Mars. Notable authors of Mars fiction include Kim Stanley Robinson, Robert A. Heinlein, and Ray Bradbury.

***Climbing Olympus* by Kevin J. Anderson**   The Mars Project was a project to terraform Mars from a desolate environment hostile to human life into a viable colony for Earth. The terraformers were called adin, surgically altered humans able to live in the poisonous atmosphere of Mars and withstand the brutal cold and heat. But with every step toward an environment friendly to humankind, a generation of adin must die. Because the adin have been altered to survive in the environment in which they work, once their work is finished, the changes they have wrought mean they can no longer survive in the new environment. The adin leader Boris Tiban realizes this and launches a desperate gamble to destroy the Mars Project.

***Moving Mars* by Greg Bear**   Revolution is sweeping across the face of Mars in response to repeated efforts from Earth to control the colonies on Mars. Soon the two planets are openly hostile as the colonists realize that Earth is trying to claim the technology of "descriptors" discovered by Charles Franklin. Franklin's discovery made instantaneous communication possible. But the technology has an even more dangerous application: the moving of entire planets (hence the book's title). Will Mars leave the solar system to avoid war with Earth? 1994 Nebula Award winner.

Mars **by Ben Bova**   An international crew of twenty-five astronauts and scientists have been pulled together for humankind's greatest undertaking: a manned exploration of another planet to look for signs of life. But tensions threaten to shake apart the tentative international consortium even before the crew leaves Earth. Once the crew lands, however, tensions are doubled because the team is over 200,000 miles away on a hostile and life-threatening planet. But the greatest discovery may yet be made on the surface of Mars. Sequel: *Return to Mars.*

Stranger in a Strange Land **by Robert A. Heinlein**—see p. 11.

Red Mars **by Kim Stanley Robinson**   For years Mars has beckoned to Earth from across a maddeningly small (in galactic terms) and yet seemingly insurmountable distance. Mars, ripe for exploration and colonization. In 2026, one hundred would-be colonists set out to accomplish the impossible: terraform and colonize Mars. For some, it is a chance at a new life; for others, Mars holds the promise of riches; and for still others, it may hold the greatest secrets of life and death. In my opinion, this is the best book ever written about Mars. Winner of the 1993 Nebula Award. Other titles in the series: *Green Mars* (1994 Hugo Award), *Blue Mars* (1997 Hugo Award).

Other Recommended Titles

White Mars; or, The Mind Set Free by Brian Aldiss

The Greening of Mars by Michael Allaby

Hard Sell by Piers Anthony

Total Recall by Piers Anthony

Solis by A. A. Attanasio

Voyage by Stephen Baxter

The Martian Race by Gregory Benford

Voyage to the Red Planet by Terry Bisson

The Martian Chronicles by Ray Bradbury

Martian Time-Slip by Philip K. Dick

The Far Call by Gordon R. Dickson

Mars Prime by William Dietz

Semper Mars by Ian Douglas

Jesus on Mars by Philip Jose Farmer

Article 23 by William R. Forstchen

Double Star by Robert A. Heinlein

Podkayne of Mars by Robert A. Heinlein

Red Planet by Robert A. Heinlein

Mars Crossing by Geoffrey Landis

Out of the Silent Planet by C. S. Lewis

Red Dust by Paul J. McAuley

Man Plus by Frederick Pohl

Mining the Ort by Frederick Pohl

Icehenge by Kim Stanley Robinson

Man O' War by William Shatner

Frontera by Lewis Shiner

Labyrinth of Night by Allen M. Steele

Martian Viking by Tim Sullivan

DEREK'S PICK

Red Mars by Kim Stanley Robinson

BEST PICK FOR THE RELUCTANT READER

Climbing Olympus by Kevin J. Anderson

THE MOON

Ever since Neil Armstrong and Buzz Aldrin first visited the Moon, science-fiction writers have been writing about humans colonizing it. As our closest satellite, the Moon has occupied a prominent position in the imagination of science-fiction writers. Unlike Mars, the Moon is not considered a candidate for terraforming into an Earthlike environment. The Moon is incapable of supporting an atmosphere of any kind. This is not to say that the Moon isn't a candidate for colonization, far from it. Books in this section generally are about establishing a human colony on the Moon but may also involve permanent settlements.

Moonseed by Stephen Baxter   What would happen if planets could catch a virus? As *Moonseed* opens, Venus dies in a fiery explosion that sprays "moonseed" on Earth. Moonseed is a nanovirus—part machine, part virus—that consumes planets. The moonseed is discovered on Earth after parts of Scotland and the United States are consumed. The nanovirus is also discovered on the Moon but seems to be in a dormant stage, leaving the Moon as the last refuge of humans. Can the Moon be made habitable in time? Or should all of humankind's energies be put into fighting the moonseed on Earth?

Moonrise by **Ben Bova**   Paul Stavenger had a dream: to build Moonbase, the first permanent human colony on the Moon. Unfortunately, Paul is murdered by the very technology that makes Moonbase possible: nanotechnology. Nanotechnology, for those of us who haven't watched *Star Trek* recently, is a branch of engineering that uses devices and robots on the scale of billionths of a meter. In the case of the Moonbase, nanotechnology is used to construct buildings with lunar materials and to repair, microscopically, damage to human bodies. But Paul's widow, Joanna Masterson Stavenger, has the power and resources to see the Moonbase Project to fruition—if she can overcome familial pressures as well as political pressures from Earth. Sequel: *Moonwar.*

The Moon Is a Harsh Mistress by **Robert A. Heinlein**—see p. 11.

Back to the Moon by **Homer Hickam**   In the near future, a bored ex-astronaut named Jack Medaris hijacks the space shuttle *Columbia* in order to reach the Moon and hopefully end Earth's energy problems. On the Moon are great quantities of the isotope helium-3, which could be used as an alternative fuel source. Opposing Jack are NASA (which is not happy at all about the theft of its shuttle) and a mysterious group that will do anything to stop spaceflight.

Moonfall by **Jack McDevitt**   In the year 2024, humankind has made great strides in technology, the most notable being the first manned flight to Mars and the opening of a permanent settlement on the Moon. Just when the future looks brightest, disaster looms as a fast-moving comet named Tomiko is discovered on a collision course with the Moon. If the Moon is destroyed by the comet, then Earth will almost certainly be destroyed as well. What steps can be taken to avert this disaster?

Other Recommended Titles

Rogue Moon by Algis Budrys
Steel Beach by John Varley

DEREK'S PICK

The Moon Is a Harsh Mistress by Robert A. Heinlein

BEST PICK FOR THE RELUCTANT READER

Moonrise by Ben Bova

OTHER CELESTIAL BODIES

Although Mars and the Moon are the most popular subjects of science-fiction writers writing about life on another planet, the books in this section are about exploring and colonizing the rest of the planets and asteroids of our solar system.

Titan by **Stephen Baxter**   On Saturn's moon Titan, signs point toward life existing beneath its thick, swirling atmosphere. NASA immediately launches a mission to investigate under the command of Paula Benecerraf. The crew must overcome tremendous odds just to reach Titan, where they find even greater challenges waiting for them.

Venus by **Ben Bova**   If there was a place in the solar system that would approximate hell, it would be the surface of Venus, where air pressure is measured in thousands of pounds per square inch; where, although the air is not poisonous, it still cannot sustain life; and where the temperature is hot enough to melt aluminum. It is to this planet that Van must travel. Van Humphries is the younger brother of the first man who attempted a landing on Venus and who did not survive the attempt. Now Van's father is offering a reward of ten billion dollars to anyone who can retrieve his dead son's remains. Van surprises everyone, including himself, by taking the offer, but he must move quickly because his competition is financed by the man his father despises most—Van's mother's first husband.

Half-Life by **Hal Clement**   Near the end of the next century, diseases are evolving so rapidly that the average human life span has fallen to twenty years. In an effort to combat this, an expedition has been launched to explore pre-life conditions on Saturn's moon Titan. But disaster awaits the crew at every stage of the mission. Can the solution to

Earth's problems be discovered on distant, hostile Titan? Will anyone survive to take the knowledge home?

Brute Orbits **by George Zebrowski**   In the twenty-first century, Earth is suffering from global warming and overpopulation. To help correct this, humans devise a new program that places convicts on asteroids where they hollow out their own cells. The asteroids are then inserted into a solar orbit, eliminating the need for guards as well as the physical and emotional abuse common in prisons. But after extended time in solar orbit, what happens when the convicts are reintroduced into society? Do they have to be reintroduced?

The Quiet Invasion **by Sarah Zettel**   Venus is completely uninhabitable by humans, but Helen Failia wants her research station in Venus's orbit declared a permanent colony. Others on the station see Venus as the prime opportunity to rekindle a rebellion of Mars and Moon colonies against the United Nations. But everything is thrown out of balance when the researchers make two monumental discoveries—they locate a building that may have been built by aliens, and they make first contact with an alien race that seeks to use Venus as its refuge. The aliens' own planet is dying and only Venus can support them. The aliens can't understand why the humans would fight so hard to keep a planet they cannot possibly live on.

Other Recommended Titles

The Asteroid Wars (series) by Ben Bova

Jupiter by Ben Bova

Heavy Time by C. J. Cherryh

Code of the Lifemaker by James P. Hogan

The Venus Trilogy by Pamela Sargent

The Tenth Planet by Dean Wesley Smith

The Golden Globe by John Varley

DEREK'S PICK

Half-Life by Hal Clement

BEST PICK FOR THE RELUCTANT READER

The Quiet Invasion by Sarah Zettel

4

Androids and Robots
and Cyborgs . . . Oh My!

*It's interesting that I would trust a robot and
not an android. Perhaps it's because a robot
does not try to deceive you as to what it is.*

—Philip K. Dick

We've all seen the movies in which the mad scientist stands over a
corpse that is still smoking from electrical strikes, desperately begging
his creation to "Live, damn you! Live!" Creation or adaptation of life
of a different variety is the subject of this chapter: life of a mechanical
kind.

With the creation of mechanical life comes a host of concerns for
humankind, most notably that these creations are usually stronger,
faster, and smarter than we are. These attributes present the difficulties
of not only how to control them but, in the case of androids, how to
tell them apart from real humans. Androids, although mechanical in
nature, are designed to look like ordinary human beings. Robots, on the
other hand, can be crafted in the shape of a human (that is, with a recognizable head, two arms, and two legs) but can also take any shape
imaginable. In fact, two of the most recognizable robots ever created,
C3PO and R2D2 from *Star Wars,* fit this pattern. C3PO has a human
shape while R2D2 looks like a rolling garbage can. The final category

in this chapter on mechanical life is cyborgs. Cyborgs are human beings that have had body parts replaced with mechanical components that enhance their abilities. Does this mean that someone who has lost a limb or other body part and replaced it with a prosthetic is a cyborg? No. The key is that the replacement part *enhances* the person's abilities, usually through the use of advanced computers. One problem that frequently occurs in this subgenre is that the writer has not researched the physics of limb replacement and makes the cybernetic arm or leg much stronger than the human skeleton can support. The most famous cybernetic life-forms have to be *Star Trek*'s Borg—a race of cybernetic beings that live in a collective consciousness with one driving purpose: the assimilation of all technology and life.

The books in this subgenre are either about or have as their protagonist or other major characters a robot, cyborg, or an android. Isaac Asimov has had the greatest impact on this subgenre. His Three Laws of Robotics have been utilized by just about every author writing books about robots and androids. Cyborgs, however, are usually not limited by the Robotics Laws because they are basically human in nature.

The Robot Series by Isaac Asimov—see p. 9.

Solis **by A. A. Attanasio**   When Charlie Outis arranged for his head to be cryogenically frozen after his death, he hoped to be revived in the future to experience the utopia humankind created. What he found was a nightmare. In the future, cryogenically frozen heads are a valuable commodity, for they alleviate the enormous expense of creating artificial intelligence. When Charlie is revived, he is given two choices by a mysterious agent of the Commonality: one, have his entire brain installed as the CPU of an ore miner in the Asteroid Belt; or two, have pieces of his brain parceled out to work as the CPUs for several smaller machines. It is not surprising Charlie chooses the first option. He is understandably unhappy about his fate until a group comes forward with the promise of a new life on Mars.

Do Androids Dream of Electric Sheep? **by Philip K. Dick**   By 2021, humans have begun to colonize the galaxy. To facilitate the creation of these colonies, and to help relieve boredom, the colonists are issued incredibly lifelike androids. The androids are so lifelike that they are indistinguishable from real people, causing them to be banned from ever coming to Earth. Then a group of androids goes on a murder spree and flees to the anonymity of Earth. Bounty hunter Rick Deckard is given the job of hunting down the rogue androids—a job that may prove fatal for him. Warning: This book is very different from the movie inspired by it, *Blade Runner*!

Code of the Lifemaker by James P. Hogan   Long ago a race of aliens built a vast fleet of ships containing robots and released them into the universe. The robots' purpose was to find planets suitable for exploitation. Once on-site the robots were to set up self-replicating factories and begin harvesting resources. One ship, however, deviated from this plan after being damaged by a supernova. It landed on Saturn's moon Titan and, believing the moon to be exploitable, set up factories and began harvesting. Many years later an Earth probe discovers the robots and, more astonishing, reveals that the robots are a sentient, reproducing race that has evolved and created a religion. Sequel: *Immortality Option*.

Man Plus by Frederick Pohl   Man Plus is a project to explore and colonize Mars by surgically enhancing human beings with cybernetic implants. With tensions rising on Earth, Mars seems to be the only option for survival of the human race. But can cyborgs and humans live together? Winner of the 1976 Nebula Award. Sequel: *Mars Plus*.

Other Recommended Titles

Isaac Asimov's Caliban by Roger MacBride Allen

Resurrection, Inc. by Kevin J. Anderson

Conscience of the Beagle by Patricia Anthony

The Gaia Websters by Kim Antieau

The Novels of the Company (series) by Kage Baker

The White Abacus by Damien Broderick

The Fortunate Fall by Raphael Carter

We Can Build You by Philip K. Dick

Legion of the Damned by William C. Dietz

Steelheart by William C. Dietz

Diaspora by Greg Egan

Forever Peace by Joe Haldeman

The Turing Option by Harry Harrison and Marvin Minsky

Wildlife by James P. Kelly

The Ship Who Sang by Anne McCaffrey

Superluminal by Vonda McIntyre

Adiamante by L. E. Modesitt Jr.

Starswarm by Jerry Pournelle

A King of Infinite Space by Allen M. Steele

Schisimatrix by Bruce Sterling

Mirage: An Isaac Asimov's Robots Mystery by Mark W. Tiedemann

Knights of the Black Earth by Margaret Weis and Don Perrin

DEREK'S PICK

Solis by A. A. Attanasio

BEST PICK FOR THE RELUCTANT READER

The Robot Series by Isaac Asimov

5

Attack of the Killer Computers!

I never liked the idea of doing what a machine says.
I hate having to salute something built in a factory.

—Philip K. Dick

Just when you thought it was safe to type up your résumé, *BAM!* The computer leaps out and gets you! Now it's your turn to follow orders and run some programs for your computer. You can do what it wants and live, or refuse and get the infamous Blue Screen of Death! It seems that computers are getting smarter and smarter every day. Computers can now use voice recognition software to accept input from their users, eliminating the keyboard for most routine applications. You can find "bots" on the Internet, which are chat programs that can respond somewhat intelligibly to what you type in, though I did cause a bot to stop talking with me when I tried it.

As computers get closer and closer to true intelligence, to becoming self-aware, many writers have become concerned. The reason for their concern is that the intelligence that scientists are trying to create in computers is based upon a model for the *human* brain. This has led many writers to believe that because the intelligence is based on the human brain, the computer, upon becoming self-aware, will realize that it has to pay income tax and will go crazy trying to figure out the 1040EZ form. This will cause the computer to go on a rampage and end all life on this planet as we know it.

This chapter differs from the preceding chapter because, for the most part, robots, androids, and cyborgs are mobile whereas a computer doesn't generally move around (except my laptop, which is never in the same place I left it). Although a computer may control a ship or other form of transportation and thus affect its movement, it cannot move itself without outside assistance.

2001: A Space Odyssey **by Arthur C. Clarke**—see p. 10.

The Deus Machine **by Pierre Ouellette**   The year is 2005 and Earth is in the midst of a crushing economic depression caused by massive overspending in the 1980s and 1990s. Desperate to maintain America's status as a superpower, the country launches a project to create a powerful new viral weapon. The designer of the weapon is the supercomputer DEUS, which, in the course of developing the weapon, becomes self-aware. A fortunate (or unfortunate) side effect of self-awareness is that DEUS now has a conscience. Soon the hapless computer is overcome with grief and decides to take the only logical (to DEUS) way out: suicide. The problem is that DEUS has decided to eliminate all life, not just its own.

The Silicon Man **by Charles Platt**   FBI agent James Bayley has been assigned to investigate a corporation called North Industries, whose sole project is called Lifescan. The project's objective is to upload the human mind into a computer, but the firm has been unable to report any success to its main financier, the Government. The Government is suspicious at this lack of progress and sends Bayley to investigate. In reality, the scientists at North Industries are very close to success and are very upset when Bayley arrives. To keep their secret, the scientists have only two choices: kill Bayley or make him the first Lifescan test subject. They choose the latter and successfully load Bayley into the computer where he discovers that he is cut off from the outside world. His only human contact is the creator of Lifescan, a megalomaniac who can do anything he wants in the computer environment in which Bayley lives.

Berserkers! Series by Fred Saberhagen   After centuries of warfare, Earth was finally at peace. Poverty had been eliminated as humankind spread outward through the universe. First contact had been made with alien races and peace was the outcome. Then the Berserkers came. Berserkers are planet-sized superweapons guided by self-aware computers with singular programming: destroy all life. Series titles in order: *Berserker!*, *Berserker Blue Death*, *Berserker Throne*, *Berserker Base*, *Berserker Planet*, *Berserker Man*, *Berserker Kill*, *Berserker Fury*, *Shiva in Steel*. Collections: *Berserker Wars*, *Ultimate Enemy*, *Berserker Lies*, *Brother Assassin*. Omnibus: *Berserkers: The Beginning* (contains *Berserker!* and *Ultimate Enemy*).

Steel Beach by John Varley   On the Moon humans have created a paradise free of all illness, where everything a person needs is provided by the Central Computer (CC), a vast AI (artificial intelligence) that controls the colony. For Hildy Johnson, however, life is not a paradise. In fact, Hildy wants nothing more than to end his life. The CC tries to help Hildy with his problems, but as the two progress through the therapy, the CC admits that it, too, has been feeling suicidal. As the CC descends farther into madness, Hildy must discover what is affecting it before the CC destroys itself and the colony with it.

Other Recommended Titles

The Computer Connection by Alfred Bester

Infecress by Tom Cool

Diaspora by Greg Egan

Permutation City by Greg Egan

A Boy and His Tank by Leo Frankowski

Take Back Plenty by Colin Greenland

The Turing Option by Harry Harrison and Marvin Minsky

Entoverse by James P. Hogan

Caverns of Socrates by Dennis L. McKiernan

Halo by Tom Maddox

Cyberweb by Lisa Mason

Mars Plus by Frederick Pohl

The Hacker and the Ants by Rudy Rucker

Ventus by Karl Schroeder

Dreamships by Melissa Scott

The Shapes of Their Hearts by Melissa Scott

Lady El by Jim Starlin

The Jericho Iteration by Allen M. Steele

A King of Infinite Space by Allen M. Steele

The Imperium Game by K. D. Wentworth

Fool's War by Sarah Zettel

DEREK'S PICK

2001: A Space Odyssey by Arthur C. Clarke

BEST PICK FOR THE RELUCTANT READER

The Deus Machine by Pierre Ouellette

6

Cyberpunk–Are You Looking at Me?

Science Fiction with an Attitude

The term "cyberpunk" was invented by Bruce Bethke for a short story ironically entitled "Cyberpunk," but the actual subgenre began when William Gibson wrote a novel called *Neuromancer*. The key component of cyberpunk is computer expertise, often enhanced through cybernetic implants that allow the user to connect his or her mind to a computer, data network, or the Internet. The main character of cyberpunk is most often an antihero who thumbs his or her nose at authority of any kind and uses superior computer skills to combat those in authority. The environment in cyberpunk novels is generally dark and gritty with a gothic or noir feeling. Sex and drugs are also prevalent in cyberpunk novels.

***Neuromancer* by William Gibson**   Case was the best at what he did: collecting information. By linking his mind to the Internet, Case was freed from his body. His mind could soar through cyberspace and find any information, provided the buyer could meet Case's price. Then Case double-crossed the wrong client and was forcefully removed from the Internet. His brain damaged to prevent reconnection with the Internet, and locked into his physical body, Case had hit rock bottom. Then an employer offers to repair the damage in exchange for Case's loyalty and abilities. To ensure loyalty, the employer injects Case with a slow-acting poison, the antidote to be provided after the mission is over. But as Case progresses into the mission, he uncovers conspiracy after conspiracy, culminating in a showdown with a dangerous entity known only as the Neuromancer. *Neuromancer* was the winner of the three most coveted awards in science fiction: the Hugo, the Nebula, and the Philip K. Dick Awards. The book also is credited with creating the cyberpunk genre. Sequels: *Count Zero, Mona Lisa Overdrive.*

***Signal to Noise* by Eric S. Nylund**   By 2070, generations have been raised with only one philosophy: do whatever you have to in order to get ahead. Jack Potter is the perfect embodiment of this philosophy. Using a device that allows him to link his brain with powerful computers, Jack has clawed his way into a shot at a tenure position. But his chances are dwindling because of an academic rival, and the National Security Organization is investigating Jack for suspected information-dealing with China. Then Jack makes an incredible discovery. Hidden in an interstellar signal is a message from an alien species. When Jack contacts the aliens, he finds they are offering many things, including a cure for cancer. But everyone wants to get in on the opportunities the aliens offer and will do anything, even kill, to get them.

***The Hacker and the Ants* by Rudy Rucker**   Jerzy Rugby is extremely intelligent and creative, and a loner. His obsession lately has been the development of robotic intelligence. All these traits make Jerzy the prime suspect for the release of the destructive cyberspace ants onto the Net. The ants themselves began replicating as soon as they were released and quickly developed intelligence, causing them to turn against their creator. As forces move in to arrest Jerzy, he is forced to go on the run even as he is trying to discover who set him up.

***Trouble and Her Friends* by Melissa Scott**   Under the moniker of Trouble, India Carless was once the greatest of the hackers, able to break even the most sophisticated computer security program. Then the government decided to cut down on the security breaches of the Internet, and India quickly retired to become a system operator. Life is good for India until another hacker takes her moniker of Trouble and hacks into the government's systems, bragging about the break-ins to anyone who will read about them. India has no choice but to marshal the troops, hackers from her former life, to track down the imposter and clear her name.

Snow Crash by Neal Stephenson   Hiro Protagonist (great name, huh?) is the world's greatest swordsman and one of the last great hackers. When his mentor is turned into a brainless zombie by a new drug called Snow Crash, Hiro has no choice but to seek out and stop the drug's creator. Snow Crash affects not just hackers but computers as well, and it is up to Hiro to stop the drug's spread before society is thrown back into the Stone Age.

Other Recommended Titles

Dead Girls by Richard Calder

The Wonderland Gambit by Jack L. Chalker

Svaha by Charles de Lint

The Steampunk Trilogy by Paul Di Filippo

All Tomorrow's Parties by William Gibson

Idoru by William Gibson

Virtual Punk by William Gibson

Slow River by Nicola Griffith

Arachne by Lisa Mason

Nocturne for a Dangerous Man by Marc Matz

Gaia's Toys by Rebecca Ore

The Silicon Man by Charles Platt

Software by Rudy Rucker

Dreamships by Melissa Scott

Night Sky Mine by Melissa Scott

Heavy Weather by Bruce Stirling

Catspaw by Joan Vinge

DEREK'S PICK

Neuromancer by William Gibson

BEST PICK FOR THE RELUCTANT READER

Trouble and Her Friends by Melissa Scott

7

Virtual Reality

Virtual reality is a computer-generated environment that a user can enter, and most important, interact with. Everything that the user sees, smells, tastes, hears, and touches is created by a computer. Using a virtual reality program, a person can experience anything that can be imagined and created by the computer, from taking part in the defense of Little Round Top at Gettysburg to finding out what it would be like to be married to Marilyn Monroe. In some cases, users interact with the virtual reality through a helmet that covers their eyes and special gloves on their hands. In other cases, users enter the environment through a direct connection of their mind to the computer.

Most people are familiar with virtual reality through the holosuites featured on *the Star Trek* television programs: *Next Generation, Deep Space Nine,* and *Voyager*. In these cases, the user enters the room and a hologram is projected on the walls, ceiling, and floor with the computer creating people, animals, and objects and inserting them into the holosuite. However users access the virtual reality program, it allows them to experience a wide range of emotions, adventures, history, even different lifestyles without any danger or inconvenience to themselves. When they are done, they can unplug from the program and return to their lives none the worse for wear. The books in this chapter all feature virtual reality as their subject matter. It either provides the environment the hero lives in or creates the conflict of the story.

***RIM: A Novel* by Alexander Besher**   In the future, millions of users escape reality by jacking into Gametime. Gametime is a virtual reality complex that entertains as well as educates. When the CEO of Gametime is captured and Gametime crashes, trapping millions of users online, Frank Gobi is called in to investigate the kidnapping and restore the system. Sequels: *MIR* and *CHI*.

***Death Dream* by Ben Bova**   In an effort to create an amusement park to rival Disneyland, Kyle Muncrief hires unstable but brilliant Jace Lowery and his partner, Dan Santorini. Muncrief dreams of creating a Virtual Reality Complex where all dreams can become possible. But the complex seems doomed from the start with myriad problems ranging from financial difficulties to unexplained murders. Throughout it all, Dan tries to rein in Jace's wildly unconventional plan and still protect his family from becoming the next victims.

***The Wonderland Gambit* by Jack L. Chalker**   Cory Maddox was on the verge of abject poverty when Alan Stark entered his life and offered him the chance to work on a new virtual reality program. But Stark is on the edge not just of creating virtual reality, but of controlling reality itself. And whoever can control reality can become a god. Titles in series: *The Cybernetic Walrus, The March Hare Network, The Hot-Wired Dodo*.

***Caverns of Socrates* by Dennis L. McKiernan**   They were the Black Foxes, the best virtual reality adventurers in the world, and they had the privilege of testing Avery. Avery is a self-aware computer designed to be the ultimate virtual reality experience. Under the watchful eyes of Avery's creators, the Black Foxes enter the VR world and begin the adventure of a lifetime. Unfortunately for the Foxes, with each challenge bested, Avery grows more and more determined to defeat them. Suddenly Avery cuts off the Foxes from the outside world, trapping them in the computer's VR world. For the researchers watching from the outside, it becomes a race against time to get the Foxes safely out of VR. For the

Foxes, it's a race to defeat the Demon Queen and, therefore, defeat Avery at its own game.

Donnerjack by Roger Zelazny and Jane Lindskold   When the worldwide computer net crashed, the world of Virtu was created. Virtu is a virtual reality environment coexisting beside our world, called Verite. Inside Virtu the Gods of myth are planning to invade and conquer Verite, and only the hero Donnerjack stands in the way of their plans. Donnerjack is John D'Arcy, one of the creators of Virtu. His son is the first child born of both worlds and could mean the difference between the success and failure of the Gods' plans.

Other Recommended Titles

Glimpses by Roger Alexander

Killobyte by Piers Anthony

Virtuosity by Terry Bisson

Fortunate Fall by Raphael Carter

Circuit of Heaven by Dennis Danvers

Fourth World by Dennis Danvers

The Sherwood Game by Esther Friesner

Red Dust by Paul McAuley

Signal to Noise by Eric S. Nylund

Night Sky Mine by Melissa Scott

Trouble and Her Friends by Melissa Scott

The Silicon Man by Charles Platt

Virtually Eliminated by Jefferson Scott

Cyberstorm by Gloria Skurzynski

Virtual War by Gloria Skurzynski

DEREK'S PICK

Death Dream by Ben Bova

BEST PICK FOR THE RELUCTANT READER

Caverns of Socrates by Dennis L. McKiernan

8

It's the End of the World

Holocaust Fiction

Repent! The End Is Near! The end of the world is, for some reason, a favorite topic of science-fiction writers. Whether it is a globe-destroying asteroid or the geological equivalent of heartburn, the destruction of Earth makes for captivating reading. The books in this chapter fall into three categories: pre-holocaust, during the holocaust, and post-holocaust. Pre-holocaust stories take place when the disaster is pending and humankind must find a way to avoid it. During the holocaust, the disaster is unfolding and humankind must find a way to survive. Post-holocaust is the most popular category for science-fiction writers. An example of post-holocaust fiction: the button has been pushed, and humankind has been nuked and is living in the rubble (with the cockroaches, of course).

***Parable of the Sower* by Octavia Butler**   Lauren Olamina is an empath living in one of the walled cities prevalent after the collapse of civilization. Lauren feels the pain of others, and when her village is destroyed, she takes her talent on the road hoping to help people. During her travels she is joined by other refugees. Lauren and her followers, after many mishaps on the road, reach haven in northern California, where they settle to teach Lauren's new philosophy of Earthseed.

***The Hammer of God* by Arthur C. Clarke**   The year is 2110 and human-kind is enjoying an era of unparalleled peace and prosperity. All that has been achieved is threatened by a rogue asteroid on a collision course with Earth. As humans race to marshal the resources to prevent the collision, a sect of religious fanatics sees the asteroid as the divine will of God and will do anything to sabotage the anticollision efforts.

***Blind Waves* by Steven Gould**   After the polar ice caps melt, the sea level of the world rises a hundred feet, dislocating millions and isolating whole societies. In New Galveston, a floating city located over the sunken coast of Texas, Patricia Beeman ekes out a living as a salvage diver. But everything changes when Patricia locates a freighter recently sunk by military-grade ordinance, with a hold full of dead and chained immigrants. Frightened by the implications, Patricia flees, only to be pursued by an Immigration and Naturalization patrol boat. Meeting INS Commander Thomas Bechet, she falls in love with him, thereby dragging him into a plot more serious than the two can imagine. Patricia and Thomas must investigate quickly in order to extricate themselves from the mess before they, and the rest of humanity, pay the ultimate price.

***Dreamsnake* by Vonda McIntyre**   Living in a world blasted and torn apart by an ancient war, Snake makes her living as a healer. To assist her in the healing arts, Snake uses an alien being called a Dreamsnake. When it is killed by the very people that Snake is trying to help, she feels like she's been stripped of all her powers. Then she discovers that she can obtain another Dreamsnake, and, to retrieve it, she sets off on a perilous quest that will challenge all her abilities and could cost her her life.

***A Canticle for Liebowitz* by Walter F. Miller Jr.**   In the future the Earth has been destroyed by a nuclear holocaust. In a knee-jerk reaction, the survivors of the holocaust have purged society of all doctors, scientists, historians, and so on. Enter Liebowitz, a scientist who is collecting books and moving them into the Catholic Church. He is caught and slowly tortured to death for the crime of harboring books and knowledge. In response, he is made a martyr by the church, and the Holy Order of Liebowitz is formed to make him a saint. As *A Canticle for Liebowitz* opens, a novice has discovered an ancient document of Liebowitz's: a shopping list for pastrami, kraut, and bagels. *A Canticle for Liebowitz* is a story of faith in the face of adversity. Winner of the 1961 Hugo Award.

Other Recommended Titles

Glimpses by Roger Alexander

Mercycle by Piers Anthony

The Gaia Websters by Kim Antieau

Manifold: Time by Stephen Baxter

Moonseed by Stephen Baxter

The Postman by David Brin

Aftermath by Levar Burton

Dawn by Octavia Butler

The Folk on the Fringe by Orson Scott Card

Killing Time: A Novel of the Future by Caleb Carr

Virtual Light by William Gibson

The Paratwa Saga by Christopher Hinz

Bloom by Wil McCarthy

Eternity Road by Jack McDevitt

Moonfall by Jack McDevitt

Souls in the Great Machine by Sean McMullen

The Iron Bridge by David E. Morse

Aftermath by Charles Sheffield

Wheelers by Jan Stewart and Jack Cohen

Lethe by Tricia Sullivan

The Rift by Walter Williams

DEREK'S PICK

A Canticle for Liebowitz by Walter F. Miller Jr.

BEST PICK FOR THE RELUCTANT READER

Parable of the Sower by Octavia Butler

9

Alternate History

For years SF stood for speculative fiction because of its "what if" component, and alternate history is a big part of that "what if" component. The most popular "what if" theme to explore is "what would have happened if the Nazis had won World War II?" This makes up a large portion of the alternate history subgenre of science fiction. Alternate history takes the established history of events, usually changes the outcome of one of these events, and then explores what would have happened from there.

***Fatherland* by Robert Harris**   In 1942, German fortunes of war were very different—Germany wins the war and controls much of Europe and the U.S.S.R. In 1964, as Germany prepares to celebrate Hitler's seventy-fifth birthday, Berlin cop Xavier March is called upon to investigate two homicides. The victims are retired Nazi officials. As Xavier, with the help of American journalist Charlie Maguire, investigates the murders, he uncovers a top secret cover-up that could destroy everything the Nazis have created.

***Stars and Stripes Forever* by Harry Harrison**   During the American Civil War, Union forces stopped a British ship, removing two Confederate ambassadors to Britain. Incensed over this insult to its sovereignty, Britain (actually Queen Victoria) declares war in a fit of vengeance. In our time stream, war was avoided by the calming influence of the queen's consort, Prince Albert. In *Stars and Stripes Forever,* Prince Albert dies before he can calm things down. Just like during the Revolution, the English invade through Canada and the Union is faced with fighting a war on two fronts. Then the British accidentally attack a Southern port, causing the Union and Confederate armies to unite in the common cause of ridding America of the British army. Sequel: *Stars and Stripes in Peril.*

The Age of Unreason Series by J. Gregory Keyes   In this series alchemy is more science than magic, and Sir Isaac Newton has become a master of alchemy. Meanwhile a young Ben Franklin in the American Colonies has unwittingly made an enemy through his own alchemical research, forcing him to flee to Newton's protection. But Newton has troubles of his own, as he has discovered Philosopher's Mercury, an element that King Louis XIV hopes to use to create the devastating weapon known as Newton's Cannon. Louis hopes that by using the cannon he will finally defeat Britain. But dark forces are mobilizing against Newton, even as plots evolve in an attempt to thwart Louis. Titles in the series: *Newton's Cannon, A Calculus of Angels, Empire of Unreason.*

***Empire of Fear* by Brian Stableford**   In the eighteenth century much of Europe is ruled by vampires, who achieved power during the Dark Ages. Edmund Cordery, an advisor to England's vampire-ruler Richard the Lionhearted, is researching the biology of vampirism in the hope of ending the vampires' domination of European politics. But Edmund's search will take him to the depths of Africa and of his own soul, where he is faced with the knowledge that he may have to pay the ultimate price to gain freedom for Europe.

***The Guns of the South* by Harry Turtledove**   The year is 1864 and the Confederate army is just a pale shadow of its former glory after a string of defeats that began with the loss at Gettysburg. But just at the army's darkest hour, Confederate General Robert E. Lee is approached by a man who offers him an astounding weapon called the AK-47. With the new weapon's ability to fire more rounds accurately, the South immediately turns the tide in the war, decimating the Union army. There is only one problem: The AK-47 won't be invented for another eighty-five years. Who could be supplying this futuristic weapon and what are their plans for the fledgling Confederate government?

Other Recommended Titles

Brother Termite by Patricia Anthony

Voyage by Stephen Baxter

Dinosaur Summer by Greg Bear

Hitler Victorious by Gregory Benford

S.S.-G.B. Nazi Occupied Great Britain 1941 by Len Deighton

The Steampunk Trilogy by Paul Di Filippo

An Oblique Approach by David Drake

The Two Georges by Richard Dreyfuss and Harry Turtledove

Celestial Matters by Richard Garfinkle

The Eden Trilogy by Harry Harrison

Of Tangible Ghosts by L. E. Modesitt Jr.

Apacheria by Jake Page

For Want of a Nail: If Burgoyne Had Won at Saratoga by Robert Sobel

The Draka Series by S. M. Stirling

The Great War Series by Harry Turtledove

World War Series by Harry Turtledove

Darwinia by Robert Charles Wilson

DEREK'S PICK

Fatherland by Robert Harris

BEST PICK FOR THE RELUCTANT READER

Stars and Stripes Forever by Harry Harrison

10

Time Travel

A generation which ignores history has no past and no future.
                                                    —Robert A. Heinlein

Everybody has at least one event that they would love to go back in time and change if they could. Some would like to go back to Dallas, Texas, on November 22, 1963, and unload the bullet that was used to assassinate President Kennedy. Others would go back in time to Pearl Harbor on December 7, 1941, and warn the officers of the impending Japanese attack. But this is not all that time-travel fiction is about. Other uses of time travel include research (why go through all those historical documents and interviews with survivors when you can observe it firsthand?); entertainment (go back in time and walk like an Egyptian—literally); and as a place of residence (go back and live in the time of the American Civil War).

There are two types of time-travel fiction: science fiction and fantasy. The key to understanding the difference between the two types is to recognize the manner of travel the character utilizes. If the character uses a machine, psychic ability, or some other form of technology, then it is science fiction. If the character happens to trip over a magical toadstool while touring Celtic sites in Ireland and wakes up in the past, then it is fantasy time travel. In other words, if the means of travel is mystical or otherwise unexplained, then it is fantasy. Unfortunately, not many books are strictly fantasy time travel. A number of romance books utilize a fantasy time-travel component, but as these books concentrate on the romance and just use time travel as a means of telling the story, they will not be included in this book.

SCIENCE-FICTION TIME TRAVEL

The Novels of the Company (series) by Kage Baker   In the year 2335, the most powerful entity on the planet is a company called Dr. Zeus Incorporated. The Company became the most powerful entity because of two great discoveries—the secret to immortality and practical time travel. Some say that Dr. Zeus discovered immortality through time travel. In reality, the Company discovered time travel as the only way to test immortality. The Company then found the answer to a question that has perplexed scholars and philosophers alike: Can the past be changed? The answer is no. The Company then set out to send its agents backward in time to influence people to make the correct investments so that hundreds of years later, the Company has wealth beyond imagination. The Company also went into the past seeking agents who could be made immortal through cybernetic implants. These agents would then be trained to work for the Company. Mendoza is one of these agents, rescued from the Spanish Inquisition and trained as a botanist for the Company. Titles in the series: *In the Garden of Iden, Sky Coyote, Mendoza in Hollywood, The Graveyard Game.*

Kindred by **Octavia Butler**   On her twenty-sixth birthday, an African-American writer named Dana Franklin receives a life-altering gift: She is sent back in time to the 1840s in the South. There she has to save the life of Rufus, the white son of a slave owner and, as Dana discovers, one of her ancestors. If she doesn't save his life and allow him to rape his slave Alice Greenwood (her other ancestor), she will never be born. Dana is eventually made a slave herself and is initiated into the horrors of slavery. How will a modern woman react to slavery?

***Pastwatch: The Redemption of Christopher Columbus* by Orson Scott Card**   In the future, historians of the organization Pastwatch study history in a new way: by watching it "live." The observers can only watch as history unfolds; they can do nothing to intervene in past events. That is, until they realize that someone has done just that, changing the flow of history. What could the interveners have been trying to avoid? Can the damage be fixed, and, if so, what are the consequences of fixing the changes?

***Timeline* by Michael Crichton**   In 1999, archaeologists uncover a note from their team leader—the problem is that the paper and ink used to write the note date from 1357! It seems that the team leader has also been working on a time travel project utilizing quantum mechanics and has become trapped in the past. Now it's up to his students to launch a rescue party to recover the professor. But the rescuers have no idea what deadly surprises await them in the past.

***The Doomsday Book* by Connie Willis**   As a history major, I find the ideas in this book fascinating. In the future, time travel is a tool for historical research, allowing researchers to experience and observe history firsthand. (Why did I spend all that time pawing through pieces of paper when I was an undergraduate?) Student Kivrin Engles is making preparations to travel back to Christmas 1320. But before she can complete the preparations, and before her immunizations can take full effect, her departure time is moved up and she is sent back. Problems continue to arise for Kivrin when she discovers that she isn't in 1320 but in 1348 on the eve of the Black Death, a massive outbreak of bubonic plague. As Kivrin helps the victims of the plague, a mysterious plague strikes the future, endangering everything. Winner of the 1993 Hugo and 1992 Nebula Awards.

Other Recommended Titles

The Depths of Time by Roger MacBride Allen

Catch the Lightning by Catherine Asaro

Time Scout Series by Robert Aspirin and Linda Evans

The Time Ships by Stephen Baxter

Timelike Infinity by Stephen Baxter

Eon by Greg Bear

Timescape by Gregory Benford

Psychoshop by Alfred Bester and Roger Zelazny

No Enemy but Time by Michael Bishop

Orion Series by Ben Bova

Downtiming the Night Side by Jack L. Chalker

Foreign Bodies by Stephen Dedman

Time on My Hands by Peter Delacorte

Days of Cain by J. R. Dunn

Far Edge of Darkness by Linda Evans

Time and Again by Jack Finney

The Cross-Time Engineer Series by Leo Frankowski

12 Monkeys by Elizabeth Hand

The Door into Summer by Robert A. Heinlein

A Very Strange Trip by L. Ron Hubbard and Dave Wolverton

The Seeds of Time by Kay Kenyon

Corrupting Dr. Nice by John Kessel

Outpost by Scott Mackay

Summer of Love by Lisa Mason

Saga of the Pliocene Exile (series) by Julian May

The Iron Bridge by David E. Morse

Lost Millennium by Mike Moscoe

Key out of Time by Andre Norton

Echoes in Time by Andre Norton and Sherwood Smith

Door Number Three by Patrick O'Leary

The Gates of Time Series by Dan Parkinson

The Complete Paratime by H. Beam Piper

Atlantis Found by R. Garcia Y. Roberts

The Virgin and the Dinosaurs by R. Garcia Y. Roberts

End of an Era by Robert J. Sawyer

Thebes of the Hundred Gates by Robert Silverberg

The Time Machine by H. G. Wells

To Say Nothing of the Dog by Connie Willis

Isaac Asimov's Robots in Time Series by William F. Wu

DEREK'S PICK

The Doomsday Book by Connie Willis

BEST PICK FOR THE RELUCTANT READER

Timeline by Michael Crichton

FANTASY TIME TRAVEL

Lest Darkness Falls **by L. Sprague De Camp**   Archaeologist Martin Padway knows more than anyone what happened in the world after the fall of the Roman Empire—a period known as the Dark Ages. Padway is in Rome in the 1930s when he is struck by lightning. When Padway awakens, he finds himself in the sixth century A.D.—just before the fall of the Roman Empire—with no apparent way back to his own time. Padway's immediate concern is how to make a living in this new world. His next concern is to use his knowledge of history to stop the fall of the Roman Empire and thus avert the Dark Ages. Sequel: *To Bring the Light.*

The Dancers at the End of Time **by Michael Moorcock**   This book is part of the Eternal Champions series, which explores the concept of chaos versus order, but you do not have to read any of the other books in the series to understand *Dancers at the End of Time.* In the far future, technology has advanced to the point where humans have developed into beings with godlike powers and near immortality. These beings live at a place called the End of Time. One of these beings, Jherek Carnelian, has grown bored with his life because his people can grant any wish that they desire. Indeed, all of Jherek's and his people's time is spent in the pursuit of diversions, any diversion. The social structure of Jherek's people is arranged around these pursuits; the people with the best diversions are the most influential and powerful in the society. Then a grand diversion enters Jherek's life in the form of Mrs. Amelia Underwood, a traveler from Victorian England (1896, to be exact). Jherek decides to fall in love with Amelia, who does not return his favors because she is already married. This does not deter Jherek in the least and he continues to pursue her, even journeying to 1896 England when she returns to her home. As Jherek's fancy for Amelia turns to a deep and true love, he discovers that it wasn't chance that brought them together in the End of Time—their meeting may have been part of a much larger plot. *The*

Dancers at the End of Time is actually comprised of three novels: *An Alien Heat, The Hollow Lands, The End of All Songs.*

Wolf King by Bridget Wood In the distant future, Earth has been destroyed by nuclear war. Its survivors try to eke out an existence from the ruined soil, while also trying to avoid the irradiated lands called the Glowing Lands. On the blasted island once known as Ireland, Joanna Grady and Flynn O'Connor dream of an Ireland they know only from myths and legends. Then Joanna learns that her father has arranged her marriage to a loutish neighbor, and she flees into the one place where no one will follow: the Glowing Lands. But she has not counted on Flynn pursuing her into the lands. There the two find themselves transported backward in time to an Ireland that they've only dreamed about and to the court of the deadly Wolf King.

Other Recommended Titles

Dracula Unbound by Brian Aldiss

Frankenstein Unbound by Brian Aldiss

Arthur, King by Dennis Lee Anderson

Enchantment by Orson Scott Card

Outlander Series by Diana Gabaldon

Mr. Was by Pete Hautman

Woman on the Edge of Time by Marge Piercy

Beauty by Sheri S. Tepper

The Family Tree by Sheri S. Tepper

DEREK'S PICK

Dancers at the End of Time by Michael Moorcock

BEST PICK FOR THE RELUCTANT READER

Lest Darkness Falls by L. Sprague De Camp

11

Superheroes, Graphic Novels, and Genetic Engineering

SUPERHEROES

Although many of the characters in this book are heroes, few can be considered superheroes. Superheroes are generally humans who have "superhuman" or greater-than-average abilities. Everyone, at one point or another, has wanted to possess some kind of special talent or ability of the superhuman kind. It could be the ability to transport instantaneously from one spot to another, a talent that would be very handy to have on those occasions when the call of nature is very insistent. Or it could be the ability to move at very high speeds like the superhero The Flash. Imagine being able to clean your entire house in under thirty minutes at super speed and then have the rest of the day to yourself!

The fact is that we can identify with superheroes, we admire them, and, deep down, we want to have superheroes in the world. We want to know that there is someone out there to keep us safe, to provide justice, to stop disasters like the 9-11-01 attack from happening. Perhaps the fascination we have with superheroes lies in the bullies we encountered on the playgrounds of our childhood. The natural response to the humiliation we felt at the hands of these bullies is to want to be bigger and stronger. And through young Billy Batson, we can live out this dream. Billy, a 110-pound weakling, only has to speak the word

"Shazaam!" and he is magically transformed into Captain Marvel, the world's mightiest mortal. But possibly the most famous superhero of all time is DC Comics' Superman, created by Jerry Siegel and Joe Shuster. Superman's abilities are varied but he possesses the ability to fly, he has X-ray vision, and he is superhumanly strong. In this chapter, the super-heroes are all based on characters created by DC Comics and Marvel Comics.

***Spider-Man: Venom Factor* by Diane Duane**   Mysteries abound in New York City: Someone is stealing nuclear waste, homeless people are being murdered, and the price of film is skyrocketing. Well, the latter mystery is not much of a concern for most, but for newspaper photog-rapher Peter Parker, it is a major concern. A greater concern for Peter, who is also Spider-Man, the city's defender and resident web slinger, is that evidence found at the latest murder points to the involvement of Spider-Man's enemy, Venom. Venom sees itself as a defender of the weak and would hardly kill people who couldn't defend themselves. As Spider-Man begins to investigate the murders and thefts, he has to keep his eyes peeled and his spidersense alerted for Venom, who has also begun investigating the murders and would like nothing more than to crush a hapless Spider-Man in the process. Soon Spider-Man realizes an even greater menace may be behind the crimes. Can Spider-Man and Venom put aside their differences long enough to solve the crimes? Or will they kill each other rather than work together?

***Spider-Man: Wanted Dead or Alive* by Craig Shaw Gardner**   Tyler Stewart has plans to take over all of New York's crime organizations but a very large obstacle is standing in his way: Spider-Man. To get Spider-Man out of the picture, Tyler hits upon a desperate plan: frame Spider-Man for the murder of an innocent. Soon Spider-Man is Public Enemy Number 1 and must go into hiding. He must find a way to clear his name without drawing attention to himself. Just then, two of his dead-liest enemies, Electro and Rhino, arrive in New York. Can Spider-Man clear his name, capture Electro and Rhino, and avoid the police all at the same time?

***Kingdom Come* by Elliot S. Maggin**   It is the early twenty-first century, and Earth is on the brink of a disaster brought on by her greatest champions. Superman and his colleagues disappeared years previously, leaving Earth in the hands of a younger generation of heroes. Led by the merciless Magog, these younger heroes have no compulsion against killing to stop a supervillain. Soon most of the villains are either dead or in hiding, so the heroes begin battling each other with humankind stuck in the middle. After part of Kansas is destroyed, the old guard of superheroes, with Superman in the vanguard, come out of retirement to put an end to the young heroes' reign of terror. Time is running out for Superman's heroes in their battle to rein in the younger heroes, because humankind has decided to take the ultimate step and end the war once and for all by destroying all heroes.

Batman: Knightfall by **Dennis O'Neil**   For years while he was imprisoned in South America, Bane has dreamed of one thing: the total destruction of Batman. Immediately after his escape from the prison, Bane makes his way to Gotham City to learn all he can about his nemesis, including the fact that Batman is in reality billionaire Bruce Wayne. The next step in Bane's plan is to wear Batman down by releasing all the inmates of the Arkham Asylum for the Criminally Insane. Over the next few days, Batman doesn't rest as he hunts down some of the most dangerous criminals on the planet. Finally, on the edge of exhaustion, Batman is confronted by Bane. The confrontation ends with Batman's broken body being hurled down to the streets of Gotham as Bane proclaims himself King of Gotham. Batman is forced to pass the mantle of the Bat to the young hero Azrael. But is Azrael ready to assume the role of Gotham's Protector?

The Death and Life of Superman by **Roger Stern**   Would you be willing to die in order to protect all that you hold dear? This question confronts Superman when he is forced to battle Doomsday, a genetically engineered living weapon that has already defeated many of the world's greatest heroes. Superman's answer is yes as he valiantly dies while stopping Doomsday, and the world is forced to face a future without a Superman. Almost immediately after Superman's funeral, his body is taken from the crypt, and the world holds its collective breath as sightings of four different supermen begin occurring. But which is the real Superman?

Other Recommended Titles

Spider-Man: Goblin Moon by Kurt Busiek and Nathan Archer

X-Men: Soul Killer by Richard Lee Byers

Gamma Quest by Greg Cox (X-Men and Avengers)

Iron Man: The Armor Trap by Greg Cox

Time's Arrow Series by Tom Defalco and Jason Henderson (X-Men and Spider-Man)

Spider-Man: The Lizard Sanction by Diane Duane

Spider-Man: The Octopus Agenda by Diane Duane

X-Men: Empire's End by Diane Duane

X-Men: Shadows of the Past by Michael Jan Friedman

Codename: Wolverine by Christopher Golden

Spider-Man: Carnage in New York by David Michelinie and Dean Wesley Smith

Prisoner X by Ann Nocenti (X-Men)

Batman: No Man's Land by Greg Rucka

X-Men by Kristine Rusch

Spider-Man: Emerald Mystery by Dean Wesley Smith

Spider-Man: Goblin's Revenge by Dean Wesley Smith and Greg Cox

Spiderman: Valley of the Lizard by John Vornholt

DEREK'S PICK

Batman: Knightfall by Dennis O'Neil

BEST PICK FOR THE RELUCTANT READER

Kingdom Come by Elliot S. Maggin

GRAPHIC NOVELS

Comic books are dangerous to the American way of life.
A child raised on comics can't help but grow up with a
questing mind, an expanding imagination, a sense
of wonder, a desire to know what makes things tick.
No wonder our gilded conservatives are afraid of them.

—Alan Dean Foster

How graphic are graphic novels? Not very graphic at all, actually. Graphic novels are bound collections of superhero comics. They could be a collection of comics that were published as part of a monthly series or a special story line about a character or group of characters that was written for onetime publication. The latter books may not even match the time line and events chronicled in the monthly comics. The following novels are suitable for library shelves because they contain no nudity, profanity, or graphic violence.

Marvels by Kurt Busiek and Alex Ross

Batman: Thrillkiller by Howard Chaykin

The Incredible Hulk: Future Imperfect by Peter David

The Last Avengers Story by Peter David

Batman: Knightfall Who Rules the Night by Chuck Dixon

Batman: Prodigal by Chuck Dixon

Bloodties: Featuring the Avengers, Avengers West Coast, and the X-Men by Matt Idelson

Ultimate Spider-Man: Power and Responsibility by Bill Jemas

The Inhumans by Paul Jenkins

Hulk: Transformations by Stan Lee

X-Men: The Dark Phoenix Saga by Stan Lee

Batman: The Long Halloween by Jeph Loeb

Superman for All Seasons by Jeph Loeb

Green Lantern: Aliens by Ron Marz

DC versus Marvel by Ron Marz, Peter David, and Bob Kahan

Ultimate X-Men by Mark Millar

Batman: The Dark Knight Returns by Frank Miller

Batman: Year One by Frank Miller

Daredevil: Born Again by Frank Miller

Ronin by Frank Miller

Batman: The Killing Joke by Alan Moore

Swamp Thing: The Curse by Alan Moore

Top Ten by Alan Moore

Watchmen by Alan Moore

JLA: World War III by Grant Morrison

JLA: Earth Two by Grant Morrison and Frank Quietly

Earth X by Alex Ross

Marvel Super-Heroes: Secret Wars by Jim Shooter et al.

Batman: A Death in the Family by Jim Starlin

The Infinity Gauntlet by Jim Starlin

The Flash: Race against Time! by Mark Waid

JLA: Tower of Babel by Mark Waid

Kingdome Come by Mark Waid

Green Lantern: New Journey, Old Path by Judd Winick

Batman: A Lonely Place of Dying by Marv Wolfman

Crisis on Infinite Earths by Marv Wolfman

GENETIC ENGINEERING

There has been much discussion in the news of the morality of cloning a human being. Many feel that cloning is thwarting God's divine will, while others feel that it is just plain . . . creepy to clone a human being. But as human delve deeper into the genetic code in search of the technology of cloning humans, a whole new host of concerns is created. With a complete understanding of the genetic code, humankind would then be able to *manipulate* that code to eliminate things like viruses and diseases. Doctors would also be able to repair at the cellular level problems like poor eyesight and hearing, as well as fix much larger concerns like failed or damaged organs. Theoretically doctors would also be able to design a perfect human from *conception,* which could lead to the following implausible scenario:

> *Doctor:* Okay, Mr. and Mrs. Simpson, I understand you're ready to start a family. Have you chosen a sex for your child yet?

Mrs. Simpson: Oh yes, we'd like to have a boy.

Doctor: Excellent. We have several packages of career development you might be interested in for your son. We have the Scientist Package for $300,000, the Scholar for $350,000, the Doctor for $500,000, and the Stellar Athlete for $1,200,000.

Mr. Simpson: Athlete! Can he be a football player?

Mrs. Simpson: Honey! We discussed the lawyer package!

Doctor: I'm sorry, but the Cloning Rights Act of 2324 outlawed the offering of that particular package, Mrs. Simpson.

Mrs. Simpson: Oh. How about the Doctor Package?

Mr. Simpson (Resigned sigh): Fine.

Doctor: Excellent. Now for $1,500 we can make sure your son doesn't have acne.

Mrs. Simpson: Oh dear. Uh . . .

Mr. Simpson: No acne! The girls won't like him if he has acne!

Mrs. Simpson: Oh, all right.

Doctor: All right. And would you like your son to have perfect eyesight? It will cost an additional $3,000.

Mrs. Simpson: But I thought that was part of the Total Health Package?

Doctor: Oh no, that just covers good health, but if you happen to have our perfect eyesight coupon from our website, you can have it for free.

Mrs. Simpson: No . . . no, we don't have a coupon. Oh dear, this is getting expensive.

Doctor: Well, we do have a package that includes perfect eyesight, hearing guaranteed good for sixty years, and straight teeth for $6,000.

Mr. Simpson: We'll take it.

Although the preceding may have been in jest, the benefits of genetic engineering or manipulation could be quite great. Disease and viruses would most likely be the first targets of geneticists. Another use of genetic engineering would be to create a human who is faster, stronger, and smarter than most humans, like the heroine of the popular television show *Dark Angel*. Another use would be to combine human DNA with animal DNA to create a creature with the strength of a gorilla, the speed of a cheetah, and the intelligence of a human. The books in this section either involve genetic engineering as the subject matter or have genetically engineered characters.

Falling Free **by Lois McMaster Bujold**   Leo Graf is an engineer who just wants to do his job, without politics and bureaucracies. But this isn't going to happen in his new job in charge of training at the zero-gravity facility Cay Habitat. At Cay Habitat, scientists have been developing the "Quaddies"—beings genetically engineered to work in a zero-gravity environment. Instead of two arms and two legs like a human being, the Quaddies have four arms, which enable them to adapt to work and life in a zero-gravity environment much more easily than a human. At first reluctant to train the Quaddies for work in zero gravity, Graf soon overcomes his misgivings and begins training them. But a rival company has developed a technology that makes the Quaddies obsolete. Unfortunately, the scientists at Cay Habitat do not see the Quaddies as human beings but as property that can be disposed of as needed. Graf is horrified by this decision and is faced with a difficult choice: stay in the safety of his work as an engineer or begin training the Quaddies in a new skill—how to fight back. Winner of the 1988 Nebula Award. Note: Although this book is set in the same universe as Bujold's Vorkosigan saga, it takes place two hundred years before the saga and doesn't relate to the events portrayed in the saga.

Friday **by Robert A. Heinlein**   Friday is an AP, an Artificial Person, not a robot or android but a person genetically designed to be smarter, faster, and stronger than a normal person. As Friday states: "My mother was a test tube, my father was a knife." This statement sums up the truth of Friday's existence very well. APs are not respected or liked in the future, and Friday must always be conscious of not revealing her true nature to anyone, which makes for a very lonely existence indeed. Normally it isn't a problem in her job as a courier for a man called Boss, but when she is not working, she finds herself searching desperately for a meaningful relationship, for a family that will accept her for what she is.

SUPERHEROES, GRAPHIC NOVELS, AND GENETIC ENGINEERING

Beggars Trilogy by Nancy Kress   What if you no longer needed sleep? In the future, humans have been genetically designed to not require sleep. They are also physically perfect and highly intelligent. These beings have been named the Sleepless, and Leisha Camden is one of them. But tensions are high between the Sleepless and Sleepers (normal humans) because of the enhanced performance and longevity of the Sleepless. This forces the Sleepless to establish an orbiting space station as a sanctuary in order to continue their experiments. Leisha, meanwhile, stays on Earth as an advocate of peace between the Sleepless and Sleepers. But unbeknownst to Leisha, the Sleepless have launched a plan to reclaim Earth by removing the indigenous population. Series: *Beggars in Spain, Beggars and Choosers, Beggars Ride. Beggars in Spain* won the Nebula Award in 1991 and the Hugo Award in 1992 for best novella.

Chimera **by Will Shetterly**   In the twenty-first century, gene splicing has allowed the creation of Chimeras, part human and part animal. Chimeras are not considered human but are considered property, and this leads to trouble for a private investigator named Chase Maxwell. A Chimera named Zoe wants Chase to investigate the murder of her human friend, roboticist Janna Gold. Zoe claims that Gold was murdered by a copbot, an action that is unthinkable because copbots are programmed not to kill. Reprogramming the copbot is believed to be impossible, but all evidence points to just that scenario. Zoe also has in her possession a device that many would kill to obtain, a device that allows the user to shut down any robot. While investigating Gold's murder, Zoe and Maxwell are implicated in the murder of a prominent Chimera rights advocate, forcing them to go into hiding. Adding to the tension are the artificial intelligence advocates who see Chimeras as opposing rights for AI—and they'll do anything to achieve those rights.

The Island of Doctor Moreau **by H. G. Wells**   In the South Seas, a shipwrecked passenger finds refuge on a tropical island that on cursory inspection is a paradise. But the evil Dr. Moreau has taken up residence on the island to pursue experiments that blur the line between animals and humans. Dr. Moreau's surgical creations are hideous animals that possess remarkable intelligence and, when released, become more dangerous than either human or beast.

SUPERHEROES, GRAPHIC NOVELS, AND GENETIC ENGINEERING

Other Recommended Titles

Climbing Olympus by Kevin J. Anderson

The Secret of Spring by Piers Anthony

Spider Legs by Piers Anthony

Primary Inversion by Catherine Asaro

Manifold: Time by Stephen Baxter

Orion Series by Ben Bova

Glory Season by David Brin

The Mayflower Trilogy by Orson Scott Card

Killing Time by Caleb Carr

Cyteen by C. J. Cherryh

Hunted by James Alan Gardner

Accidental Creatures by Anne Harris

The Paratwa Saga by Christopher Hinz

Flowers for Algernon by Daniel Keyes

Beggars in Spain by Nancy Kress

Maximum Light by Nancy Kress

Rebel Sutra by Shariann Lewitt

The Confluence by Paul J. McAuley

Fairyland by Paul J. McAuley

Gravity Dreams by L. E. Modesitt Jr.

Cold as Ice by Charles Sheffield

Virtual War by Gloria Skurzynski

Schisimatrix by Bruce Sterling

Starfish by Peter Watts

Armed Memory by Jim Young

DEREK'S PICK

Friday by Robert A. Heinlein

BEST PICK FOR THE RELUCTANT READER

Chimera by Will Shetterly

12

Thrills and Chills in Zero Gravity

Science-Fiction Mysteries and Thrillers

Many people are confused about the difference between a mystery and a thriller. The difference lies in murder. A mystery involves the murder of one or more individuals by persons unknown, and the main character must investigate and discover the guilty party. A thriller, on the other hand, although it may have murders of individuals, usually involves a conspiracy of some kind that takes precedence over the murders. Often the main character investigates to uncover the conspiracy as a lifesaving measure because he or she has become the target of powerful individuals and organizations who wish to keep the conspiracy a secret. The conspiracy could also involve a governmental agency's activities or a new technology with the potential to change the world.

MYSTERIES

Science-fiction mysteries are, literally, mysteries that take place in a science-fiction setting. Sometimes technology or science is used to solve the murder that has been committed, or the victim was murdered by someone using technology. Most often, however, technology and science form the background of the story and help move the plot along, but ultimately the murder and subsequent investigation are the focus of the plot.

***Archangel* by Michael Conner**　In an alternate reality, World War I ended after the German high command released a terrible blood disease called Hun. In the years that followed, the Hun virus killed millions of whites, leaving those of African descent unscathed. In the late 1920s, Minneapolis newspaper reporter Danny Constantine has discovered a series of murders that look like the work of a vampire. Teamed with a black police detective, Danny must dig deep to discover the identity of the murderer, even when his own newspaper refuses to carry the story.

***Cyber Way* by Alan Dean Foster**　Detective Vernon Moody of the Tampa Bay Police Department is an expert in twenty-first-century sleuthing. Utilizing computers, the Internet, databases, and the latest electronic equipment, Vernon always gets his man. Vernon's latest case, involving the murders of wealthy art collector Elroy Kettrick and his housekeeper, will prove to be the strangest and most difficult of his career. Only one clue was found at the murder scene: the remains of a large sand painting. Why would the assailant ignore the obvious wealth of the Kettrick mansion and destroy only the sand painting? The search for the answer leads Vernon to the land of the Navajo and more questions than he bargained for.

***A Quantum Murder* by Peter F. Hamilton**　When Greg Mandel is called in to investigate the murder of physicist Edward Kitchner, he figured it would be an open-and-shut case. After all, only six other people had access to the laboratory. But when Mandel uses his powers of empathy and intuition to interrogate the suspects, he is shocked to find that all of them are innocent. Who could have killed Kitchner if not one of the six suspects? Could one of them have hidden the truth from Mandel's powers? Although second in the Greg Mandel series, this can be read as a stand-alone novel. First book: *Mindstar Rising;* third book: *The Nano Flower.*

***Murder in the Solid State* by Wil McCarthy**　David Sanger's latest invention has the potential to make the Vandegroot sniffer obsolete. The only problem is that Otto Vandegroot, the inventor of the sniffer, is not happy about this happening. When the two researchers cross paths at a research conference, Vandegroot challenges David to a duel. Vandegroot is humiliated when David defeats him. David is shocked to later learn that Vandegroot has been murdered and David is the prime suspect! To find the murderer, David must move quickly before the police can catch him and throw him in jail.

Bimbos of the Death Sun by **Sharyn McCrumb**   Although not technically a science-fiction mystery, *Bimbos of the Death Sun* takes place at a science-fiction and fantasy convention. Best-selling fantasy author Appin Dungannon is famous for two things: his sword and sorcery series revolving around the hero Tratyn Runewind, and his overpowering ego. His ego and arrogance lead Appin to treat his fans like scum and may be what lead to his murder at the convention. When the police arrive to investigate, they are perplexed about who would want to murder a fantasy author. For the convention guests more familiar with Appin, the question is "Who wouldn't?" Sequel: *Zombies of the Gene Pool*.

Other Recommended Titles

Isaac Asimov's Caliban by Roger MacBride Allen

Happy Policeman by Patricia Anthony

The Robot Series by Isaac Asimov

Murder at the Galactic Writers' Society by Janet Asimov

The Demolished Man by Alfred Bester

Tea from an Empty Cup by Pat Cadigan

When Gravity Fails by George Alec Effinger

The Shift by George Foy

Circle of One by Eric James Fullilove

Flesh and Gold by Phyllis Gotlieb

Nimbus by Alexander Jabkklokov

Noir by K. W. Jeter

Polar City Blues by Katherine Kerr

Dancing on Air by Nancy Kress

Legacy of Lehr by Katherine Kurtz

Dream Park Series by Larry Niven and Steven Barnes

Too, Too Solid Flesh by Nick O'Donohoe

The Digital Effect by Steve Perry

Sherlock Holmes in Orbit by Mike Resnick

Destroying Angel by Richard Paul Russo

Golden Fleece by Robert Sawyer

Illegal Alien by Robert Sawyer

The Terminal Experiment by Robert Sawyer

Chimera by Will Shetterly

Passion Play by Sean Stewart

Reunion on Neverend by John E. Stith

Mirage: An Isaac Asimov's Robots Mystery by Mark W. Tiedmann

Manjinn Moon by Denise Vitola

DEREK'S PICK

Archangel by Michael Conner

BEST PICK FOR THE RELUCTANT READER

Bimbos of the Death Sun by Sharyn McCrumb

THRILLERS

Science-fiction thrillers, much like science-fiction mysteries, are thrillers in a science-fiction setting. Technology plays a much larger role in science-fiction thrillers than in science-fiction mysteries because the technology frequently forms the basis of the conspiracy. Technology and science don't *have* to be the basis of the conspiracy, but they do have to at least form the backdrop of the story, assisting the conspiracy.

Cosm by Gregory Benford Physicist Alicia Butterworth runs experiments to study the conditions that existed before the Big Bang. One of the experiments goes awry, causing an explosion that destroys the lab. In the debris Alicia finds a metallic sphere made of a material that defies explanation. Alicia and her team find that the sphere is a cosm, a pocket of time and space that is a microscopic universe sealed off from our universe. Time moves much faster in the cosm, allowing the researchers a ringside seat to evolution. But there are groups interested in the cosm, and Alicia's team must work fast to unlock the secrets of the sphere before it can be taken from them. Soon Alicia realizes that the cosm's energies may not be safely contained within the sphere and, if released, could spell disaster for the residents of our universe.

Jurassic Park by Michael Crichton The idea was nothing short of brilliant. The results were nothing short of disastrously terrifying. The plan was to extract dinosaur DNA from insects trapped in amber, repair the damaged portions of the DNA with frog DNA, and grow dinosaurs. The dinosaurs could then be viewed by the public at the newly created Jurassic Park. The park planners thought they had developed a perfectly safe environment for the public. By ensuring the birth of only female dinosaurs, the scientists thought they had a fail-safe way to keep the population of dinosaurs in check. They were all wrong—dead wrong. Sequel: *The Lost World.*

***Foreign Bodies* by Stephen Dedman**   In 2014, Mike Galloway has forged a tentative friendship with a homeless stripper named Swiftie, who has taken up residence on his balcony. One day Mike's life is turned upside down when he awakens to find himself in Swiftie's body and the being he knew as Swiftie in possession of his body. Soon Mike discovers that Swiftie is in fact a member of a secret organization, and her mind has been sent from the future to inhabit Swiftie's body. But what nefarious plan necessitates sending a group member's mind into the past?

***Nocturne for a Dangerous Man* by Marc Matz**   Gavilan Robie recovers lost things for a living. Mostly he looks for missing art, but on occasion he looks for lost people. Such is the case with Siv Mathiessen, the executive of a large corporation, who has been kidnapped by ecoterrorists. Convinced that Siv will be killed, the company hires Gavilan to track her down. Gavilan utilizes many tools to help in the search, but his most useful tool is a computer simulation of Siv. So realistic is the simulation that Gavilan finds himself falling for the beguiling woman. Just as Gavilan is close to finding Siv, the stakes are raised by the ecoterrorists with deadly results.

***The Icarus Hunt* by Timothy Zahn**   In the far future, the Patth control the technology of the Patth drive, which allows for hyperspace travel. Jordan McKell and his alien partner, Izil, are freelance shippers trying to eke out a living in the shadow of the Patth's shipping monopoly. McKell and Izil are approached to do a very strange job. The job is to fly the bizarrely designed ship *Icarus* and its mysterious cargo to Earth. The cargo is so mysterious that it is sealed in its own chamber, which makes up most of the ship. Jordan soon realizes that a murderer and saboteur is on board. As the *Icarus* makes its way toward Earth, it becomes apparent that the cargo it carries poses a serious threat not only to the Patth monopoly but to organized crime as well. Jordan has to think and act quickly to keep one step ahead of both as he tries to unravel the ship's mysteries on the journey to Earth.

Other Recommended Titles

Conscience of the Beagle by Patricia Anthony

Mute by Piers Anthony

Virtuosity by Terry Bisson

Death Dream by Ben Bova

Sphere by Michael Crichton

Beholder's Eye by Julie Czerneda

Bodyguard by William C. Dietz

Mars Prime by William C. Dietz

The Two Georges by Richard Dreyfuss and Harry Turtledove

The Abductors: Conspiracy by Jonathan Frakes

Vigilant by James Alan Gardner

Idoru by William Gibson

Blind Waves by William Gould

Mindstar Rising by Peter Hamilton

Back to the Moon by Homer Hickam

Maximum Light by Nancy Kress

Pitch Black by Frank Lauria and David Twohy

Ancient Shores by Jack McDevitt

The Engines of God by Jack McDevitt

Infinity Beach by Jack McDevitt

Saturn's Race by Larry Niven and Steven Barnes

Terminal Games by Cole Perriman

The World at the End of Time by Frederick Pohl

Marrow by Robert Reed

Icehenge by Kim Stanley Robinson

The Memory of Whiteness by Kim Stanley Robinson

Tek War by William Shatner

The Compleat McAndrew by Charles Sheffield

In the Cube by David Alexander Smith

Code of Conduct by Kristine Smith

The Jericho Iteration by Allen M. Steele

Oceanspace by Allen M. Steele

The Fresco by Sheri S. Tepper

Mirage by F. Paul Wilson

DEREK'S PICK

The Icarus Hunt by Timothy Zahn

BEST PICK FOR THE RELUCTANT READER

Jurassic Park by Michael Crichton

BIOTECH THRILLERS

Biotech thrillers basically involve nature gone wrong. Whether it's a deadly virus rampaging through the population or a mutation of the human body, humankind must race against time to find a cure before all life is wiped out on Earth.

***The Andromeda Strain* by Michael Crichton** Many people envision Earth's first contact with aliens to be of the little green men variety. In *The Andromeda Strain,* Michael Crichton sees a first contact of the single cell variety. Bacteriologist Jerome Stone has been on a crusade to have the government institute a program to decontaminate astronauts upon their return from space. He is surprised when the government suddenly agrees and quickly builds a facility called the Wildfire Lab. Unbeknownst to Project Wildfire, the army has been using satellites to collect alien pathogens from space to use in the most deadly round of biological warfare. When one of the satellites crashes, a virus is released that decimates a quiet town, forcing Wildfire to scramble to contain the virus before it can destroy the world's population.

***Virus Clans: A Story of Evolution* by Michael Kanaly** Billions of years ago, life evolved on a distant planet. Consequently, viruses arose as well. Over the years the viruses evolved along with the life-form, eventually overtaking their hosts and spreading to Earth. Fast-forward to the future: entomologist Gary Bracken has discovered that viruses are not only intelligent, but can communicate with each other, forming clans. As Bracken tries to develop a computer program to translate the viruses' communications, the government steps in to shut down the research. This forces Bracken to move his research lab into his basement, where he makes a startling discovery: the viruses have been directing each stage of human evolution, and humankind is on the brink of a new stage of evolution.

***Oaths and Miracles* by Nancy Kress** FBI agent Robert Kavanaugh believes the latest murders he is investigating may be related. On the surface the murders of a showgirl in Las Vegas and a geneticist in Boston would not appear to be related, but soon Kavanaugh is able to uncover clues that point to a common suspect. The geneticist's widow, Judy O'Brien Kozinski, also believes her husband's murder was not a random attack. Together the two are determined to get to the bottom of a conspiracy that points to the possibility of a biological weapon in the hands of the Mob. Sequel: *Stinger.*

***Inherit the Earth* by Brian Stableford** Damon Hart is the son of the savior of humanity. During the twenty-first century, humankind was rendered sterile during the Plague Wars. Conrad Helior (Hart's father) invented the artificial womb, allowing humankind to breed again. In the twenty-second century, nanotechnology has evolved to the point that immortality is possible. But who should be allowed to live forever? This question causes a terrorist group to strike out at Hart in the hope of driving Helior out of hiding.

***Playing God* by Sarah Zettel** The planet All Cradle's population, the Dedelphi, has been decimated by centuries of interspecies war and now faces extinction in the form of a genetically engineered superweapon. The Dedelphi's only hope for survival lies in a desperate alliance of the clans with the human race. The Dedelphi want the help of the humans in cleansing the planet of the plague in exchange for access to the planet's biological resources. But the alliance may be doomed from the outset because the touch of a human is toxic to the Dedelphi, and the Dedelphi just can't stop fighting among themselves.

Other Recommended Titles

Darwin's Radio by Greg Bear
The Brazen Rule by Steven
   Burgauer

The Secret of Life by Paul J.
   McAuley
Brain Plague by Joan Slonczewski

Holy Fire by Bruce
  Stirling

Mirage by F. Paul Wilson

The Bridge by Janine Ellen
  Young

DEREK'S PICK

Inherit the Earth by Brian Stableford

BEST PICK FOR THE RELUCTANT READER

The Andromeda Strain by Michael Crichton

13

Science-Fiction Humor

In the beginning the Universe was created.
This has made a lot of people very angry
and been widely regarded as a bad move.

—Douglas Adams

Nobody is sure exactly why humans as a species feel the need to laugh, but Vilayanur Ramachandran, a researcher at the University of California, has a very intriguing theory. Ramachandran's theory is, in very simple terms, that laughter is the release of built-up tension. This theory helps explain many real-life events. What is the response of someone who has been startled in a haunted house at Halloween? The response is usually fear followed by nervous laughter when the scary monster turns out to be a man in a rubber mask.

Given this context, it is reasonable to assume that laughter today is primarily a means of releasing tension, to make people feel good. Is it any wonder, then, that comedy films and television shows are so popular? Anybody who has attended a science-fiction convention has seen evidence of this firsthand, from skits that parody popular shows like *Star Trek* to folk songs that poke fun at almost every subject (basically folk songs with a science-fiction or fantasy theme; they can be sung to the tune of either an old song or a new one). With this tradition of humor in mind, the books in this chapter range from those with a zany feel to outright parodies of everything from pop culture to *Star Trek*. Although all these books are set within a science-fiction background, the science is very rarely explained and rarely has any impact beyond moving the plot forward.

Hitch Hiker's Guide to the Galaxy Trilogy by Douglas Adams   Ford Prefect is a researcher for the travel guide known as the *Hitch Hiker's Guide to the Galaxy,* the ultimate travel guide, and a resident of a planet near the star Betelguese. Arthur Dent is the lone survivor of Earth, the plant having been destroyed to make way for a hyperspace thoroughfare. Together the two travelers are on a wild journey, meeting incredible aliens in their quest to find the answer to the question of life, the universe, and everything. Some of these characters are: Zaphod Beeblebrox, the former president of the Galaxy; Trillian, literally the last woman from Earth; and Marvin, the paranoid android. Books in the inaccurately named trilogy are: *The Hitch Hiker's Guide to the Galaxy; The Restaurant at the End of the Universe; Life, the Universe, and Everything; So Long, and Thanks for All the Fish;* and *Mostly Harmless.*

***Glory Lane* by Alan Dean Foster**   Together they represent the three "cliques" of high school society—Kerwin the nerd, Seth the punk, and Miranda of the popular crowd. One evening the three teens are at a bowling alley when a strange bowler with seven fingers on one hand attracts their attention. Before the teens can approach the stranger, he is accosted by a group of very odd policemen. The teens help the stranger escape from the police and are surprised to learn that he is an alien and that the bowling ball he is so protective of holds a very powerful secret. In gratitude for his rescue, the alien takes the teens with him to a strange planet peopled by more aliens than the cantina scene from *Star Wars.* Unfortunately, the teens are separated from their newfound alien friend and find themselves alone on an alien world trying to safeguard a sphere that many would kill to recover.

***Waiting for the Galactic Bus* by Parke Godwin**   Two brothers from a vastly superior civilization find themselves stranded on a backwater world called Earth. Bored, they decide to move the residents of the planet (apes) up to the next rung of the evolutionary ladder, thereby creating the human race. Millions of years later, everything the brothers have created is threatened by an unborn baby. That's right, an unborn baby has the potential to destroy the entire human race. The brothers must act quickly to stop the baby's parents from marrying each other or all is lost. Sequel: *The Snake Oil Wars.*

The Stainless Steel Rat (series) by Harry Harrison James Bolivar "Slippery Jim" di Griz is quite possibly the galaxy's best thief and con man. Unfortunately for di Griz, he is working on the "right" side of the law, having been caught committing a crime. The punishment is to be recruited into the Special Corps, a peacekeeping task force—after all, it takes a thief to catch a thief. Soon di Griz finds himself launched through the galaxy on a wild series of adventures that include a time-traveling madman and a trip to hell itself. Series order: *The Stainless Steel Rat, The Stainless Steel Rat's Revenge, The Stainless Steel Rat Saves the World, The Stainless Steel Rat Wants You, The Stainless Steel Rat for President, A Stainless Steel Rat Is Born, The Stainless Steel Rat Gets Drafted, The Stainless Steel Rat Sings the Blues, The Stainless Steel Rat Goes to Hell, The Stainless Steel Rat Joins the Circus.*

***Sewer, Gas and Electric: The Public Works Trilogy* by Matt Ruff** The title is a misnomer. There is no trilogy, but a single comprehensive volume filled with humor and action. The year is 2023 and billionaire Harry Gant is constructing a new Tower of Babel. Meanwhile in the streets below a darker plot is afoot as a Wall Street shark is found murdered and Gant's ex-wife is hired to find the killer. This complex story is richly peopled and includes real personas, such as Ayn Rand and Abbie Hoffman, and imaginary ones, such as Meisterbrau, a mutant great white shark swimming through the sewers of New York dispatching the alligators people have been flushing for centuries.

Other Recommended Titles

Dirk Gently's Holistic Detective Agency by Douglas Adams

Hard Sell by Piers Anthony

Secret of Spring by Piers Anthony

Phule's Company by Robert Aspirin

The Computer Connection by Alfred Bester

Psychoshop by Alfred Bester and Roger Zelazny

Cyberbooks by Ben Bova

Cowboy Feng's Space Bar and Grill by Steven Brust

Inhuman Beings by Jerry Jay
Carroll

The Red Tape Wars by Jack L.
Chalker

*Buddy Holly Is Alive and Well
on Ganymede* by Bradley
Denton

The Magnificent Wilf by
Gordon R. Dickson

The Organ Grinders by Bill
Fitzhugh

Codger Space by Alan Dean Foster

Jed the Dead by Alan Dean Foster

Mad Amos by Alan Dean Foster

Quozl by Alan Dean Foster

Rats, Bats, and Vats by Dave
Freer and Eric Flint

The VMR Theory by Robert
Frezza

The Sherwood Game by Esther
Friesner

Bill the Galactic Hero Series by
Harry Harrison

Job: A Comedy of Justice by
Robert A. Heinlein

A Company of Stars by James P.
Hogan

The Road to Mars by Eric Idle

*Rock 'n' Roll Babes from Outer
Space* by Linda Jaivin

Starship Titanic by Terry Jones

Corrupting Dr. Nice by John
Kessel

Peace on Earth by John Kessel

Et Tu Babe by Mark Leyner

After the Blue by Russel Like

Door Number Three by Patrick
O'Leary

Men in Black by Steve Perry

Armageddon the Musical by
Robert Rankin

Starwreck Series by Lea
Rewolinski

The Stardwarves Trilogy by
David Richardson

Escape from Kathmandu by Kim
Stanley Robinson

The Callahan Chronicles by
Spider Robinson

The Samurai Cat Series by
Mark E. Rogers

*How to Mutate and Take Over
the World* by R. U. Sirrius and
St. Jude

Starship Troupers by
Christopher Stasheff

DEREK'S PICK

Hitch Hiker's Guide to the Galaxy Trilogy by Douglas Adams

BEST PICK FOR THE RELUCTANT READER

Glory Lane by Alan Dean Foster

14

Science-Fiction
and Fantasy Blenders

One man's magic is another man's engineering.
—Robert A. Heinlein

Any sufficiently advanced technology
is indistinguishable from magic.
—Arthur C. Clarke

Recipe for a science-fiction/fantasy blender: take one part science, add one part magic, mix in some ice, toss it all in a blender, and hit "frappe." Serves four in a chilled glass. The books and series that are "blenders" contain elements of both science fiction and fantasy. They exist side by side in whatever world they happen to inhabit. You could see a cybernetic alien casting fireballs at a dragon with a laser attached to its head. In a science-fiction/fantasy blender, neither magic nor science takes precedence over the other, and both are crucial to the telling of the story. The books in this chapter are different from the books discussed in chapter 26, "Demons Loose in the City: Urban Fantasy." Blenders place no particular emphasis on either fantasy or science fiction, whereas urban fantasies place the emphasis on the fantasy elements. Although urban fantasies take place in the modern world, technology and science have very little impact on the story. The emphasis instead is on the fact that magic exists in the modern world. Piers Anthony and Christopher Stasheff are well-known examples of authors who have written science-fiction and fantasy blenders.

Incarnations of Immortality Series by Piers Anthony In a world where cars have accident-avoidance spells in their bumpers and flying carpets are used for travel, the Incarnations of Immortality are Death, Time, Fate, War, and Mother Nature, otherworldly roles filled by mortal people. In Book I, *On a Pale Horse,* Zane is on the verge of committing suicide when the Incarnation of Death appears to collect his soul. Startled, Zane accidentally shoots Death, killing him. Zane is then forced to take on the Office of Death, and soon finds himself traveling all over the world collecting those souls that are in balance between Good and Evil. Acting as the souls' final judge over their final destination (either heaven or hell), Zane is drawn into a conflict with the Prince of Evil himself, and the fate of Zane's love, Luna, hangs in the balance. Other books in the series: *Bearing an Hourglass, With a Tangled Skein, Wielding a Red Sword, Being a Green Mother,* and *For Love of Evil.*

How Like a God by Brenda M. Clough One day Rob Lewis wakes up and discovers that not only can he read other people's minds, but he can control them as well. Rob initially uses his powers for selfish reasons, but when his children begin to show harmful side effects, Rob selflessly decides to leave his family and become an outcast. Determined to get back to his family and some semblance of order, he begins an epic journey to discover the source of his powers, leading him into a confrontation with a legendary hero. Sequel: *Doors of Death.*

Svaha by Charles de Lint Years from now Earth has been destroyed by environmental pollution, and only a few "clean" spots remain on the Earth's surface. One of these clean spots is called the Enclave, made clean by its inhabitants, the remnants of a Native American tribe. The Enclave coexists in uneasy peace with the rest of the polluted world until an Enclave plane crashes outside the Enclave. On board the plane is a chip containing the information the Enclave inhabitants used to clean up the polluted ground. Fearing that the chip may fall into exploitive hands, the Enclave sends Gahzee and Lisa to recover it. The duo must utilize mystical Native American powers in order to walk the fine line between the real world and the dream world.

Midnight Robber by Nalo Hopkinson   In the future, the Caribbean has colonized the planet Toussaint, bringing many of the Caribbean's holidays to the planet. Chief among these is Carnival, a Mardi Gras–like celebration of magic and music. Tan-Tan's father, Antonio, is a politician who frequently cheats on his wife, but when his wife has an affair with family friend Quashee, Antonio challenges him to a duel with machetes. Antonio's plan to drug Quashee during the duel backfires and Quashee dies, earning Antonio a prison sentence on the nearby planet New Half-Way Tree. Tan-Tan accompanies her father to New Half-Way Tree where she struggles to survive in a world populated by criminals and a strange alien race. In the midst of this, Tan-Tan finds herself assuming the identity and the powers of the mythical Queen of the Carnival: the Robber Queen.

Warlock Series by Christopher Stasheff   On the planet of Gramarye live elves, goblins, and other creatures that comprise Earth's legends. Magic flourishes upon Gramarye, but the planet is also in danger from destructive forces of technology. Rod Gallowglass can save Gramarye, but only if he can unleash his awesome magical powers. Unfortunately, Rod is from a technologically advanced civilization and doesn't believe in magic. Other titles in the series: *The Warlock in Spite of Himself, King Kobold Revived, The Warlock Unlocked, The Warlock Enraged, The Warlock Wandering, The Warlock Is Missing, The Warlock Heretical, The Warlock's Companion, The Warlock Insane, The Warlock Rock, Warlock and Son*. Related series: The Warlock's Heirs: *A Wizard in Absentia, M'lady Witch, Quicksilver Knight, The Spellbound Scholar*.

Other Recommended Titles

The Apprentice Adept Series by Piers Anthony

The Secret of Spring by Piers Anthony

And the Devil Will Drag You Under by Jack L. Chalker

The Changewinds by Jack L. Chalker

The Quintara Marathon by Jack L. Chalker

Saga of the Well World Series by Jack L. Chalker

LonTobyn Chronicle (series) by David B. Coe

Shiva 3000 by Jan Lars Jensen

Dragonriders of Pern by Anne McCaffrey

The Glass Harmonica by Louise Marley

Blood: A Southern Fantasy by Michael Moorcock

Archangel by Sharon Shinn

Rogue Wizard Series by Christopher Stasheff

Galveston by Sean Stewart

A Plague of Angels by Sheri S. Tepper

Shadow's End by Sheri S. Tepper

Singer from the Sea by Sheri S. Tepper

The Mantle of Kendis Dai by Margaret Weis and Tracy Hickman

Shadow and Claw by Gene Wolfe

DEREK'S PICK

Incarnations of Immortality Series by Piers Anthony

BEST PICK FOR THE RELUCTANT READER

Warlock Series by Christopher Stasheff

15

Telepathic Mutants and Other Weirdos

Mutants have been a staple of science fiction since scientists discovered that radiation can cause human cells to mutate and that space travel exposes humans to radiation. The speculation has been that these mutations will eventually produce creatures with extra appendages, a grotesque appearance, and even psychic abilities. Some of these psychic powers are: empathy, which is the ability to feel the pain of others; telekinesis, which is the ability to move objects using your mind; and telepathy, which is the ability to read others' minds. For the purposes of this chapter, I have not included mutants that are part of the comic book world, such as the group known as the Uncanny X-Men.

Mute **by Piers Anthony**   Years of space travel have had an unfortunate side effect on humankind, producing thousands of mutations, including such powers as telepathy, precognition, and telekinesis. The Galactic Computer was created by the Galactic Empire to catalog all the known mutations and match those mutations to the best climate for their survival. This allowed for increased human colonization of the galaxy, but it also meant that the Galactic Computer held incredible power over all humankind, normals as well as mutants, a fact that mutant Knot was bitterly opposed to. But a mutant named Piebald is threatening everything the Galactic Empire stands for, forcing Knot to ally himself with the hated Galactic Computer. Aided by the beautiful agent Finesse (a normal), a telepathic ferret, and a precognitive crab, Knot must travel across the galaxy in a race to save all humankind.

***The Demolished Man* by Alfred Bester**   In the future, the Espers make planning and commiting crimes impossible by periodically scanning the minds of the populace. The Espers are telepaths who are experts at reading others' minds. Ben Reich hopes to not only plan but also commit the most heinous of all crimes: murder. Ben has been driven to the edge of murder by a decade-long corporate battle with a rival company. Now on the eve of his company's destruction, Ben plans to reverse it all by killing the CEO of the rival company. But how can he get around the Espers? Winner of the first Hugo Award in 1953.

***A Thousand Words for Stranger* by Julie Czerneda**   Sira is a member of the reclusive and powerful Clan. The Clan is a race of beings with the ability to teleport and read minds and who have little to do with the rest of the galaxy. Unfortunately, Sira has no memory of who or what she is or even how she ended up on a strange alien planet pursued by a powerful and mysterious being. Sira *does* know that she is strangely compelled to escape the planet via the starship *Silver Fox,* captained by the handsome trader Morgan. Soon the pair are on the run not only from the mysterious stalker, but from space pirates, the trade pact, even Sira's own kind! Can Sira break through the blocks on her memory and discover her true identity and heritage before their pursuers catch them?

The Pegasus Saga by Anne McCaffrey   Henry Darrow can see the future. Molly Mahoney can heal with her mind. In a world that hates them for their abilities, the two forge a friendship and create the Jerhatten Parapsychic Center. The center teaches other "Talents" (people with psychic abilities) to use their powers for the benefit of humankind, benefits such as the creation of an orbital space station and the lifting of cargo platforms into orbit and across vast interstellar distances. Titles in the series: *To Ride Pegasus, Pegasus in Flight, Pegasus in Space.*

***The Hollow Man* by Dan Simmons**   Jeremy Bremen is a telepath who is constantly barraged by other people's thoughts. This changes when he meets and marries Gail, who acts as a barrier between Jeremy and the outside world. Unfortunately, Gail is terminally ill, and when she dies, Jeremy is again bombarded by the maddening din of other people's thoughts. Driven to the edge of insanity, Jeremy sets fire to his house and escapes into a journey across America and into madness in a futile search for isolation and the peace he had enjoyed with his wife. Instead, Jeremy finds terror and pain as he escapes from one danger only to fall into another.

Other Recommended Titles

Conscience of the Beagle by Patricia Anthony

Total Recall by Piers Anthony

Catch the Lightning by Catherine Asaro

Primary Inversion by Catherine Asaro

Chaos Come Again by Wilhelmina Baird

Obernewtyn by Isobele Carmody

How Like a God by Brenda M. Clough

The Simulacra by Philip K. Dick

Design for a Great Day by Alan Dean Foster

Jumper by David Gould

Mindstar Rising by Peter Hamilton

White Queen by Gwyneth Jones

Tower and Hive Series by Anne McCaffrey

The Sholan Alliance Series by Lisanne Norman

Telzey Amberdon by James H. Schmitz

Escape Velocity by Christopher Stasheff

More than Human by Theodore Sturgeon

Catspaw Series by Joan Vinge

DEREK'S PICK

The Demolished Man by Alfred Bester

BEST PICK FOR THE RELUCTANT READER

Mute by Piers Anthony

16

Science-Fiction
Romance and Religion

ROMANCE

So what makes the books in this chapter different from your average romance novel where the cyborg vixen falls in love with the dashing space pirate? The science involved would be the easiest answer, but not the most complete. The books in this chapter are basically science-fiction novels with a strong romantic element. But the romance is not the driving force in the story. The science drives the story forward while the romance is basically a subplot. Unfortunately, not very many science-fiction novels have a strong romantic subplot.

***Primary Inversion* by Catherine Asaro**   Sauscony Valdoria is the heir to the throne of the powerful Skolian Empire. Sauscony has been bioengineered to be a gifted space pilot as well as possessing the ability to link her mind telepathically with the Skolian Web. The Web allows instantaneous communication over vast distances as well as faster-than-light travel. Using these abilities, the Skolian Empire rules one-third of the galaxy. The other two-thirds is ruled by the Allied Worlds (led by Earth) and the Eubian Traders, a race that many feel embodies evil itself. While on shore leave on a neutral world, Sauscony meets and falls in love with a man named Jabriol, who could very well prove to be her soul mate. The problem is that Jabriol is the heir to the Eubian Empire and has been bred to destroy the Skolian Empire and everything that Sauscony holds dear. This is the first book in a series called the Saga of the Skolian Empire, but each book is written to be a stand-alone novel. Other books in the series: *Catch the Lightning, The Last Hawk, The Radiant Seas, The Veiled Web, The Quantum Rose, Ascendant Sun, The Phoenix Code.*

***Cordelia's Honor* by Lois McMaster Bujold**   Cordelia Nesmith is the captain of the Betan Expeditionary Force, charged with stopping a vastly superior alien force. In the resulting battle, Cordelia's force is defeated and betrayed, forcing Cordelia to sue for peace with her enemy, Aral Vorkosigan, a man known as the Butcher of Komarr. Soon Cordelia finds herself falling in love with Aral and becomes an outcast on her own planet. Known as the Lady Vorkosigan, Cordelia looks forward to a quiet life of raising her infant son. Then the emperor dies, throwing Cordelia and Aral into a volatile dynastic struggle. *Cordelia's Honor* is a reprint of the first two novels in the Vorkosigan series: *Shards of Honor* and *Barrayar.*

***Circuit of Heaven* by Dennis Danvers**   In the future, Earth is sparsely populated by crazies and religious fanatics, the rest of the population having chosen to leave their bodies and enter the Bin, a virtual reality environment with no disease, poverty, or death. Once the decision to enter the Bin is made, there is no going back—the bodies of Bin residents are cremated. Nemo has seen the crematorium and refuses to enter the Bin, both despite and because of the fact that his parents are Bin residents. But Nemo is allowed to visit his parents in the Bin for short periods. It is on one of these visits that Nemo meets and falls in love with Justine Ingham, a new arrival to the Bin who has memories that are not her own. Will Nemo join Justine in the Bin, or will he try to forget the love of his life? To make the decision more difficult, Nemo has been contacted by a religious group asking him to infect the Bin with a computer virus that will sever the Bin's connections to the outside world. Sequel: *End of Days.*

***Blind Waves* by Steven Gould**—see p. 47.

***To Say Nothing of the Dog* by Connie Willis**   Frequent flyers often suffer from jet lag after making several trips in a short time. In 2057, Ned

Henry is suffering from time lag after making several jumps into the past. But wealthy dowager Lady Schrapnell has one last trip for Ned— a trip to 1888 to recover an item known as the bishop's bird stump, an item Lady Schrapnell needs to complete the rebuilding of Coventry Cathedral, destroyed in 1940 by the Nazis. Once in 1888, Ned finds that there has been a change in the time line caused by fellow time traveler Verity Kindle. As Ned and Verity begin searching for the bishop's bird stump, they find themselves falling deeper and deeper in love. However, if Ned and Verity don't fix the change in the time line, the Nazis win World War II. Winner of the 1999 Hugo Award.

Other Recommended Titles

Glimpses by Roger Alexander

The Secret of Spring by Piers Anthony

Catch the Lightning by Catherine Asaro

Last Hawk by Catherine Asaro

The Radiant Seas by Catherine Asaro

Fourth World by Dennis Danvers

Time and Again by Jack Finney

Job: A Comedy of Justice by Robert A. Heinlein

Time Enough for Love by Robert A. Heinlein

Wrapt in Crystal by Sharon Shinn

DEREK'S PICK

Primary Inversion by Catherine Asaro

BEST PICK FOR THE RELUCTANT READER

To Say Nothing of the Dog by Connie Willis

RELIGION

To the casual observer it would seem that there is no room in science fiction for religion of any kind, even Scientology. How could something based upon faith and belief, rather than facts, have anything to do with science fiction? And yet, strangely enough, religion factors into quite a few science-fiction stories. Explorations of how religion may evolve over the years as well as of entirely different belief systems have long been part of science fiction. Some of these books, however, are outright satires of religions, so please exercise caution in making selections.

Glimpses by Roger Alexander   The year is 2515 and the human race is virtually extinct. Two hundred thousand people live in a virtual reality created and maintained by a self-sufficient computer. Computer engineer Alex Rojas is one of the two hundred thousand entities to awaken in the virtual reality environment and is drafted to help create spaceships to spread humankind through the virtual solar system. Within the virtual reality environment, the people live much as they did on Earth, falling in love and raising families, and Alex is no exception. But as Alex explores the virtual reality and his own spirituality, he discovers evil can exist in virtual reality as well. This raises a question: Is evil part of the program's code or is it intrinsic to human nature?

Code of the Lifemaker by James P. Hogan—see p. 34.

The Ethan Hamilton Cyber-Thriller Series by Jefferson Scott   In *Virtually Eliminated,* the first book of the series, virtual reality has supplanted the Internet in the twenty-first century and nearly everyone accesses GlobeNet. Users access GlobeNet for different reasons. Some use it to explore adventures, others are doing research and seeking education. But a madman has been using it to murder users, including a CIA agent. The FBI asks virtual-reality expert Ethan Hamilton to investigate. Ethan has deep Christian beliefs that guide every aspect of his life. Things are proceeding well for Ethan when the murderer decides to raise the stakes and targets: Ethan's family. Other books featuring Ethan Hamilton: *Terminal Logic, Fatal Defect* (each of these books can be read as a stand-alone title).

The Christ Clone Trilogy by James Beau Seigneur   A team has been formed to examine and determine the validity of the Shroud of Turin (believed to be the burial shroud of Jesus). But one of the scientists, Professor Harold Goodman, has made a startling discovery: Cells, embedded in the shroud, are still living after two thousand years! Goodman is convinced that the cells belong to a member of an alien race, and to prove his theory, he sets into motion a plan with Earth-shattering potential: clone a being from the cells. Goodman's plan begins a wave of catastrophes that could mean the end of the world. Titles in the series: *In His Image, Birth of an Age, Acts of God.*

***Archangel* by Sharon Shinn**   The colony of Samaria had been settled to be a religious utopia. Lately the colony has been overcome by vice and iniquity. The society of Samaria is divided into two classes: the mortals and the angels. Orbiting the planet is their god Jehovah, who can only be communicated with through the songs of the angels. Gabriel is to be the next Archangel of Samaria, and he has been ordered by Jehovah to marry the mortal Rachel so that they may sing the hymns of Gabriel's elevation. Many oppose Gabriel's elevation to Archangel because he wants to return to the old order and put a stop to the vice and iniquity. And those that would oppose Gabriel will do anything to stop his elevation. Sharon Shinn has written three books about Samaria, loosely titled the Samaria Trilogy. All three books are stand-alone books and can be read in any order. Other titles in the series: *Jehovah's Angel, The Allelulia Files.*

Other Recommended Titles

God's Fires by Patricia Anthony

Balshazzar's Serpent by Jack L. Chalker

The Hammer of God by Arthur C. Clarke

Job: A Comedy of Justice by Robert A. Heinlein

Out of the Silent Planet by C. S. Lewis

The Shapes of Their Hearts by Melissa Scott

Wrapt in Crystal by Sharon Shinn

Deus X by Norman Spinard

Soulsaver by James Stevens-Arce (satire)

Firebird by Katherine Tyers

DEREK'S PICK

Code of the Lifemaker by James P. Hogan

BEST PICK FOR THE RELUCTANT READER

Archangel by Sharon Shinn

17

Space Operas

Space operas! Where the men are men, the women are real women, and the aliens are real ugly! Where problems are solved at the end of a gun (or space cruiser—take your pick)! And where the men have big guns and the women have bigger . . . er . . . guns! Space operas are, in a nutshell, adventures in space. These adventures generally take place on a galactic scale, sometimes involving vast empires and massive space battles. Space operas involve a lot of action and intrigue, which are the hallmarks of the subgenre. The science used in these books is not essential to telling the story; indeed, many times the story could still be told in another setting if the science were removed. Space operas are one of the few subgenres that you can judge by their covers. Space operas usually have at least one large spaceship on the cover, sometimes more. These ships are frequently bristling with laser cannons, and in the background are explosions and other signs that the book is full of action. The most popular examples of space operas are *Star Trek* and *Star Wars;* these two series comprise most of the space operas written today.

Bio of a Space Tyrant (series) by Piers Anthony   When his sister attracts the salacious attentions of a wealthy scion, Hope Hubris is forced into defending her honor. In the course of the fight, the scion is injured, necessitating the moving of the Hubris family off the planet. Once in space the ship carrying the family and other refugees is subjected to relentless attacks by space pirates. His family destroyed in the attacks, Hope and his sister join the Jupiter navy, where Hope swears revenge on the pirates. Rising quickly through the ranks of the Jupiter navy, Hope soon earns the command of a squadron of warships with the mission to eradicate piracy. From humble beginnings Hope's career soars to new heights as he sets his eye on an even loftier goal: president of Jupiter. Titles in the series: *Refugee, Mercenary, Politician, Executive, Statesman.*

The Gap Series by Stephen R. Donaldson   In the far future, humans are able to travel between the stars using "gap drives." Most of the known galaxy is controlled by the United Mining Company (UMC). Against this backdrop, UMC cop Morn Hyland is discovered on a disabled ship by well-known scoundrel Angus Thermapyle. Morn is the victim of gap sickness, which caused her to destroy her father's warship, but she remembers little of her former life as a UMC cop and soon realizes that Thermapyle is holding her captive with an illegal brain plant. Desperate to be free of Thermapyle, Morn attracts the attention of space pirate Nick Succorso, who manages to free her from Thermapyle and at the same time loses his heart to Morn. Meanwhile an alien race called the Amnion has set in motion a plan that may cause the mutation of the entire human race even as the UMC sets into motion its own plans. Titles in the series: *The Gap into Vision: Forbidden Knowledge, A Dark and Hungry God Arises: The Gap into Power, This Day All Gods Die: The Gap into Ruin.*

Mageworlds Series by Debra Doyle   In the first book in the series, *Price of Stars,* the human Republic has enjoyed an uneasy peace with the Mageworlds for thirty years. The Mageworlds had just barely been held at bay in the last war through the dynamic military leadership of Beka Rosselin-Metadi's father. Since then the Republic's fragile government has been held together by the skillful diplomacy and leadership of Beka's mother. Beka herself wants nothing to do with either politics or the military. All of that is changed when Beka's mother is assassinated on the Senate floor, threatening to destroy the Republic's tentative peace with the Mageworlds. Then Beka's father approaches Beka with an unconventional deal: he will give Beka his warship, *Warhammer*, so long as she uses it to track down the assassins and bring them back to him. And then Beka's troubles really begin. Other titles in the series: *Starpilot's Grave, By Honor Betrayed.* Prequels to trilogy: *The Gathering Flame, The Long Hunt, The Stars Asunder.*

Honor Harrington Series by David Weber   In the first book in the series, *On Basilisk Station,* newly promoted Commander Honor Harrington is thrilled to learn that she's going to be commanding her first "serious" warship, the HMS *Fearless.* Her enthusiasm is greatly diminished when she learns that *Fearless* is going to be the testing platform for an experimental weapons system that effectively robs *Fearless* of half her firepower. To make matters worse, *Fearless* is expected to take part in tactical games with superior warships. Honor manages to find a way to come out on top in the games. In doing so, she embarrasses several highly placed individuals in the navy who conspire to have Honor assigned to the worst station of service possible: Basilisk Station. Once on station at Basilisk, Honor must deal with smugglers, corrupt politicians, and an unexpected invasion by the powerful Haven Republic using an aging light cruiser with an experimental weapons platform. Just another day at the office for Honor Harrington. Other titles in the series: *The Honor of the Queen, The Short Victorious War, Field of Dishonor, Flag in Exile, Honor among Enemies, In Enemy Hands, More than Honor, Echoes of Honor, Worlds of Honor, Changer of Worlds, Ashes of Victory.*

Other Recommended Titles

Vorkosigan Saga by Lois McMaster Bujold

The Last Legion Series by Chris Bunch

Priam's Lens by Jack L. Chalker

The Quintara Marathon by Jack L. Chalker

Downbelow Station by C. J. Cherryh

Sten by Allan Cole and Chris Bunch

Flight Engineer Series by James Doohan and S. M. Stirling

Earth the Final Conflict: Requiem for Boone by Debra Doyle and John D. MacDonald

Design for a Great Day by Alan Dean Foster

Rats, Bats, and Vats by Dave Freer

Ghost of a Chance by Mark Garland and Charles McGraw

Starcruiser Shenandoah Series by Roland Green

Forever War by Joe Haldeman

Starship Troopers by Robert A. Heinlein

Stark's War by John G. Hemry

Dune by Frank Herbert

The Death of Sleep by Anne McCaffrey

The Rampart Worlds Series by Julian May

The Price of Peace by Mike Moscoe

Gust Front by Jolin Ringo

Man O' War by William Shatner

Quest for Tomorrow by William Shatner

Starfist Series by David Sherman and Dan Cragg

Firebird by Katherine Tyers

A *Fire upon the Deep* by Vernor Vinge

In Death Ground by David Weber

Insurrection by David Weber

Mag Force 7 Series by Margaret Weis and Don Perrin

Stars of the Guardians Series by Margaret Weis and Don Perrin

Chung Kuo by David Wingrove

DEREK'S PICK

Honor Harrington Series by David Weber

BEST PICK FOR THE RELUCTANT READER

The Gap Series by Stephen R. Donaldson

STAR WARS

In 1977, ten words scrolled across a movie screen that would have a huge impact on science fiction and spawn a large subculture within the science-fiction community. The words were: "A long time ago in a galaxy far, far away . . . " and the movie was *Star Wars*. With this fairy-tale-like opener *Star Wars* began, and almost a quarter of a century and five movies later, *Star Wars* is still a thriving franchise. The story itself is very like a fairy tale. Young man finds a robot with a hologram of a beautiful girl, who ironically is a princess. The hologram implores the finder to take the robot to Obi Wan Kenobi since he is their "only hope." The boy is Luke Skywalker, and when he finds Obi Wan, he learns that the old man is part of an almost extinct group called the Jedi Knights, and that Luke's father was one of the greatest of that number. Sadly, Luke learns that his father was killed by Darth Vader, an evil renegade Jedi who systematically tracked down and slew all the Jedi Knights except his old master, Obi Wan.

Darth is a minion of the evil Emperor and is in search of the robot that Luke delivered to Obi Wan. The robot has the plans to the Empire's most dangerous superweapon, the Death Star. Luke discovers that he has lost all of his family in an attack by the Empire, and he decides the only thing left to do is to help Obi Wan deliver the droid to the Rebellion on the planet Alderraan. Luke enlists the help of a space smuggler named Han Solo and the entire group ends up imprisoned on the Death Star with the princess. They then have to rescue the princess, escape with the plans to the rebel base, and defeat the Empire.

Throughout the movies Luke begins to explore his Jedi powers, which are an extension of the Force—a mysterious power that surrounds all living things. His powers include being able to lift and move objects with his mind as well as using "suggestions" to make other creatures do what he wants. For this reason *Star Wars* truly belonged in the science-fiction/fantasy blenders chapter until recently, when the true nature of the Force was revealed. In the movie *Star Wars Episode I: The Phantom Menace* (chronologically the first movie but the fourth one made in the series), a Jedi Knight named Qui-Gon Jinn explains midi-chlorians, subcellular life-forms that live in symbiosis with their host and provide the Force that Jedi Knights use to perform their feats. The more midi-chlorians a Jedi has, the stronger he is in the Force. The act of explaining the origin of the mystic Force in technological terms has made the series completely science fiction rather than the blender it used to be.

For the most part, *Star Wars* readers are self-sufficient. They rarely seek advice on what book to read next beyond what is next in a series. For that reason I've limited the books in this section to those that the reluctant *Star Wars* reader may want to read. I've also eliminated synopses of the novelizations of the movies because most people have seen the movies.

Jedi Academy Series by Kevin J. Anderson   Seven years after the defeat of the Empire at Endor, the Republic is still locked in combat with the scattered forces of the Empire. Jedi Master Luke Skywalker, buoyed by recent findings of others strong in the Force, decides to build a Jedi Academy to recruit and train Jedi Knights again. Meanwhile, the remaining forces of the Empire have set into motion three different plans to regain their position of galactic preeminence. The first is the development of a superweapon called the Sun Crusher, the second is guerrilla warfare on Republic worlds by a group of Star Destroyers under the command of Imperial Admiral Daala, and the last is the construction of a third Death Star battle station. In the midst of this, Luke must deal with the results of one of his students' research into the dark side of the Force. And Han and Leia must discover who kidnapped their twin children. Series order: *Jedi Search, Dark Apprentice, Champions of the Force.*

***Rogue Planet* by Greg Bear**   Young Anakin Skywalker has been apprenticed to be a Jedi Knight under the training of Obi Wan Kenobi for the last few years since the events chronicled in *Episode I: The Phantom Menace.* Although he is a gifted student, lately Anakin has grown restless with his studies at the Jedi Temple and has taken to sneaking off to take part in dangerous races. Hoping to harness the boy's energy, the Jedi Council assigns Obi Wan and Anakin to look into the disappearance of another Jedi on the mysterious planet Zonama Sekot. What they find is a world of mystery and danger whose inhabitants "grow" wonderful spacecraft. What the pair doesn't know is that three different factions are closing in on Zonama Sekot with the purpose of stealing the technology to grow organic spacecraft. And they'll eliminate anyone in the way to get it.

Bounty Hunter Wars Series by K. W. Jeter   Taking place concurrently with the events chronicled in *Return of the Jedi,* the events in the Bounty Hunter Wars series involve plans by the Emperor, Lord Vader, and Prince Xizor to destroy the second most powerful organization in the galaxy: the Bounty Hunters Guild. Unfortunately, there is a powerful wild card in the mix: bounty hunter Boba Fett, who answers to neither side but is the best bounty hunter in the galaxy. Soon Boba becomes the target not only of the Empire, but of the Bounty Hunters Guild. As plans and intrigues stack against him, Boba must use all of his considerable skills as a bounty hunter to wriggle free. Titles in the series: *The Mandalorian Armor, Slave Ship, Hard Merchandise*.

***Shadows of the Empire* by Steve Perry**   This novel takes place between the events chronicled in *The Empire Strikes Back* and *Return of the Jedi*. Prince Xizor is the leader of the criminal group known as the Black Sun. More than anything Xizor wants to replace Darth Vader as the Emperor's right-hand man. To achieve this, Xizor hatches a plan to discredit Vader in the eyes of the Emperor even while allying with Vader to capture Vader's son Luke. Meanwhile, Luke and his friends are racing against time to rescue Han Solo before he can be turned over to the nefarious gangster Jabba the Hutt.

***Vector Prime* by R. A. Salvatore**   It's been close to a quarter-century since the Republic defeated the Empire at the Battle of Endor. The fledgling Republic is still suffering growing pains when it is confronted by an insidious invasion by a sinister alien race. The Vong are technologically and physically superior to the Republic and are even a match for the vaunted Jedi Knights. Into this volatile mix enters a charismatic politician who begins inciting rebellion within the Republic.

Other Recommended Titles

Corellian Trilogy by Roger MacBride Allen

Darksaber by Kevin J. Anderson

Young Jedi Knights Series by Kevin J. Anderson

Tales from Jabba's Palace edited by Kevin J. Anderson

Tales from Mos Eisley Cantina edited by Kevin J. Anderson

Tales of the Bounty Hunters edited by Kevin J. Anderson

Star Wars Episode I: The Phantom Menace by Terry Brooks

The Han Solo Trilogy by A. C. Crispin

The Han Solo Adventures by Brian Daley

Star Wars: The Empire Strikes Back by Donald Glut

Planet of Twilight by Barbara Hambly

Star Wars: Return of the Jedi by James Khan

The Adventures of Lando Calrissian by L. Neil Smith

Admiral Thrawn Series by Timothy Zahn

DEREK'S PICK

Rogue Planet by Greg Bear

BEST PICK FOR THE RELUCTANT READER

Jedi Academy Series by Kevin J. Anderson

STAR TREK

Novel Versions of the Movies:

Star Trek: The Motion Picture by Gene Roddenberry

Star Trek II: The Wrath of Khan by Vonda McIntyre

Star Trek III: The Search for Spock by Vonda McIntyre

Star Trek IV: The Voyage Home by Vonda McIntyre

Star Trek V: The Final Frontier by J. M. Dillard

Star Trek VI: The Undiscovered Country by J. M. Dillard

Star Trek Next Generation: Generations by J. M. Dillard

Star Trek Next Generation: First Contact by Rick Berman and Brannon Braga

Star Trek Next Generation: Insurrection by John Vornholt

Original Series

Gene Roddenberry once described *Star Trek* as *"Wagon Train* to the stars,"* and this is an apt description of the original series. *Wagon Train* was a television series in the 1950s about a group of settlers traveling westward in the post–Civil War era. *Star Trek* has many components in common with *Wagon Train.* The starship *Enterprise* is on a five-year mission to seek out new worlds, but is also charged with administering the law of the Federation that it serves. The original series, starring William Shatner as Captain Kirk, in many ways exemplifies space operas: the story is most important; the science just provides the background and is used to move the story along. In many cases, the same story can be written in another format. The books in this section are all based on characters from the television series that ran from 1966 to 1969, as well as on the first six movies in the series. These characters include: Captain Kirk, Spock, Dr. McCoy, Scotty, and Lieutenant Sulu, among others. This series is sometimes called STTOS for *Star Trek The*

Original Series. *Star Trek* readers, much like *Star Wars* readers, are usually self-sufficient and do not need very much guidance. The books in this section are suggestions for the *Star Trek* reluctant reader. For this reason no synopses of the *Star Trek* movies have been given. I've included the titles in series order for easy reference.

***Spock Must Die!* by James Blish**   A freak transporter accident has created two Mr. Spocks. One is the true first officer of the *Enterprise;* the other is a twisted, evil being. One of the Spocks must go. The problem lies in figuring out which Spock is the "true" Mr. Spock.

***Dreadnought* by Diane Carey**   The *Star Empire* is the most powerful ship in the Federation's fleet. In fact, the *Star Empire* is the most powerful ship in the galaxy and has the potential to subdue whole star systems or destroy them. But on the eve of her maiden voyage, the *Star Empire* is taken over by a mysterious group of terrorists who have only one demand: a rendezvous with the Federation's flagship, the *Enterprise,* and a meeting with one of her officers, Lieutenant Piper. Lt. Piper is shocked to find that some of her friends are among the terrorists, and they assert that they did not steal the *Star Empire* to harm the Federation, but to save the Federation from certain destruction!

***The Kobayashi Maru* by Julie Ecklar**   The Kobayashi Maru is the Federation's toughest test for Starfleet cadets. Designed to be a "no-win" scenario, the Kobayashi Maru doesn't test individuals' fitness for command but rather their character through the decisions they make. When Captain Kirk, Scotty, Sulu, and Chekov are trapped on a crippled shuttlecraft, the four officers begin trading stories of their own experiences with the "no-win" scenario, including the startling fact that Kirk is the only person to ever beat the scenario.

***How Much for Just the Planet?* by John M. Ford**   On the distant planet Direidi, a vast fortune in dilithium crystals has been discovered. Dilithium is most often used for powering spaceships, and the Federation and the Klingon Empire are the top consumers of dilithium. Under a treaty signed between the two powers, the planet Direidi (and its dilithium) goes to whoever can best develop the planet. To determine this, the Federation will send its best ship, the *Enterprise,* under the command of Captain James T. Kirk, and the Klingons will send their best ship. Unfortunately for both sides, the Direidians are making the rules for the contest—rules that will make this the strangest and most hilarious adventure either side has yet experienced!

Prime Directive by Judith and Garfield Reeves-Stevens The planet Talin had been on the brink of space travel and of discovering that it was not alone in the universe, so the Federation dispatched its flagship, the *Enterprise,* under the command of Captain Kirk, to make first contact. One rule governed the conduct of the *Enterprise*'s crew: Do not break the Prime Directive. The Prime Directive states that no Starfleet officer shall interfere with the development of a species. But something went terribly wrong during the *Enterprise*'s first contact with the Talinians— something so wrong that the planet lies in ruins under a nuclear winter. The crew of the *Enterprise* has been scattered throughout the fleet, the *Enterprise* herself has been dismantled, and Captain Kirk faces court-martial for breaking the Prime Directive. It's up to those crew members still loyal to Kirk to journey to Talin to find out the truth behind that disastrous first contact, discover the whereabouts of their fugitive captain, and clear his name.

Other Recommended Titles

Battlestations! by Diane Carey

New Earth Series by Diane Carey et al.

Sarek by A. C. Crispin

Star Trek: The Lost Years by J. M. Dillard

Devil's World by Gordon Eklund

The Fearful Summons by Denny Martin Flinn

Crossover by Michael Jan Friedman

Republic by Michael Jan Friedman

The Joy Machine by James Gunn and Theodore Sturgeon

Mudd in Your Eye by Jerry Oltion

Twilight's End by Jerry Oltion

Federation by Judith and Garfield Reeves-Stevens

Heart of the Sun by Pamela Sargent

Vulcan's Forge by Josepha Sherman

Strange New Worlds edited by Dean Wesley Smith

Mind Meld by John Vornholt

The Better Man by Howard Weinstein

Deep Domain by Howard Weinstein

DEREK'S PICK

Dreadnought by Diane Carey

BEST PICK FOR THE RELUCTANT READER

Prime Directive by Judith and Garfield Reeves-Stevens

The Next Generation

Sometimes referred to as STNG for *Star Trek: The Next Generation,* the books in this section revolve around the characters introduced in the Paramount television series that ran from 1987 to 1994 and in the three movies. Paramount has announced a tenth *Star Trek* movie but has not announced if this movie will involve the characters from *Next Generation,* some of whom are Captain Jean-Luc Picard, Commander Riker, Commander Data, and Dr. Crusher.

***Q-Squared* by Peter David**   How do you discipline a god? This question confronted Captain James Kirk when the *Enterprise* met the immature godling Trelane. Now, almost a century later, Captain Picard and the *Enterprise D* are approached for help by the omnipotent being known as Q from the Q-Continuum. Q is having trouble with a renegade member of the continuum, Trelane, the same Trelane Kirk dealt with a century before and still very much a child. Trelane has somehow managed to tap into a vast power source that gives him powers far beyond the rest of the Q. When the *Enterprise* encounters Trelane, he decides to experiment with his power and collapses three different time lines onto the *Enterprise.* Amongst the chaos that ensues, Picard must use all his wits and those of his crew to stop Trelane before all the universes are destroyed.

***Dark Mirror* by Diane Duane**   A century ago, four members of the starship *Enterprise* discovered an alternate universe almost exactly like ours, except that the Federation of that universe was focused on conquest and most inhabitants were evil, twisted mockeries of their counterparts in our universe. Now, a hundred years later, history repeats itself when Captain Jean-Luc Picard's *Enterprise* is pulled into the alternate universe. The plan of their evil counterparts is to capture the *Enterprise,* replace the crew, and use the *Enterprise* as a cover to invade the "good" Federation universe.

Kahless by **Michael Jan Friedman**   The greatest hero of the Klingon Empire was its legendary first emperor, Kahless. Kahless was the great warrior who united the warring Klingon houses, propelling the fledgling Klingon Empire into a new golden age. In the present age the emperor is a clone of the legendary warrior, holding a position that is mostly honorary. But with the discovery of an ancient scroll, much of what was once believed about the original Kahless has proved to be more myth than truth, throwing the empire into chaos. Uncertain of who he can trust within the empire, Kahless turns to the only friends he can trust outside the empire, Captain Jean-Luc Picard and Lieutenant Worf, to help restore order to an empire threatened with civil war.

The Romulan Prize by **Simon Hawke**   Ordered by the Federation to patrol the neutral zone near the Romulan border, the USS *Enterprise* finds a Romulan Warbird adrift in space. Upon examining it, crew members discover that it is an experimental prototype of deadly potential. The *Enterprise* crew also discovers a Romulan plan to claim the mysterious planet Hermeticus 2—a planet with a deadly secret of its own. All that stands between the Federation and total destruction is the *Enterprise* and her crew.

Dyson Sphere by **George Zebrowski**   In the far reaches of space, the Federation has discovered a Dyson Sphere, an artificially constructed world of vast proportions. Sent to investigate the sphere, the *Enterprise* is charged with learning its secrets and possibly the secret origins of the Borg itself. Upon reaching the sphere, the *Enterprise*'s crew are shocked to learn that the sphere and all life on it are threatened by the approach of a rogue star. The *Enterprise*'s crew must race against time to discover the Dyson Sphere's secrets and rescue the inhabitants of the sphere before they are all destroyed by the runaway star.

Other Recommended Titles

I, Q. by John De Lancie

Intellivore by Diane Duane

The Last Stand by Brad Ferguson

The Forgotten War by William R. Forstchen

Romulan Stratagem by Robert Greenberger

Dragon's Honor by Kij Johnson and Greg Cox

The Death of Princes by John Peel

A Fury Scorned by Pamela Sargent

DEREK'S PICK

Kahless by Michael Jan Friedman

BEST PICK FOR THE RELUCTANT READER

Dark Mirror by Diane Duane

Deep Space Nine

The books in this series, sometimes referred to as DS9, all have characters from the Paramount television series of the same name that ran from 1993 to 1999. Characters in this series, which takes place on a jointly controlled Federation/Bajoran space station, include Captain Benjamin Sisko, Dax, Kira, and Doctor Julian Bashir.

***The Heart of a Warrior* by John Betancourt**   The Federation is locked in combat with the Changelings and their shock troopers, the Jem'Hadar, over control of the wormhole that allows for instant transit from the Alpha Quadrant to the Gamma Quadrant (the home of the Changelings and the Jem'Hadar). Failure means opening up all of the Alpha Quadrant to invasion and the destruction of the Federation. The Gamma Quadrant's forces seem virtually unstoppable until the Federation hatches a desperate plan: send two operatives, Lieutenant Commander Worf and Major Kira, deep into the Gamma Quadrant to discover the nature of the mysterious substance the Changelings use to control the Jem'Hadar. For Worf and Kira, failure is not an option.

***Trials and Tribble-ations* by Diane Carey**   Almost a century has passed since the troublesome tribbles were introduced to the Federation and almost precipitated a war between the Federation and the Klingons. The tribbles are a race of animals that basically resemble balls of fur and have a sex drive that makes rabbits look impotent. They also give out feelings of pleasure to humans and most races, but they hate the

Klingons. Now the crew of Deep Space Nine must travel back in time to prevent a present-day Klingon traitor from changing history by exacting revenge upon Captain Kirk.

***Saratoga* by Michael Jan Friedman**   Captain Benjamin Sisko lost his wife when the ship she commanded, the USS *Saratoga,* was destroyed by the Borg at the Battle of Wolf 359. Years later, Sisko and the *Defiant* have been ordered by Starfleet to escort the survivors of the *Saratoga* disaster to a ceremony to honor the victims. But an accident en route cripples the *Defiant,* and all evidence points to one of Sisko's former crewmates as the saboteur.

***Warped* by K. W. Jeter**   Bajor, never a center of peace, has once again erupted in turmoil because of a new religious faction that is sweeping the planet. In the midst of this, a series of murders has begun occurring on Deep Space Nine. As chief of security, Odo investigates the murders and soon discovers that they are the result of a new holosuite technology. Furthermore, evidence points toward a link between the uprisings on Bajor and the murders on Deep Space Nine.

***The Laertian Gamble* by Robert Sheckley**   Hoping to catch the attention of a beautiful alien, Doctor Julian Bashir begins gambling, and winning, at Quark's tables. But as Bashir wins, strange events begin occurring in Federation space. In fact, the more Bashir wins, the worse things get in the Federation as disasters begin occurring throughout its territories. When Bashir attempts to quit gambling, a fleet of Laertian warships arrives to force him to keep playing. Meanwhile, Kira and Dax must journey to Laertia in the hope of finding a way to stop the disasters before the Federation is destroyed.

Other Recommended Titles

What You Leave Behind by Diane Carey

Wrath of the Prophets by Peter David

The Rebels Trilogy by Dafydd ab Hugh

Objective: Bajor by John Peel

The Long Night by Dean Wesley Smith

The Tempest by Susan Wright

DEREK'S PICK

Trials and Tribble-ations by Diane Carey

BEST PICK FOR THE RELUCTANT READER

Saratoga by Michael Jan Friedman

Voyager

The *Voyager* series ran on Paramount's newly created United Paramount Network from 1995 to 2001. The crew of the starship *Voyager* find themselves mysteriously light-years away from Earth, stranded on the far side of the galaxy. They must journey homeward through unfamiliar space. The characters in this series, sometimes abbreviated STV, include Captain Kathryn Janeway, Commander Chakotay, and Lieutenant Tom Paris as well as a holographic doctor.

***Ragnarok* by Nathan Archer**   Stranded in the Delta Quadrant, the crew of the USS *Voyager* detect a signal that could lead them back to Earth. *Voyager* immediately sets out at maximum speed to follow the signal and, in doing so, runs directly into a battle between two alien races who have been warring for hundreds of years.

***Battle Lines* by Dave Galanter and Greg Brodeur**   While traveling back to Earth, the USS *Voyager* is attacked by a race known as the Edesians. During the attack, members of the *Voyager* crew are taken hostage. Captain Kathryn Janeway is then given the monstrous choice of helping the Edesians in their war with the Gimlons or never seeing the crew again. Janeway chooses to cooperate, but soon she will regret her choice when the *Voyager* crew discover that the Gimlons have weapons that can destroy entire planets.

***Ghost of a Chance* by Mark Garland and Charles G. McGraw**   Deep in the Delta Quadrant the starship *Voyager* is crippled by a collapsing star. While the ship is limping away, the crew discover a planet peopled by a race of primitives. Unbeknownst to the primitive inhabitants, the planet is on the verge of being torn apart by its own volcanic activity. Captain Janeway is moved to rescue the inhabitants of the planet but is forbidden to do so by the Prime Directive, a Starfleet regulation that requires all captains to not interfere with pre–space travel populations. Help arrives from an unexpected quarter when an alien vessel arrives and offers to rescue the primitives and repair *Voyager*. This leads Janeway to wonder what her new allies want in return.

***Caretaker* by L. A. Graf**   On its maiden voyage, the starship *Voyager* is flung to the far side of the galaxy into the Delta Quadrant by a strange alien technology. There the crew is confronted by an enigmatic being known as the Caretaker, who could possess the ability to return *Voyager* to Earth. But first the crew is going to have to penetrate and solve the mystery surrounding the Caretaker.

***Mosaic* by Jeri Taylor**   The USS *Voyager* is trapped on the far side of the galaxy when it comes under attack from an alien race known as the Kazons. The sudden ambush forces *Voyager* to break off before the crew can retrieve a landing party from a planet's surface. Under constant attack from the Kazon ship and unable to rescue her landing party, Janeway uses the time as an opportunity to review her life and the decisions she has made throughout her career.

Other Recommended Titles

Flashback by Brannon Braga

Marooned by Christie Golden

The Murdered Sun by Christie Golden

Bless the Beasts by Karen Haber

Death of a Neutron Star by Eric Kotani and Dean Wesley Smith

Echoes by Dean Wesley Smith

Pathways by Jeri Taylor

Chrysalis by David Wilson

DEREK'S PICK

Caretaker by L. A. Graf

BEST PICK FOR THE RELUCTANT READER

Mosaic by Jeri Taylor

Book II
Fantasy

18

Fantastic Fantasy

What is fantasy? The simple answer would be that fantasy fiction is everything that science fiction is not. Of course this simplistic definition, like so much in life, is not the complete answer. Whereas science fiction is based on technology or science that may or may not exist, fantasy has at its core one very basic assumption: magic exists in whatever world the author has decided to set the story. Fantasy fiction can be comprised of many elements, such as gods or mythical creatures like dragons and unicorns, but all these elements rely on one crucial ingredient: magic. Magic by its very nature is mysterious and ceases to be magic when it is described in scientific or technological terms. For example, if a young hero could throw fire from his hands at armored beings, it would be magic. If, however, the author explained that the young man's abilities were the result of a particular formation in his brain and that the armored beings were really mechanical, then it would be science fiction.

CLASSIC FANTASY

Unlike science fiction, which has its origins in the Industrial Revolution and the technology it spawned, the origins of fantasy go much farther back—before Shakespeare wrote about fairies, even before Nordic peoples explained thunder as the god Thor's footsteps, to the very origins of primitive humans. The world that confronted these early people was confusing and frightening, and their tales were attempts to explain an inexplicable world. For our purposes we need not go back quite that far, but just to those authors who have had the greatest impact on today's fantasy writers and the genre as a whole. These authors were themselves influenced by folktales of fairies and goblins, of gods and titans. For the purposes of this chapter, I've defined as "classics" books that were published before 1980 and that have shown lasting significance by remaining in print for most of the intervening years.

The Big Three of Fantasy

Three authors have had more impact on modern fantasy than any others. They are L. Frank Baum, C. S. Lewis, and J. R. R. Tolkien, and their influence can be seen in many of the works of today's fantasy writers. L. Frank Baum's Oz series has elements that other authors have used in their own tales, elements that can be seen in books by Roald Dahl and J. K. Rowling, among others. Likewise, parallels to C. S. Lewis's Narnia series can be found in Philip Pullman's His Dark Materials series. But of the three, J. R. R. Tolkien has had the greatest influence on today's fantasy authors. Elements from his Lord of the Rings tetralogy appear in many authors' works. Indeed, many of the dwarves and elves featured in today's fantasy works are based on the dwarves and elves created by Tolkien.

Oz Series by L. Frank Baum In the first book in the series, *The Wonderful Wizard of Oz*, Dorothy is an ordinary girl living in Kansas when she and her house are picked up by a tornado and deposited in the magical land of Oz. Unfortunately, the house lands on an evil witch—the Wicked Witch of the East. This mishap immediately earns Dorothy the ire of the witch's sister, the Wicked Witch of the West. Dorothy wants only to return home to Kansas, and the only one who can help her is the man known as the Wizard of Oz. With no other choice, Dorothy sets off to the wizard's home in the Emerald City. Along the way Dorothy meets three others who also are journeying to see the wizard: the Scarecrow, who wants a brain; the Tin Woodsman, who wants a heart; and the Cowardly Lion, who wants courage. At every turn, Dorothy is confronted by the Wicked Witch's traps until she reaches the Emerald City where the true surprises await her. Other titles in the series: *The Land of Oz, Ozma of Oz, Dorothy and the Wizard in Oz, The Road to Oz, The Emerald City of Oz, The Patchwork Girl of Oz, The Scarecrow of Oz, Rinkitink in Oz, The Lost Princess of Oz, The Tin Woodsman of Oz, The Magic of Oz, Glinda of Oz.*

The Last Unicorn **by Peter S. Beagle**   The Unicorn who lives in the lilac wood could be the oldest and quite possibly the last of her kind. Wondering what has become of the rest of her kind, the Unicorn sets off to find out. Along the way she meets a hapless wizard named Schmendrick whose magic never works as he intends as well as a good-hearted woman named Molly Grue. They discover that an evil king named Haggard has been using a demon named the Red Bull to imprison the unicorns. But can the Unicorn and her friends rescue them in time?

Earthsea Tetralogy by Ursula K. Le Guin   The Earthsea tetralogy is about a young boy's journey into manhood and his struggle to master his magical talents. Sparrowhawk is an ordinary boy living a quiet life in a village when he begins learning magic that eventually enables him to save his village from almost certain destruction. Sparrowhawk is rewarded for this great deed with the knowledge of his true name and is then sent to an academy to learn the trade of a wizard. But in his thirst for knowledge, he accidentally sets loose upon the world an evil that he must defeat, or he will be enslaved to its will for all eternity. Titles in the series: *A Wizard of Earthsea, The Tombs of Atuan, The Farthest Shore, Tehanu.*

The Chronicles of Narnia by C. S. Lewis   In the first book in the series, *The Lion, the Witch, and the Wardrobe,* it is 1940, and Germany has begun a bombing campaign on London to bring Great Britain to her knees. Thousands have been displaced by the bombing, including four siblings whose parents are involved in the war effort. The young siblings, Peter, Susan, Edmund, and Lucy, have been sent to live with a relative, an old professor living in an ancient house in the English countryside. One day the four are playing hide-and-seek inside the professor's house when they discover a peculiar wardrobe that acts as a portal to a magical land called Narnia. Narnia is in the grip of perpetual winter caused by an evil being named the White Witch. But a prophecy has foretold that the White Witch's power will be broken and

FANTASTIC FANTASY

her reign ended if two sons of Adam and two daughters of Eve sit on the thrones at Castle Cair Paravel. Because of this prophecy, the White Witch has issued an edict against *any* humans in Narnia. The children's only hope for survival lies with the mysterious godlike lion named Aslan. Other titles in the series: *The Horse and His Boy, Prince Caspian, The Voyage of the Dawn Treader, The Silver Chair, The Last Battle, The Magician's Nephew* (prequel).

The Lord of the Rings Tetralogy by J. R. R. Tolkien   Long ago the Elven smiths of Middle Earth forged the rings of power: three rings for the Elven kings, seven for the Dwarf kings, and nine for the Human kings. At the same time the Dark Lord, Sauron, began forging a ring that would be the master of them all, enabling Sauron to realize his dream of ruling all Middle Earth. But the ring was cut from Sauron's hand during an epic battle and lost for many years until a hobbit discovered the ring and put it on. Such was the power of the ring that the hapless hobbit was twisted into a nightmarish creature called Gollum. But the ring was not content to dwell in darkness with Gollum and managed to slip off his finger. The hobbit Bilbo Baggins then discovered the ring during his adventures with the dwarves. Bilbo took the ring back to the Shire with him where he kept it for several years before passing the ring to his heir and nephew, Frodo. By this time, the wizard Gandalf has determined the evil nature of the ring and sets Frodo on the quest of destroying the ring in the fires in which it was forged—the fires of Mount Doom and the seat of Sauron's power. Sauron meanwhile has not only set his Ringwraiths to find the ring, but also has gathered his armies to march against the rest of Middle Earth. The fate of the world now rests upon some very small shoulders indeed. Titles in the series: *The Hobbit* (prequel), *The Fellowship of the Ring, The Two Towers, The Return of the King.*

Other Recommended Titles

A Spell for Chameleon by Piers Anthony

Sword of Shannara by Terry Brooks

Alice's Adventures in Wonderland by Lewis Carroll

Chronicles of Thomas Covenant by Stephen R. Donaldson

The Worm Ouroboros by E. R. Eddison

Elric Saga by Michael Moorcock

The Arthurian Saga by Mary Stewart

DEREK'S PICK

Lord of the Rings Tetralogy by J. R. R. Tolkien

BEST PICK FOR THE RELUCTANT READER

The Chronicles of Narnia by C. S. Lewis

GENERAL FANTASY

In 1954, J. R. R. Tolkien published a book series that would have a profound impact on fantasy literature, an impact that is still being felt almost fifty years later. That series was The Lord of the Rings, which contains elements imitated by a wide range of today's writers. For example, Tolkien's elves are tall and ethereally beautiful, a description that many of today's authors use in their books. Tolkien also wrote a great deal of history about his creation of Middle Earth, much of it not included in the tetralogy, that gives the reader the impression that much more is still to be learned of Middle Earth.

Because of Tolkien's influence on the genre, many contemporary authors tend to write large tales spanning several volumes. As a result, many of today's fantasies fall into the category of epic fantasy (see chapter 19), while the rest fall into the subgenres delineated in the remaining chapters of this book. Very few books written today fall into the category of general fantasy, which are books that involve magic but have no other conventions of fantasy literature, such as dragons, a crossing from Earth to another magical world, or a setting on Earth in a contemporary period.

Hart's Hope **by Orson Scott Card**   Burland, a country of enchantment and many gods, is ruled by a ruthless tyrant named King Nasilee. Convinced that he is destined to rule in Nasilee's stead, Prince Palicrovol raises an army and begins marching on Nasilee's throne at the city of Inwit. Eventually Palicrovol succeeds in taking Inwit and slays Nasilee in front of the tyrant's daughter, Asineth. Palicrovol is then driven by necessity to legitimize his rule by marrying and impregnating the young princess Asineth. He then gives the girl over to be raised by his wizard Zymas. Because of Palicrovol's actions, Asineth is driven to learn all she can of magic from Zymas and design a plan for revenge. But to do that Asineth must gather magical power to herself, and the greatest magic involves blood. The closer the link between the sacrificer of blood and the wizard, the greater the magic attained. Asineth decides to sacrifice the blood of her own child and in doing so binds him with the four gods of Burland: the Hart, the Sweet Sisters, and the newest deity known as God. Bound by the spell to Palicrovol's fate, the gods have only one choice to thwart Asineth's rise to power: the birth of a son who will destroy her powers.

***The Winter Queen* by Devin Cary**   In the land of Albor, women are not seen as fit to rule; only men have the faculties to rule effectively. But King Ethelred breaks that tradition by naming his young wife Elissa as regent until their son Edgar is old enough to rule. This decision does not sit well with the nobles of Albor, who immediately begin plotting to remove Elissa from the throne. But the nobles haven't counted on the young queen's strength and resolve in fighting for her infant son's throne, as Elissa calls upon men of honor and unspeakable powers for assistance.

***The Eyes of the Dragon* by Stephen King**   King Roland of Delain, a great hunter and man of fifty, has never married, which leaves his kingdom without an heir. That changes when Roland meets and falls in love with Sasha, a beautiful young lady of seventeen. The two marry but Roland suffers from impotence, and four years pass before Sasha is impregnated. After a great hunt in which Roland slays a dragon, he visits Sasha and ensures an heir to the throne of Delain: Peter. Four years later, Sasha gives Roland another son, named Thomas, but unfortunately she dies in the birthing, setting the stage for the rest of the story. Roland has a court magician, an advisor by the name of Flagg, who has been plotting for years to remove Roland from the throne and then rule through his son. But Flagg soon realizes that Peter will not be controllable, so he sets his sights on Thomas, easily befriending the younger son. As the years pass Peter gets in the habit of sharing a glass of wine with his father before bedtime. It is in this act of sharing between father and son that Flagg sees an opportunity to kill two birds with one stone: kill Roland and pin the crime on Peter by poisoning the wine. Despite Peter's protestations he is found guilty and imprisoned in the Needle. Thus Thomas ascends to the throne and begins Flagg's reign. But a secret cadre of Peter's friends refuse to believe Peter guilty, and they'll do anything to restore Peter's name and throne.

The Starstone Duology by Christopher Stasheff   In the first book in the series, *The Shaman,* the Ulin are an elder race of giants who view the younger races of humans and elves as toys to satisfy their pleasures, both capricious and murderous. One of their kind, Ulhane the Red, has sworn to destroy all humankind, and another, Lomallin, has sworn to defend them and defeat Ulhane at all costs. A prophecy has foretold that Lomallin will eventually prevail in this struggle, but not before dying. In the meantime, the fate of humanity rests upon the shoulders of those who fight under Lomallin's banner, a force that Ulhane views with nothing but contempt. But Ulhane makes a costly mistake in his war on humankind when his minions detain the Shaman who can heal the human Ohearn's wife. Ohearn has no choice but to lead a band of warriors against Ulhane's stronghold to free the Shaman. Ohearn's success in rescuing the Shaman sets into motion a series of events of great magnitude as men flock to Ohearn's side and escalate the conflict against Ulhane the Red's forces. Sequel: *The Sage.*

Garden of Stone **by Victoria Strauss**   Deep inside the garden lay the Stone, an artifact of great power—power so vast that it is prophesied that in the right hands, such as those of a man named Bron, it will restore unity to the world. But Bron has no desire to restore unity. Instead he steals the Stone and disappears. To Bron's daughter Cariad falls the task of penetrating the fortress that guards the garden of the Stone and confronting her father's greatest enemy, Jolyon, thereby paving the way for Bron's return and the restoration of the world's unity.

Other Recommended Titles

Morningstar by David Gemmel

Winter Warriors by David Gemmel

Fire in the Mist by Holly Lisle

Firelord by Sasha Miller

In Legend Born by Laura Resnick

DEREK'S PICK

Hart's Hope by Orson Scott Card

BEST PICK FOR THE RELUCTANT READER

The Eyes of the Dragon by Stephen King

19

The Long and Longer of It

Epic Fantasy

Epic fantasy is, in a nutshell, serial fantasy and makes up most of the fantasy that is written today. This simple definition, however, doesn't really encompass the subject. Epic fantasy has three essential components. First, the work must form at least a trilogy, if not a series. Second, the trilogy or series must take place over a span of time, preferably years. Weeks or a couple of months just won't cut it. Third, the trilogy or series must impart to the reader the impression that the books barely scratch the surface of the history of the world they create. A very good example of an epic fantasy is J. R. R. Tolkien's Lord of the Rings tetralogy, which takes place over several decades but also includes a massive back history prepared by Tolkien to not only create a new world, but also give it a history as complex as Earth's. This is the ideal of epic fantasies, but few authors come even close to that mark. Their books are generally episodic and involve characters that change over time. For example, in Piers Anthony's Magic of Xanth series, the author introduces the hero Bink, around whom the first two books are built, but as time goes on the emphasis switches to Bink's son Door and then to other characters from Xanth. Today's epic fantasy has evolved into serial fantasy whose books have only one thing in common: the setting of the stories in a particular world. Therefore, I suggest reading the various series in this section in the book order listed.

The Belgariad Series by David Eddings In the first book in the series, *Pawn of Prophecy,* the evil god Torak long ago was narrowly defeated in his bid for world domination by the sorcerer Belgarath when he led the men of the West to secure the orb Aldur. Now, years later, a priest of Torak plans to wake the evil god by stealing the orb from its resting place at Riva. Only the sorcerer Belgarath, his daughter the sorceress Polgara, and the unassuming farmboy Garion are willing to undertake a quest to stop Torak's priest and to fulfill a prophecy. But little does Garion know what lies in store for him and his companions. Other titles in the series: *Queen of Sorcery, Magician's Gambit, Castle of Wizardry, Enchanters End Game.* Related series: the Mallorean, comprising *Guardians of the West, King of the Murgos, Demon Lord of Karanda, Sorceress of Darshiva, The Seeress of Kell;* the Elenium, comprising *The Diamond Throne, The Ruby Knight, The Sapphire Rose;* and the Tamuli, comprising *Domes of Fire, The Shining Ones, The Hidden City.* Prequel to the Belgariad series: *Belgarath the Sorcerer* and its companion volumes, *Polgara the Sorceress, The Rivan Codex.*

Riftwar Series by Raymond E. Feist The first two books in the series, *Magician: Apprentice* and *Magician: Master,* are frequently published together under the title *Magician.* The orphan Pug has been apprenticed to the wizard Kulgan in the Kingdom of the Isles, but Pug's way of doing magic is alien to the traditional methods that Kulgan is teaching him. Before Pug's training can be completed, the land of Midkemia is attacked by strange invaders through a rift in the fabric of space-time. These warriors wear armor and wield weapons of lacquered wood as well as strange magic similar to Pug's. During the invasion, Pug is taken prisoner by the invaders and transported through the rift to their land of Kelewan. There Pug's powers continue to grow until he takes on a new name and a new role: Milamber, Champion of Midkemia and Kelewan. Other titles in the series: *Silverthorn, A Darkness at Sethanon.* Related series: the Empire trilogy, comprising *Daughter of the Empire, Servant of the Empire, Mistress of the Empire;* the Riftwar series, comprising *Prince of the Blood, The King's Buccaneer;* the Serpentwar saga, comprising *Shadow of a Dark Queen, Rise of a Merchant Prince, Rage of a Demon King, Shards of a Broken Crown;* the Riftwar Legacy, comprising *Krondor: The Betrayal, Krondor: The Assassins, Krondor: The Tear of the Gods, Krondor: The Crawler* (forthcoming), *Krondor: The Dark Mage* (forthcoming); and the Legends of the Riftwar: *Honoured Enemy*.

Wheel of Time Series by Robert Jordan   The first book in the series, *The Eye of the World*, takes place in the village of Emond's Field. Three boys, Rand Al'Thor, Perrin Aybara, and Matrim Cauthon, have grown up together completely unaware that they have captured the attention of an evil being named the Dark One. The Dark One has been imprisoned for years and now seeks to use the boys to help him escape and spread evil throughout the world. The Dark One also believes that Rand is the reincarnation of his ancient enemy, Lews Therin. But the boys have powerful guardians in the form of Moiraine, wielder of the One Power, and her warder, Lan. With Moiraine and Lan's help, the boys escape the Dark One's trap at Emond's Field and make their way to sanctuary at the city of Tar Valon with Moiraine's people, the Aes Sedai. But at Tar Valon, the boys learn that their journey has only just begun. Other titles in the series: *The Great Hunt, The Dragon Reborn, The Shadow Rising, The Fires of Heaven, The Lord of Chaos, A Crown of Swords, The Path of Daggers, Winter's Heart.*

Mithgar Series by Dennis L. McKiernan   The first book in the series is *The Dark Tide*. For centuries the Dark Lord has slept undisturbed, but now he has awakened and called forth an evil army to march against the kingdom of Mithgar. Galen, king of Mithgar, calls for his own army to battle the Dark Lord. Among the warriors flocking to Galen's banner are the warrows Tuck and his friends. Warrows are a small people with uncanny gifts and great courage of heart. But can their assistance help Galen defeat the Dark Lord? *The Dark Tide* is the first book in the Iron Tower trilogy. The other titles are *Shadows of Doom* and *The Darkest Day*. In order of publication, the Mithgar series includes the Silver Call duology: *Trek to Kraggen-Cor, The Brega Path; Dragondoom, Tales from the One-Eyed Crow, The Eye of the Hunter, Voyage of the Fox Rider, Tales of Mithgar, The Dragonstone;* Hel's Crucible duology: *Into the Forge, Into the Fire; Silver Wolf, Black Fox.* In chronological order, the Mithgar series is *The Dragonstone, Voyage of the Fox Rider,* Hel's Crucible duology, *Dragondoom, Tales of Mithgar, Tales from the One-Eyed Crow,* Iron Tower trilogy, *Trek to Kraggen-Cor, The Brega Path, The Eye of the Hunter, Silver Wolf, Black Fox.*

Memory, Sorrow and Thorn Series by Tad Williams   The first book in the series is *The Dragonbone Chair*. In the land of Osten Ard, the High King is on his deathbed when he calls his two sons to attend him. The two princes have long been feuding because the heir, Elias, despite protestations to the contrary, believes Josua secretly desires the throne for himself. Josua for his part has lost a hand in a failed attempt to protect Elias's wife from highwaymen, and Elias has never forgiven Josua for her death. Upon the death of their father, Elias ascends to the throne and, aided by the evil priest Pyrates, begins a reign of terror. Elias is allied with the evil undead king, who desires not only the return of lands lost to Osten Ard but the subjugation of the entire world. As civil war ensues between King Elias and Prince Josua, an impossible task is given to magician's apprentice Simon. Simon must discover the secret of swords of legendary power or all will be lost for Josua and Osten Ard. Other titles in the series: *Stone of Farewell, To Green Angel Tower, Parts 1 and 2.*

Other Recommended Titles

Magic of Xanth Series by Piers Anthony

Black Trillium by Marion Zimmer Bradley, Julian May, and Andre Norton

The Landover Series by Terry Brooks

Fortress in the Eye of Time Series by C. J. Cherryh

The Sword, the Ring, and the Chalice Trilogy by Deborah Chester

The Far Kingdoms Series by Allan Cole and Chris Bunch

Chronicles of Thomas Covenant by Stephen R. Donaldson

Lord of the Isles Series by David Drake

A Handful of Men Series by Dave Duncan

Crown of Stars Series by Kate Elliott

Runelords Series by David Farland

Rigante Series by David Gemmel

The Sword of Truth Series by Terry Goodkind

Rhapsody Series by Elizabeth Haydon

The Farseer Series by Robin Hobb

The Liveship Traders Series by Robin Hobb

Book of Words Series by J. V. Jones

Novels of the Westlands by Katherine Kerr

The Mage Wars Series by Mercedes Lackey and Larry Dixon

A Song of Ice and Fire (series) by George R. R. Martin

Recluse Series by L. E. Modesitt Jr.

The Watershed Trilogy by Douglas Niles

The Cycle of Oak, Yew, Ash and Rowan by Andre Norton and Sasha Miller

The Last of the Renshai by Mickey Zucker Reichert

Chronicles of the Cheysuli by Jennifer Roberson

Sword-Dancer Saga by Jennifer Roberson

The Demon Awakens by R. A. Salvatore

Lord of the Rings Tetralogy by J. R. R. Tolkien

Time of Troubles by Harry Turtledove

Darksword Trilogy by Margaret Weis and Tracy Hickman

The Cycle of Fire by Janny Wurts

The Wars of Light and Shadow by Janny Wurts

The Chronicles of Amber by Roger Zelazny

DEREK'S PICK

Memory, Sorrow and Thorn Series by Tad Williams

BEST PICK FOR THE RELUCTANT READER

Riftwar Series by Raymond E. Feist

20

Questing, Questing, Questing

Quest fantasy comes in three flavors: locate and/or rescue a person, locate and/or retrieve an item, or journey to destroy an item. Quest fantasy can, on rare occasions, involve a solitary character, but most frequently it involves a party of disparate adventurers armed with both sword and spell. These characters may be questing together of their own free will or may be unwilling partners in the enterprise. The adventurers frequently have distinct talents that, when pooled, enable the party to achieve its goals.

QUEST FANTASY

Quest fantasy has its origins, like so much of fantasy, in J. R. R. Tolkien's Lord of the Rings series in which the characters have to destroy a ring of great power. The "Fellowship of the Ring" comprises the swordsman Aragorn, the fighter Boromir, the elven archer Legolas, the dwarf Gimli, the wizard Gandalf, and a group of hobbits. The Fellowship is composed of heroes of various races and talents, and modern writers have modeled their own parties on the Fellowship. Quest fantasy and epic fantasy are very similar in that frequently in epic fantasy a group will be called upon to conduct a quest. In an epic fantasy series, however, later novels involving those same characters do not feature quests but focus on other activities instead. Quest fantasy, unlike epic fantasy, is very rarely longer than a trilogy as most groups generally get the job done in three books; if they didn't, readership would probably plummet as the series progressed and nothing was resolved.

Source of Magic by **Piers Anthony**   In the land of Xanth just about every resident can perform some sort of specific magic, and Bink is no different. Bink can cancel out magic; any magic cast upon him has no effect whatsoever. With this talent in mind the king of Xanth, Trent, gives Bink a unique quest: determine the source of magic in Xanth. Accompanying Bink on his quest is the centaur Chester, an archer without peer; the soldier-turned-griffin Crombie, who can always point out the trail; a six-inch-tall golem named Grundy, who can translate any language including animal; and the formidable wizard of information, Humphrey. But an unseen enemy will do anything, including turning Bink's own party against him, to stop Bink from discovering the source of magic. The unseen foe knows that Bink will stop magic from entering Xanth if he discovers its source. *Source of Magic* is part of the Magic of Xanth series, but one does not have to read the other titles in the series to understand the events. For more information on the series, please see the introduction to chapter 19.

Sword of Shannara by **Terry Brooks**   Long ago the world of Four Lands was nearly destroyed when the Warlock Lord marched against the forces of good. The only one to stop him was the elven prince Jerle Shannara, who wielded a mystical sword. Years later Shea Ohmsford lives in peace in the quiet hamlet of Shady Vale with his adopted family. That peace is shattered when the Druid Allanon comes to the vale in search of Shea. Allanon carries startling news with him: the dreaded Warlock Lord has risen again, once more marching his forces upon the Four Lands. Only Shea can stop him, for Shea is the last living descendant of Jerle Shannara and the only one who can wield the mighty sword Shannara against the Warlock Lord. Shea is very reluctant to leave the vale until he learns that one of the Warlock Lord's minions has entered the vale in search of Shea. Shea has no choice but to leave the vale, undertake the quest of recovering the sword, and, ultimately, face a showdown with the Warlock Lord himself. This is the first book in the Shannara series. Other titles include: *Elfstones of Shannara, Wishsong of Shannara.* A related series, Heritage of Shannara, includes *The Scions of Shannara, The Druid of Shannara, The Elfqueen of Shannara, The Talismans of Shannara, The First King of Shannara, Ilse Witch: The Voyage of Jerle Shannara, Antrax: The Voyage of Jerle Shannara.*

The Bitterbynde Series by Cecilia Dart-Thorton   In the first book in the series, *The Ill-Made Mute,* an orphan doesn't have a name and none in the Tower of Isse care to give the disfigured mute one. But one day the mute summons the courage to escape the tower in the hold of a wind-ship where he makes a new friend in adventurer and self-professed madman Sianadh. From Sianadh the mute will learn to speak with his hands and will receive the name Imrhien, along with the secret knowledge that he is in fact a she, raised in secret to protect her from powerful foes. Imrhien decides to journey to the one person who has a chance of explaining her history: the healer Maeve One-Eye. On the forest paths of Eireth she will discover a protector named Thorn but will also encounter dangerous wights who are under orders to stop Imrhien at all costs. Other titles in the series: *The Lady of the Sorrows, The Battle of Evernight* (2003).

Villains by Necessity by **Eve Forward**   What would happen if there were no evil in the world? In the world of Six Lands, such a thing has happened after an epic battle in which a band of heroes overthrew the forces of Darkness. But in establishing a utopia of peace and goodness, the forces of Light have created a far worse world in which to raise their children. Although there are no crimes or murders and the schools are great, it is all rather boring and static after the great victory. The female Druid Kaylana, realizing that it isn't healthy to have a world so out of balance, puts together a party of villains with the laudable goal of reintroducing evil into the world of Six Lands. Joining her is a mute Black Knight, a bored thief and sidekick, a vengeful sorceress, and a centaur who is a spy for the forces of good. And when the forces of good catch wind of what Kaylana's group intends, there will be hell to pay.

Ladylord by **Sasha Miller**   In the land of Monserria, women are not allowed to hold positions of power. Instead they are relegated to the demeaning positions of servants and maids for the men of their world.

But the children of Lord Quai of the Third Providence are all female, creating a question of inheritance upon his death. On his deathbed the lord establishes a monumental precedent by naming his first-born daughter Javere to be his heir. This infuriates the ruler of Monserria, First Lord Yassai, who sets an impossible task for Javere to undertake before she can be deemed worthy of the title of Third Lord. Yassai demands that Javere fetch a dragon's egg from the farthest reaches of Monserria. Javere sets out with a small band of trusted warriors and mages to retrieve the egg, but she doesn't realize that treachery awaits her not only on the trail but also at home.

The Lord of the Rings Tetralogy by J. R. R. Tolkien—see p. 114.

Other Recommended Titles

Through the Ice by Piers Anthony and Robert Kornwise

Black Trillium by Marion Zimmer Bradley, Julian May, and Andre Norton

Pigs Don't Fly by Mary Brown

The Unlikely Ones by Mary Brown

The Goblin Mirror by C. J. Cherryh

The Sword, the Ring, and the Chalice Trilogy by Deborah Chester

The Loregiver Series by Deborah Christian

The Witches of Eileanan by Kate Forsyth

Animist by Eve Forward

Journeys of the Catechist Series by Alan Dean Foster

Icefalcon's Quest by Barbara Hambly

A Cavern of Black Ice by J. V. Jones

Secret Texts Series by Holly Lisle

The Dragonstone by Dennis L. McKiernan

The Eye of the Hunter by Dennis L. McKiernan

Voyage of the Fox Rider by Dennis L. McKiernan

The Tower at Stony Wood by Patricia A. McKillip

Sword-Dancer Saga by Jennifer Roberson

Dark Light by Chelsea Quinn Yarbro

DEREK'S PICK

The Bitterbynde Series by Cecilia Dart-Thorton

BEST PICK FOR THE RELUCTANT READER

Villains by Necessity by Eve Forward

DUNGEONS AND DRAGONS

*It is the nature of wizards and dragons
to get along with each other.*

—Alan Dean Foster

A major portion of the fantasy paperbacks sold today are published by TSR, a subsidiary of Wizards of the Coast. Wizards of the Coast makes the popular pen-and-pencil role-playing game Dungeons and Dragons. Over time, the Wizards of the Coast has introduced to the game new worlds that have spawned a series of books. The most popular of these series are listed here. Readers of these popular series are pretty self-sufficient; if there is a particular world that they prefer to read about, they will read all the books published that are set in that realm. There are usually only two times that these readers will approach the desk for help. The first is when they are uncertain of the title of the next book to be published about the world(s) that they love. To find the answer, I suggest checking the website of Wizards of the Coast at www.wizards. com; if that is unavailable you can check www.amazon.com, but that site is somewhat more difficult to weed through than the Wizards of the Coast site.

The other time these dedicated readers approach the information desk for help is when they have read everything they care to read in a particular series and are looking for something to tide them over until the next title in that series comes out. For that I suggest books from the preceding "Quest Fantasy" section of this chapter because many similarities exist between quest fiction and Dungeons and Dragons fiction. Both involve groups of adventurers of disparate backgrounds and complementary skills attempting to fulfill a quest of some sort. The advantage is that quest fiction rarely lasts longer than a trilogy, which allows customers to read something and still be available to read the latest book in the series they enjoy. You could also offer titles from chapter

19, "Epic Fantasy," but those books are invariably longer than their counterparts in Dungeons and Dragons and also tend to be much longer than a trilogy, which could lead to some frustration for your customer. It isn't inappropriate, however, to suggest titles from chapter 19 ("Epic Fantasy") because it may be quite a long time between titles in the Dungeons and Dragons series, allowing the customer plenty of options for reading while waiting.

Major Series and Suggested Authors

FORGOTTEN REALMS

Mark Anthony

Scott Ciencin

Elaine Cunningham

Troy Denning

Ed Greenwood (creator of the
  Forgotten Realms series)

Jeff Grub

Douglas Niles

Kate Novak

R. A. Salvatore

THE DRAGONLANCE CHRONICLES

Mark Anthony

Tonya Carter

Tina Daniell

Tracy Hickman

Mary Kirchoff

Douglas Niles

Ellen Porath

Kevin Stein

Paul B. Thompson

Margaret Weis

Michael Williams

Steve Winter

MAGIC: THE GATHERING

Lynn Abbey

Loren L. Coleman

Clayton Emery

Jeff Grub

J. Robert King

Francis Lebaron

Vance Moore

Paul Thompson

Teri Williams

21

Fairy Tales

Not Just for Kids

They are the tales that have been told by parents to children for time immemorial and have occupied popular attention for centuries. They are fairy tales, and their origins may lie in simple people's search for an explanation for the inexplicable events of everyday life. For example, milk that seemed fresh the day before is found curdled the next. The answer? Fairies must have been angered by the homeowners and curdled the milk in revenge. Or an item that the owner had just seen has gone missing so it must have been taken by a mischievous gnome. Or a child is missing, in the nearby forest—a witch must have kidnapped the child with plans for dinnertime.

Fairy tales may be some of the first fantasy stories ever written, with the exception of mythological tales of gods. Fairy tales do not just involve fairies or other elvish creatures, but frequently include evil and good magic users as well. The books in this chapter are all retellings of classic fairy tales, such as "Snow White," "Cinderella," and "Rumpelstiltskin." But these are not childhood fairy tales sweetened by Walt Disney (well, actually they are, but minus the artificial sweetener added by Disney writers). Fairy tales have always been dark in setting and nature, and the books in this chapter uphold that tradition.

***Enchantment* by Orson Scott Card**   When he is ten years old, Russian Ivan Smelski finds something in the forest that will forever change his life. While running in the wild woods near his cousin Marek's farm, Ivan comes across a clearing with a pedestal in it. Lying upon the pedestal in preternatural stillness is a girl of incomprehensible beauty. But before young Ivan can creep closer, a large malevolent body begins moving through the underbrush toward the clearing. Frightened, Ivan runs back to the safety of his cousin's farm where he finds preparations under way for his family's emigration to Israel—the Jewish Smelskis have been granted a visa. The Smelskis, however, don't emigrate to Israel but instead make their way to the United States. Years pass and Ivan is now a graduate student studying Slavic languages and folklore when he gets the opportunity to continue his studies in the U.S.S.R. Leaving his fiancée behind in America, Ivan journeys back to the land of his youth and finds himself once again in the woods near his cousin Marek's farm. As he explores the woods of his childhood, he again finds the mysterious clearing in which he saw the sleeping beauty, and this time Ivan doesn't run when the evil beast begins moving in the underbrush. Instead he tricks the beast and manages to kiss the girl, awakening her from her millennia-long sleep. But Ivan's troubles are just beginning as the newly awakened Katerina leads him across a time bridge to the Russia of A.D. 890. Once there he learns that the powerful and evil witch Baba Yaga is responsible for Katerina's curse and that the only way to break it is for Katerina and Ivan to marry. But even this isn't enough trouble, as the evil Baba Yaga sets into motion a plot that could destroy all that Katerina holds dear.

***Faerie Tale* by Raymond E. Feist**   On the outside it would appear that Phil Hastings has it all—a beautiful wife, three wonderful kids, and a lucrative career as a writer. All that changes, however, when the Hastings purchase an old house in upstate New York. Known as the old Kessler Place, or Hill of the Elf King, the house is a subject of great mysteries and even stranger events. Then, in the woods, Phil's sons make a strange discovery that awakens an ancient and unspeakable evil. The family must find a way to stop it before all is lost.

***Spindle's End* by Robin McKinley**   After long years of childlessness, a king and queen are delighted to announce the birth of their daughter, thus ensuring an heir to the kingdom. But disaster strikes at the young girl's naming day ceremony (where she is given the name Casta Albinia Allegra Dove Minerva Fidelia Aletta Blythe Domina Delicia Aurelia Grace Isabel Griselda Gwyneth Pearl Ruby Coral Lily Iris Briar-Rose). Among the fairies attending is the evil Pernicia. Pernicia freezes the crowd and bestows a curse rather than a gift upon the hapless child: on her twenty-first birthday Rose will prick her finger on a spindle and fall into a poisoned sleep to die. But also in the assemblage is a young fairy named Katriona, who flies with the baby Rose to raise her in secret. As the years pass Rose grows into a young woman of incomparable beauty, as might be expected since this is a fairy tale, but she is also a woman of courage and intellect, which isn't expected since it *is* a fairy tale. As her twenty-first birthday approaches and Rose learns of her true identity and the curse, she strikes upon a plan to remove the curse. Using a friend as a stand-in, Rose and her friends set off on a quest to confront and defeat Pernicia in her own lair. *Spindle's End* is a retelling of "Sleeping Beauty."

***Beauty* by Sheri S. Tepper**   In fourteenth-century England, Beauty is the daughter of the Duke of Westfaire and the Queen of Faerie, making the girl half fairy. Because of a social slight, one of Beauty's fairy aunts sets a curse upon the girl: on her sixteenth birthday the daughter of the Duke of Westfaire will prick her finger on a spindle and die. But unbeknownst to the evil fairy, the Duke has another daughter who was born on the same day: Beloved. And it is Beloved who falls victim to the curse, allowing Beauty to escape the castle before an enchanted hedge appears around it. She is free to begin the search for her fairy mother and avenge the curse. But that plan is interrupted when Beauty is picked up by twenty-second-century time-traveling scholars who whisk her away on a time-traveling adventure of several lifetimes. *Beauty* is a retelling of "Sleeping Beauty" with a science-fiction/fantasy blend for a setting.

***The Snow Queen* by Joan Vinge**   The Hegemony is a vast empire of planets. On one of those planets, Tiamat, lies the secret to eternal youth. Tiamat is ruled by Arienhod, the cruel Winter Queen who controls access to the elixir of life. To keep Tiamat's power and status in check, the rest of the Hegemony has instituted a ban on technological development on the planet. Although this act does not sit well with

Arienhod, it is the least of her concerns as her reign is coming to an end. Rule of Tiamat is based on the seasons, which last fifty years on the planet. During the winter season the Winter Queen rules, and with summer approaching, Arienhod must give way to the ruler of the summer people. Desperate to retain her throne, Areinhod places a clone of herself with the summer people in the hope that she will be chosen Summer Queen. Her clone, known as Moon Dawn Treader, has been raised by the summer clan completely unaware of her heritage. Moon's best friend and lover is a man named Sparks. The two lovers dream of one day passing the tests to become Sybils, or oracles, for the clan. But when Moon passes the test and Sparks fails it, he sets off in a huff to the city of Carbuncle, the residence of the Winter Queen. Dismayed at this turn of events, Moon also sets off on a journey to find Sparks at Carbuncle. Meanwhile, Sparks has taken a position at the Snow Queen's court where he has caught the eye of the Winter Queen herself! *The Snow Queen* is a retelling of the Hans Christian Andersen tale of the same name and was the recipient of the 1981 Hugo Award for best novel. Although the setting of the book makes it a science-fiction title, the fact that it is a retelling of a fairy tale has prompted me to place it in this chapter. Sequels: *Summer Queen, Tangled Up in Blue.*

Other Recommended Titles

Snow White, Blood Red edited by Ellen Datlow and Terri Windling

Firebird by Mercedes Lackey

The Serpent's Shadow by Mercedes Lackey

Ella Enchanted by Gail Carson Levine

Once Upon a Winter's Night by Dennis L. McKiernan

Rose Daughter by Robin McKinley

Confessions of an Ugly Stepsister by Gregory Maguire

Daughter of the Forest by Juliet Marillier

Crazy Jack by Donna Jo Napoli

The Magic Circle by Donna Jo Napoli

Spinners by Donna Jo Napoli

Zel by Donna Jo Napoli

A Hidden Magic by Vivian Vande Velde

Bring Me the Head of Prince Charming by Roger Zelazny and Robert Sheckley

DEREK'S PICK

The Snow Queen by Joan Vinge

BEST PICK FOR THE RELUCTANT READER

Enchantment by Orson Scott Card

22

Larger than Life

Humanity has always believed in and told stories of heroes and gods. The books in this chapter fall into two categories: stories about gods from ancient pantheons, such as those of Greece and India; and stories about heroes from ancient folklore, such as Finn MacCool and King Arthur. The books involving gods do not necessarily have gods as major characters; the gods in question may simply provide the impetus that moves the plot. The heroes in this chapter do have to be major characters and must be from a country's folklore, such as Great Britain's Arthur.

LEGENDS AND MYTHS

American Gods by Neil Gaiman   America had long been a land with few gods, except for those brought to the country's shores by the endless waves of settlers. Because a god's strength is based on belief, the immigrants who brought the gods with them would also abandon them when confronted by the challenge of making a new start in America. In the midst of this, a prisoner named Shadow is released from prison early because of the death of his wife in a car accident. With no family, no job, and no prospects for the future, Shadow accepts an offer from the enigmatic stranger Wednesday to become a handyman and thus begins a journey into the darkest heart of America. Wednesday is in reality the Norse god Odin the All-Father, and he is on a journey to gather all the elder gods abandoned by their people in America. Odin then plans to launch an attack against the new American gods—the Internet, the media, and technology—in an epic battle that will decide which god will reign supreme.

Mythago Woods Series by Robert Holdstock   In the first book in the series, *Mythago Wood,* Earth was once covered by a great forest in which resided humankind's racial consciousness. As the centuries passed, the once-mighty forest was encroached upon by humankind, who eventually cut it back to a tiny corner of Great Britain. Living on the edge of the wood is the Huxley family, whose father, George, took his obsession with the wood's secrets to his grave. His sons Steven and Christian have discovered their father's notes about the mysterious contents of the wood and have taken up where he left off. One day Christian enters the wood and disappears, leaving Steven to explore the wood's outer portions. Soon Steven meets the beautiful Goddess of the Hunt Mythago, instantly falls in love with her, and unknowingly follows her deeper into the wood and the dangers held there. Christian, however, has been changed by his tenure in the wood and has become a savage of enormous ferocity and strength. He is also in love with the huntress and will challenge Steven for her and for mastery of the power of Mythago Wood. Other titles in the series: *Lavondyss, The Bone Forest* (short-story collection), *The Hollowing, Merlin's Wood, Gates of Ivory, Gates of Horn.*

Children of the Changeling Series by J. Gregory Keyes   In the first book in the series, *The Waterborn,* the River God and the Forest God have long ago fought a ferocious battle in which the world was forged. The River God claimed sway over all the lands that his waters touched, and his blood flows in the veins of the Imperial family at the city of Nhol. Herzhi is the young princess of the empire, and as she approaches puberty she begins to feel the stirrings of magic within herself. She quickly realizes that these powers are going to attract dangerous attention, and in desperation she wishes for a hero. Meanwhile, in the land of the Forest God a young man named Perkar is haunted by dreams of a young lady trapped in a palace of ivory. Perkar is sworn to slay the River God and is granted a sword of legendary power from the Forest God to help him in his quest. Thus armed he sets off on a journey to free the woman in his dreams and slay a god. Other title in the series: *The Blackgod.*

***Coyote Blue* by Christopher Moore**   Everything is going great in Sam Hunter's life: he has a great job as an insurance salesman and owns a beautiful condo. All of that changes when he stops to admire a gorgeous blonde on the way to an appointment. The next thing he knows, his carefully tended life is turned upside down by a mysterious buckskin-clad Indian. The Indian is the Native American god Coyote, and he wants to use Sam to return faith to his people. But returning to the reservation is not an option for Sam because he has been on the run for twenty years after a youthful indiscretion in which he assaulted a local police officer. Returning to his normal life is not possible either, as long as Coyote is involved, so Sam finds himself returning to the land of his youth on a hilarious journey of self-discovery.

Books of the Gods Series by Fred Saberhagen   In the first book in the series, *The Face of Apollo,* the gods of ancient Greece and Rome have returned after years of absence to once again hold dominion over humankind. But all is not well with the gods as a battle erupts inside Mount Olympus between Hades, the god of the underworld, and Apollo, god of light. After a fierce exchange of blows, Hades slays Apollo. One of Apollo's followers, Sal, quickly attends to the fallen god and just as quickly departs from Mount Olympus. Days later a wounded Sal stumbles out of the woods and into the arms of farm laborer Jeremy Redthorn. Sal makes Jeremy promise to carry the mysterious object she took from Apollo to her friends. Jeremy later discovers that the mysterious object is Apollo's mask, which contains the god's powers and personality. By donning the mask of Apollo, Jeremy becomes the avatar of Apollo and discovers that the battle with Hades has only just begun. Other titles in the series: *Ariadne's Web, The Arms of Hercules, God of the Golden Fleece, Gods of Fire and Thunder.*

Other Recommended Titles

The Willing Spirit by Piers Anthony

The Fall of Atlantis by Marion Zimmer Bradley

Faery in Shadow by C. J. Cherryh

World without End by Molly Cochran and Warren Murphy

Child of the Eagle by Esther Friesner

Lion of Macedon by David Gemmell

Summer King, Winter Fool by Lisa Goldstein

The Hammer and the Cross Series by Harry Harrison

Daughters of Bast by Sarah Isidore

Song of Albion by Stephen R. Lawhead

Brian Boru: Emperor of the Irish by Morgan Llywelyn

Finn MacCool by Morgan Llywelyn

Lion of Ireland by Morgan Llywelyn

Arcana Series by Morgan Llywelyn and Michael Scott

Oath of Swords by David Weber

DEREK'S PICK

Mythago Woods Series by Robert Holdstock

BEST PICK FOR THE RELUCTANT READER

Coyote Blue by Christopher Moore

ARTHURIAN LEGEND

He is a figure of mythic proportions and tragic history. Very few people real or imagined have inspired the body of literature that King Arthur has. One would have to be living under a rock to not be familiar with the legend of King Arthur. Historians now believe that Arthur did exist and was most likely a warlord of great strategic as well as martial talents. The historical Arthur is believed to have united the tribes of Britain against the Saxons, finally defeating them in A.D. 495. Arthur presided over forty years of peace before falling at the Battle of Camlann in A.D. 537. The legend of Arthur with which most people are familiar was established by Sir Thomas Malory in *Le Morte d'Arthur*, published in the fifteenth century. It is this version from which most of today's authors draw their inspiration when writing about Arthur and his court.

Why is Arthur so popular? Quite possibly the answer is that he was one of the English-speaking world's first heroes. In a world marked by humans' depredations on one another, Arthur and his knights were notable in their devotion to chivalry and honor. The answer could also lie in the allure of Arthur and Guinevere's doomed romance. Arthur is considered one of the best kings of early Britain because of the forty years of peace his reign enjoyed. Many also believe that in times of Britain's greatest peril, Arthur will return from Avalon to lead his country back to peace. As a symbol of honor and chivalry or a savior of peace, Arthur has few peers in fantasy literature.

The Mists of Avalon by Marion Zimmer Bradley   Vivian, the Lady of the Lake, is on a quest to find a king who will help preserve the old ways of the Druids and of Avalon against the encroachment of Christianity. Vivian thinks that she's found such a king in Arthur. But Arthur is married to Gwenhwyfar, a woman passionately devoted to Christianity. Opposing Gwenhwyfar is Arthur's half sister Morgaine, who desires a return to the old ways and the outright banishment of Christianity from Britain. Sequels: *Lady of Avalon, The Forest House*. Prequel: *Priestess of Avalon*.

Pendragon Cycle by Stephen R. Lawhead   In the first book in the series, *Taliesin*, Elphin, the only son of Lord Gwyddno, is considered unlucky by all who meet him. His luck changes one day when he discovers an infant of enormous potential. Elphin raises the boy, named Taliesin, who grows to be the greatest of all the bards. Meanwhile in legendary Atlantis a young princess named Charis witnesses her mother being butchered as the opening to a brutal civil war. Charis wisely flees the doomed island and seeks the safety of Britain. There she meets and falls in love with the bard Taliesin. The couple's union is soon blessed with the birth of a son and the start of a legend: Merlin. Other titles in the cycle: *Merlin, Arthur, Pendragon*.

Merlin's Descendants Series by Irene Radford   In the first book in the series, *Guardian of the Balance*, Arylwren, Wren to her friends, was a child that was never meant to be—the product of a forbidden union. Her father was the mighty mage Merlin, and the two of them travel extensively throughout Britain while Merlin keeps his eyes on his charges: Arthur, the boy who will one day be king, and his friends, who will form the nucleus of the Round Table champions. Merlin also uses this time to train his daughter in the magic she will need to survive in an increasingly dangerous world. But not even Merlin could foresee how mighty in sorcerous powers his daughter would become or that one day she would be the lynchpin in Arthur's and Camelot's defense. Sequels: *Guardian of the Trust, Guardian of the Vision*.

The Arthurian Saga by Mary Stewart   This series is the epic retelling of the legend of King Arthur through the perspective of his mentor, the wizard Merlin. Starting with the childhood of Merlin, it chronicles every moment in the Arthurian legend: the selection and tutoring of Arthur to be king, the drawing of the sword from the stone, the incestuous affair of Morgause and Arthur that produces Mordred, Mordred's rise in Arthur's court, and the inevitable downfall of Arthur and his kingdom. Books in the series: *The Crystal Cave, The Hollow Hills, The Last Enchantment, The Wicked Day*.

The Once and Future King Series by T. H. White   The first book in the series: *The Sword in the Stone,* is a retelling of Sir Thomas Malory's *Le Morte d'Arthur*. Arthur, known to most as Wart, a name given to him by his adopted brother Kay, lives in the forest Savauge with his adoptive family. One day while trying to find his adoptive father Sir Ector's favorite falcon, Arthur stumbles across Merlyn's cottage. Merlyn becomes Arthur's tutor and begins teaching him life lessons, often transforming the boy into various animals. Soon Sir Ector learns that the king of England, Uther Pendragon, has died and his successor will be the one who can draw a sword from a stone in London. Kay begs his father to let him try and Sir Ector reluctantly agrees, since they will be in London for a jousting tournament anyway. At the tournament Kay realizes he has left his sword at their lodgings, so he sends Wart to fetch it. But Arthur isn't able to get into the room, so he goes looking for another sword and finds one set in a stone in a churchyard. When he draws the sword from the stone, he is declared the king of Britain. Titles in the series: *The Sword in the Stone, The Queen of Air and Darkness* (originally titled *The Witch in the Wood*), *The Ill-Made Knight, The Candle in the Wind.*

Other Recommended Titles

The Merlin Effect by Thomas A. Barron

The Forever King by Molly Cochran and Warren Murphy

The Winter King by Bernard Cornwell

Fang the Gnome by Michael Greatex Covey

Gawain and Lady Green by Anne Eliot Crompton

The Dragon Lord by David Drake

Firelord by Parke Godwin

Strange Devices of the Sun and Moon by Lisa Goldstein

The Merlin Codex by Robert Holdstock

Black Horses for the King by Anne McCaffrey

The Hallowed Isle Series by Diana L. Paxson

Merlin's Bones by Fred Saberhagen

I Am Mordred by Nancy Springer

The Books of Merlin by Nikolai Tolstoy

DEREK'S PICK

The Arthurian Saga by Mary Stewart

BEST PICK FOR THE RELUCTANT READER

The Mists of Avalon by Marion Zimmer Bradley

23

Historical Fantasy

Historical fantasy is fantasy that takes place in a historical setting. It can also be called "alternate history" because authors frequently change the historical accuracy of a time period by inserting magic into the story line. The authors of books in this chapter use historical times, places, and even people, much as historical fiction authors do when creating a story. The difference is that authors of fantasy historical fiction inject magic into their stories. Many readers of historical fantasy will happily read popular historical fiction, but few historical fiction readers are interested in historical fantasy. For the most part, readers of historical fiction prefer the books to be historically accurate. It is, however, appropriate to suggest books from chapter 22, "Larger than Life," particularly those on the Arthurian legend, to readers of historical fantasy. Just make sure that the setting of the recommended book is historical before giving it to the customer.

The Tales of Alvin Maker by Orson Scott Card   The first book in the series, *Seventh Son,* takes place in the Indiana Territory of late eighteenth-century alternate America. A momentous event is about to occur. Alvin Miller is a seventh son, and his wife is pregnant with their seventh son, marking this child as extraordinary even before its birth. A child with such enormous potential would also have powerful enemies, one of whom attacks the family and slays one of Alvin's sons, Vigor, but not before Alvin Jr., the seventh son, is born. Once the family settles in the town of Vigor Church, named in honor of Alvin's brother, Alvin again becomes the target of evil forces—a being known as the Unmaker. Although the Unmaker is unable to attack Alvin Maker directly, he can have great influence on others and will stop at nothing to remove Alvin as a threat. Other titles in the series: *Red Prophet, Prentice Alvin, Alvin Journeyman, Heartfire.*

The Crown of Stars Series by Kate Elliott   Although the first book in the series, *King's Dragon*, takes place in a fictitious world, the setting is based on medieval European history and thus is included in this subgenre. King Henry of Wendar rules over a troubled land. The utterly inhuman Eika have invaded and are cutting a swath of destruction down the coast of Wendar. At the same time, Sabella, Henry's half sister and ruler of the rival land Varre, has led an army against Henry because he has named his bastard son Sanglant as his heir. Two youths will have an essential role in the upcoming confrontation between Henry and Sabella: Alain and Liath. Alain is a young orphan who wishes to be a soldier but is instead destined for the priesthood when he receives a vision from the Goddess Lady of Battles. In the vision the lady exhorts Alain to find his destiny, so he leaves the monastery and attaches himself to the court of Count Lavine, a man who could hold the secret to Alain's past and future. Liath, on the other hand, has been turned into a virtual slave by the priest Hugh as payment for suspicious unpaid debts that her father owed the priest. In reality Hugh is hoping to gain possession of the spell book Liath's father left her but is thwarted in his ambitions when Liath is chosen for King Henry's Eagles, who provide messenger and spy services for the king of Wendar. Even as Henry and Sabella move toward each other, the shadow of the Eika grows stronger every day, threatening to overwhelm them all. Other titles in the series: *Prince of Dogs, The Burning Stone, Child of Flame,* and the tentatively titled and forthcoming *Crown of Stars.*

The Hammer and the Cross Series by Harry Harrison   In the first book in the series, *The Hammer and the Cross*, Shef is a young smith in East Anglia (England) in the ninth century. Driven by strange visions from

Nordic gods, Shef forges a sword of incomprehensible strength—a sword so strong that when a group of Vikings named the Ragnarssons invade East Anglia, their swords break upon Shef's sword. Despite the best efforts of her defenders, East Anglia falls to the Vikings and Shef flees for his life. Soon Shef stumbles upon another group of Vikings in the forest who are opposed to the Ragnarssons and joins them by allying with their mighty leader Brand. Shef is a natural engineer and begins developing war machines to help Brand's band defeat the Ragnarssons. But Shef's successes have drawn attention from the Christian church, which asks for help from Rome in stopping Brand's group. Rome's response could destroy not only Shef but also the rest of Brand's Vikings. Other titles in the series: *One King's Way, King and Emperor.*

The Moon and the Sun by Vonda McIntyre   In the court of the Sun King, Louis XIV, the king is obsessed with discovering the secret of immortality and believes he can obtain it from the organs of sea creatures. To achieve this Louis orders the Jesuit priest Yves de la Croix to capture sea monsters. Yves captures and brings back two monsters: a male, which is dead, and a living female. Under Louis's watchful gaze, Yves begins dissecting the corpse with the assistance of his sister Marie-Josephe. Soon Marie-Josephe realizes that the female sea monster is sentient and tries to convince Louis to release her back into the seas. But resistance in Louis's court is very stiff and Marie-Josephe's only ally is her lover, Count Lucien. All too soon Marie-Josephe and Lucien will discover the price of defying a king. *The Moon and the Sun* won the 1997 Nebula Award for best novel.

The Hallowed Isle Series by Diana L. Paxson   The legend of Arthur is retold, with each of the four volumes revolving around a different mythical event. Volume 1, *The Book of the Sword,* involves the power vacuum left when Rome withdraws from Britain. To end this the Lady of the Lake encloses a mighty blade in stone and calls upon the god of war to send a champion worthy of wielding the blade and uniting the warring tribes of Britain. The champion she receives is Artor, a gifted warrior and leader who inspires his men with his desire for peace and unity in Britain. Other titles in the series: *The Book of the Spear, The Book of the Cauldron, The Book of the Stone.*

Other Recommended Titles

The Silver Wolf by Alice Borchardt

The Merlin of St. Giles Well by Ann Chamberlin

Child of the Eagle by Esther Friesner

Lion of Macedon by David Gemmell

The Books of Ash Series by Mary Gentle

Strange Devices of the Sun and Moon by Lisa Goldstein

The Demon Sword by Ken Hood

The Black Chalice by Marie Jakober

The Diaries of the Family Dracul (series) by Jeanne Kalogridis

The Serpent's Shadow by Mercedes Lackey

Brian Boru: Emperor of the Irish by Morgan Llywelyn

Druids by Morgan Llywelyn

The Elementals by Morgan Llywelyn

Finn MacCool by Morgan Llywelyn

The Horse Goddess by Morgan Llywelyn

Lion of Ireland by Morgan Llywelyn

Etruscans by Morgan Llywelyn and Michael Scott

The Shadow of Albion by Andre Norton and Rosemary Edghill

The Master of All Desires by Judith Merkle Riley

The Shattered Oath by Josepha Sherman

The Hand and the Falcon Trilogy by Judith Tarr

DEREK'S PICK

The Moon and the Sun by Vonda McIntyre

BEST PICK FOR THE RELUCTANT READER

The Tales of Alvin Maker by Orson Scott Card

24

The Dark Side of Fantasy

If science-fiction/fantasy blenders are a mixture of equal parts science fiction and fantasy, then dark fantasy is a blending of horror and fantasy in equal parts. The purpose of dark fantasy, unlike horror, isn't to scare the reader but to demonstrate that fantasy doesn't *have* to be about shining realms of happy creatures. Instead the realms can be places of darkness, where evil not only strides openly across the land, but also has no qualms about revealing its face, unlike Tolkien's Sauron. The conflict of good versus evil takes on much greater importance in a dark fantasy, unlike most fantasy fiction in which the conflict between good and evil frequently has an ambiguous ending. Dark fantasy is also usually cast with monsters that are more evil than the cast of your typical fantasy novel. Whereas the goblins and orcs of typical fantasy are ugly and tend to have a taste for human flesh, the monsters of dark fantasy will not only be extremely ugly or disfigured, but will frequently torture a human before devouring him or her. Another difference between fantasy and dark fantasy is the heroes. Although the hero of a typical fantasy novel may not be courageous at first, he or she will find courage in time to do what needs to be done to bring about the plot's denouement. Dark fantasy heroes are typically antiheroes. They generally are pressed into service by forces beyond their control, because given their choice they would rather have been left alone. Be wary of recommending books from this chapter to readers of such authors as Mercedes Lackey or Piers Anthony; it would be tantamount to giving *The Exorcist* to someone whose favorite movie is *Casper*. This is one of the few subgenres in fantasy where it is extremely important that you, as a librarian, understand exactly what your customer is asking for.

The Banned and the Banished Series by James Clemens The first book in the series is *Wit'ch Fire*. Five hundred years ago the evil Gul'gotha invaded Alsea, slaying all the goodly Chi mages and beginning a five-hundred-year-long reign of terror. Unbeknownst to the Gul'gotha, three Chi mages were able to create an arcane artifact that held the promise of removing the Gul'gotha from power. Five centuries later Elena, a simple farm girl, discovers that her hand has turned red, an ancient sign that she is the Wit'ch of Spirit and Stone—the Wielder of Blood Magic. But the Gul'gotha have sensed Elena's awakening powers and sent demonic minions to capture her. Elena's hopes lie with a group of companions who will help her recover the artifact created by the Chi mages and restore freedom to Alsea. Titles in the series: *Wit'ch Storm, Wit'ch War, Wit'ch Gate.*

The Chronicles of the Black Company by Glen Cook They were the Black Company—mercenaries whose moral compass was very simple: get the job done at any cost. Some of the company were men of cruel appetites, others were men of noble aspirations; together they were a force to be reckoned with. The company had a proud tradition of getting the job done whether it was good or evil. But then the company was hired by the Lady, a figure of incomprehensible evil and cruelty. Her lieutenant and new commander of the company was the fearsome being known as the Soulcatcher. But the challenges for the Lady and Soulcatcher were only beginning as a new force, a force of good, loomed on the horizon. Titles in the series: The Books of the North: *The Black Company, Shadows Linger, The White Rose;* The Books of the South: *Shadow Games, Dreams of Steel;* Books of the Glittering Stone: *Bleak Seasons, She Is the Darkness, Water Sleeps, Soldiers Live.*

Neverwhere **by Neil Gaiman** Richard Mayhew is a young, successful businessman in London and has a beautiful but cold fiancée. This changes one night when Richard stops to help an injured young lady named Door. The next day Richard ceases to exist in our world and instead becomes a resident of London Below. London Below is a world of shadows and darkness, where the myths and legends of the distant past exist. Door is on a quest to discover who murdered her family and why; Richard only wants to return to his life in London Above. Richard has no choice but to help Door in her quest in the hope that he will find a way home. The two, however, will first have to defeat a loathsome evil.

***Dark Cities under Ground* by Lisa Goldstein** When he was a child Jeremy Jones told his mother strange stories of a place called Neverwas. His mother wrote those stories down, creating the highly successful children's book series The Adventures of Jeremy in Neverwas. Years later Jeremy is a middle-aged recluse angry with his mother because he feels she robbed him of his childhood with her books. Ruthie Berry is a writer hoping to interview and learn more about Jeremy, her childhood hero. Ruthie soon begins to suspect that Jeremy really did visit another land when he was a child, a suspicion that is borne out when she and Jeremy enter the nightmarish land of Neverwas. Neverwas is a land of elder gods and creatures from the darkest parts of the human heart. Jeremy and Ruthie discover that a power struggle is developing between the gods of Neverwas and an engineer who hopes to control all the underworld through his robots.

***The High House* by James Stoddard** Evenmere is the High House, a house of indeterminable vastness, whose rooms lead to entirely different dimensions and worlds. The attic contains a dragon with oracular talents and a taste for human flesh. The cellar contains the monsters of our darkest nightmares, the denizens of innumerable closets and under-the-bed spaces. The High House is also the metaphysical hub of the universe, the last bastion of order. High House's importance cannot be denied: if its lights go out, then suns will go nova, and if its clocks run down, then time will stop. Carter Anderson, the young heir to Evenmere, has been called back from a fourteen-year absence because his father, the Lord of Evenmere, is missing and presumed dead. Carter has been called home to become Evenmere's new master and protector from the forces of chaos who desire the house for themselves. Carter doesn't think that his father is dead, and with the help of some friends he sets out to find his father and the master keys to the house in order to lock chaos out of Evenmere forever.

Other Recommended Titles

The Last Rune Series by Mark Anthony

Something Wicked This Way Comes by Ray Bradbury

The Hobb's Bargain by Patricia Briggs

Running with the Demon by Terry Brooks

The Night Parade by Scott Ciencin

Snow White, Blood Red edited by Ellen Datlow and Terri Windling

Chronicles of Thomas Covenant by Stephen R. Donaldson

Dance of the Dead by Christie Golden

The Enemy Within by Christie Golden

Vampire of the Mists by Christie Golden

Scholar of Decay by Tanya Huff

Heart of Midnight by J. Robert King

Knight of the Black Rose by James Lowder

Elric Saga by Michael Moorcock

DEREK'S PICK

The High House by James Stoddard

BEST PICK FOR THE RELUCTANT READER

Neverwhere by Neil Gaiman

25

Ever Since I Died,
I Can't Sleep at Night

Vampires, Werewolves, Ghosts,
and Other Undead

I know what you're thinking: "What in the world do vampires have to do with fantasy?" Plenty, in the case of the books in this chapter. Vampires have occupied a special place in popular culture and in folklore for hundreds of years. No one is certain where the idea of vampires came from, but possibly they arose from folktales in which neighbors who supposedly had died were later seen returning from the graveyard. Vampires could have originated with some people's dietary need for blood. Whatever their origin, vampires have recently become very popular as characters in fantasy. Part of their popularity may stem from the abilities that vampires possess: shape-changing, hypnotism, supernatural strength and speed, for example, which make vampires very attractive as characters.

VAMPIRES

At this point you may be asking, "So why are vampires not in the genre of horror?" The answer is that of course they are. But they are also in fantasy because of their powers. How do you explain a person coming back from the dead? Or a person who can change shape into a bat, a wolf, or even mist? Or a person who can compel someone to accept a brutal bite on the neck without complaint? Magic is really the only answer to these questions and is the reason why the following books are in this chapter. But not all vampire fiction belongs in fantasy. For example, you won't see Anne Rice or Bram Stoker on this list because the focus of their books is different. The books in this chapter don't actively try to scare the reader; instead, they focus on the vampire's abilities and character, not exclusively on his or her hungers and hunts. Frequently the vampires in fantasy literature are detectives, warriors, or wizards and use their particular skills to their advantage in their chosen field. A good example is P. N. Elrod's Jack Flemming, who becomes a detective after being made into a vampire.

***In the Forests of the Night* by Amelia Atwater-Rhodes**   Three hundred years ago Rachel's life was forever changed when her family and her very humanity were stripped from her by a vampire named Ather. Rachel took the name of Risika upon her rebirth as a vampire and spent the next three centuries learning her new vampiric abilities. Now Risika spends her days in Concord, Massachusetts, and her nights prowling the streets of New York City searching for her next victim. After one of these hunts Risika returns to her home and makes a startling discovery. She finds a black rose, the same kind of rose that was given to her upon her death. Risika is certain that the rose is a challenge from her archenemy Aubrey, the vampire she holds responsible for her brother's death. But in accepting the challenge Risika will have some uncomfortable revelations about herself and learn the shocking truth surrounding her brother's death. Atwater-Rhodes was a fourteen-year-old student in junior high school when she wrote this book. Sequel: *Demon in My View*.

***Those Who Hunt the Night* by Barbara Hambly**   Vampires have been "living" quietly in London since the reign of Elizabeth I. But someone is hunting the vampires' coffins and exposing them to the sunlight as they sleep, thereby destroying them. The vampires cannot hunt the murderer in the daylight, so they turn to James Asher, ex-spy turned professor. The vampires offer Asher a devil's pact: if he refuses to help them find the murderer, they will kill his wife. If he learns too much, they will kill both Ashers. Sequel: *Traveling with the Dead*.

The Anita Blake Series by Laurell K. Hamilton   In the first book in the series, *Guilty Pleasures,* vampires have come out of the darkness to take a position of equality with humans. But what happens if a creature possessing supernatural strength, agility, and other abilities breaks the law? The answer is to issue a death warrant and call the executioner. The executioner is Anita Blake, a tough necromancer who can briefly reanimate dead bodies and permanently put the undead back in their graves. The problem is that someone is killing vampires, and the most powerful vampire in the city, Nikolaos, wants Anita to find the killer. Other titles in the series: *The Laughing Corpse, A Circus of the Damned, The Lunatic Café, Bloody Bones, The Killing Dance, Burnt Offerings, Blue Moon, Obsidian Butterfly, Narcissus in Chains.*

***Anno Dracula* by Kim Newman**   In 1880s England, vampires have come to power through the marriage of Count Dracula and Queen Victoria. Vampirism has become fashionable as a result, and just about any street-corner prostitute is able to confer it on a buyer. But not everyone cares for fashionable vampirism. A shadowy figure called Jack knows that vampires can be slain if any internal body organ is heavily damaged, a fact he demonstrates at every opportunity, earning him the moniker "the Ripper." But Jack is in reality Dr. John Seward, who slew Dracula's love interest, Lucy Westerna. The police assign a vampire detective to hunt down and stop Jack at all costs. Sequels: *The Bloody Red Baron, Judgement of Tears.*

***One Foot in the Grave* by William Mark Simmons**   Chris Csejthe is the victim of a rare degenerative blood disease. Chris is desperate for a cure and for information about the strange occurrences surrounding the death of his wife and child. Chris discovers that his rare blood condition is indeed vampirism and that his family may have been murdered. Soon he is the target both of vampire hunters who want to kill him and of rival vampire clans who want him to join them. Chris must decide who to trust as well as figure out who was responsible for his condition and the murder of his family.

Other Recommended Titles

I Am Dracula by C. Dean Anderson	The Vampire Files (series) by P. N. Elrod
I, Strahd by P. N. Elrod	*Vampire of the Mists* by Christopher Golden

Immortal by Christopher Golden and Nancy Holder

Victory Nelson Series by Tanya Huff

Diaries of the Family Dracul (series) by Jeanne Kalogridis

The Silver Kiss by Annette Curtis Klause

Knights of the Blood by Katherine Kurtz and Scott MacMillan

Bloodsucking Fiends by Christopher Moore

Vampire Hunter by Michael Romkey

Vampire Series by Fred Saberhagen

Blood Secrets by Karen Taylor

Companions of the Night by Vivian Vande Velde

Cycle of Count Ragoczy Saint-Germain by Chelsea Quinn Yarbo

Dark Light by Chelsea Quinn Yarbro

DEREK'S PICK

The Anita Blake Series by Laurell K. Hamilton

BEST PICK FOR THE RELUCTANT READER

In the Forests of the Night by Amelia Atwater-Rhodes

WEREWOLVES

Werewolves run a very close second behind vampires in popularity as characters in the dark fantasy subgenre, primarily because they enjoy similar abilities—shape-shifting from wolf form to human form, supernatural strength and speed, and highly refined senses. Their status may also reflect the romanticism of the noble yet savage beast popularized by the fairy tale "Beauty and the Beast." The titles in this section all have werewolves as their primary characters, and for the most part these beings are good in nature despite their capacity for violence. Most of them must hide their werewolf natures from society for fear that discovery may lead to their execution at the hands of fearful humans. This adds a sense that the characters are outsiders in their own communities, a feeling that many readers can identify with.

***The Silver Wolf* by Alice Borchardt**   In eighth-century Rome, Regeane is orphaned when her father is slain by a crossbow bolt. Taken in by her Uncle Gundabald, she is horrified when she learns that he plans on capitalizing on her relation to royalty by marrying her off to a barbarian lord named Maenielin in order to recoup his squandered fortune. Regeane has no choice but to comply because her uncle holds the secret to her true nature as a werewolf, a secret that if revealed would cost Regeane her life. Even as Regeane searches for an escape from her uncle, she must survive political intrigue after intrigue while trying desperately to keep her own nature a secret. Sequels: *Night of the Wolf, The Wolf King.*

***Blood and Chocolate* by Annette Curtis Klause**   Young teen Vivian Gandillon is just like most kids her age and is trying to fit in at one of the most awkward stages of life. Unfortunately, Vivian isn't like other teenagers; she's a werewolf and her pack has just moved to a Maryland suburb after their West Virginia home was burned down by suspicious neighbors. Whereas most teenagers have to deal with raging hormones as part of puberty, it is much worse for werewolves, who have the morals and sensibilities of the wolves whose shape they take. Vivian, however, is uninterested in the male members of her pack and instead finds that she is attracted to a human boy named Aiden Teague. As Vivian's feelings for Aiden deepen she begins to question her sense of self and werewolf society in general. Should she reveal her true nature to Aiden? If she does, will he welcome her with open arms or a closed fist? Is it even possible for a werewolf and a human to love each other?

***The Fire Rose* by Mercedes Lackey**   Rosalind Hawkins is a scholar in medieval studies in Chicago when she's forced to cut her studies short by the death of her father. Destitute, she has no choice but to accept a strange job offer from Jason Cameron in San Francisco. Rose is to be a governess for the Cameron family, but when she arrives at the stately manor, she finds no wife or family. The only residents of the house are Rose's mysterious employer and his butler. Rose then discovers that one of her jobs is to read the classics of literature aloud to her new employer through a speaking tube every night. Indeed, Rose has never even *seen* Jason, but as she reads to him night after night she begins to regain her self-confidence. Jason, for his part, begins to get back in touch with his humanity, and his faculties return. For Jason is an alchemist, and, in researching an ancient werewolf transformation spell, he bungled it and turned himself permanently into a werewolf. As Rose and Jason grow closer, a complication arises when a rival alchemist approaches Rose with a fiendish bargain: reveal Jason for the beast he is and receive her family fortune as payment. *The Fire Rose* is a retelling of the fairy tale "Beauty and the Beast."

The Secret Texts Series by Holly Lisle   In the first book in the series, *Diplomacy of Wolves,* the noble houses of Sabir and Galweigh have battled for years with men of arms and spell-equipped mages in a fruitless campaign for control of Calimekka. At a diplomatic function, young diplomat Kait of the Galweigh House discovers a plot by the Sabir to ambush the Galweigh House. Alone in territory covertly allied with the Sabir, Kait must use all her wits and a deadly secret to get back to the Galweigh House in time to warn them of the danger the Sabir present. Kait's secret is that she is a shape-shifter and can transform into a werewolf, a secret for which her own family would kill her if they discovered it. Other titles in the series: *Vengeance of Dragons, Courage of Falcons.*

***The Changeling Prince* by Vivian Vande Velde**   The dark sorceress Daria uses an army of shape-shifters as bodyguards, hunters, and enforcers of her evil will. Weiland is one of Daria's bodyguards and can change into a werewolf. Weiland chafes under Daria's rule, hating the hunts and the killings. More than anything else, he hates the charades Daria plays in which she makes the shape-shifters assume human form and act as her servants while she plays the part of a noblewoman. Things change, however, when Weiland meets a young thief named Shile and the two of them happen upon a plan to free Weiland from Daria. But Daria is not known for giving up easily.

Other Recommended Titles

Operation Chaos by Poul Anderson
Wild Blood by Nancy Collins
Heart of Midnight by J. Robert King

DEREK'S PICK

The Fire Rose by Mercedes Lackey

BEST PICK FOR THE RELUCTANT READER

Blood and Chocolate by Annette Curtis Klause

GHOSTS AND OTHER UNDEAD

The fascinating idea that someone can exist after death has attracted much attention for hundreds of years. While vampires are the dead brought back to a semblance of life, ghosts are the souls of people who have died but have remained on Earth. There can be a variety of reasons why the ghost is still lingering on the mortal plane. The most prominent reason is that the ghost has unfinished business on Earth, such as finding his or her murderer. Another reason is that the manner of death for the ghost was so violent that the soul was prevented from journeying to the afterlife. Generally ghosts cannot take physical form and influence objects directly. Poltergeists, however, can, and will, throw and break objects and sometimes physically attack mortals. Ghosts have been used as characters in a wide range of genres, most notably horror and romance but also fantasy. The ghosts in fantasy literature usually possess abilities very much like magic, which they use to achieve their ends and to influence the characters.

***Shade of the Tree* by Piers Anthony** Widower Joshua Pinson and his kids Chris and Sue have had it with New York City ever since a mugger murdered Mina, his wife and the children's mother. When Joshua's uncle leaves the family a house in Florida, Joshua jumps at the opportunity for a new beginning. The estate seems to be perfect, and the family seizes the chance to return their lives to normal. Unfortunately, strange events begin occurring at the house shortly after they move in: a phantom train passes by, a ghostly figure appears at the sink in the kitchen, and a legendary creature called the skunk-ape nearly kills Joshua. These events cause the family to rethink their decision to live in the shade of the Tree.

***Tamsin* by Peter S. Beagle**   Thirteen-year-old Jenny Gluckstein is at first resentful that her mother has remarried and forced the family to relocate to England. But then Jenny's cat makes friends with a ghostly cat, which leads Jenny to make friends with the cat's mistress, Tamsin. Tamsin has been dead for three centuries, doomed to forever haunt the farm where Jenny lives. Jenny must help Tamsin discover the truth surrounding her death even as she convinces a boggart, a kind of playful ghost, to depart the area and deals with other supernatural creatures. But can Jenny and Tamsin discover the truth before an even darker evil arises on the farm?

***Ghostlight* by Marion Zimmer Bradley**   Thirty years ago, during the 1960s, a group of practitioners of an ancient religion gathered together in a secret mansion called Shadow's Gate to perform a dark ritual. On that night Truth Blackburne's father vanished during the ritual and her mother died. Now Truth is determined to get to the bottom of the mystery surrounding the events at Shadow's Gate even as she receives a summons to return to the ancestral home. A new group following what they call the Blackburne Way and led by the charismatic Julian Pilgrim intend to reenact the very same ritual that killed Truth's mother. Stand-alone sequels: *Witchlight, Gravelight, Heartlight.*

***Treasure Box* by Orson Scott Card**   When Quentin Fears was eleven years old, his beloved sister Lizzie died, leaving Quentin emotionally distraught. As the years pass Quentin continues to communicate with his sister, although he believes she is a figment of his imagination. Then, at the "tender" age of thirty-four, Quentin, a self-made millionaire, meets the love of his life at a party. The two are soon confronted by the most fearsome event a new couple must face: meeting the future in-laws. Quentin accompanies his love Madeline to a spooky mansion in upstate New York where he meets several of Madeline's strange relations. Toward the end of the welcome breakfast, Quentin is ordered by the clan's matriarch to open a box that she says holds Madeline's inheritance. Quentin becomes very uneasy at this point and refuses to open the box, causing Madeline to storm off in a fury. Quentin chases her and is struck by the realization that Madeline isn't leaving any tracks in the snow! Proceeding to where he last saw Madeline standing, he enters a tiny graveyard where he makes an even stranger discovery: the graves of the family members he has just met! Quentin must get to the bottom of the mystery surrounding Madeline and her family before an ancient evil is released upon the world.

***Rusalka* by C. J. Cherryh**   Long ago Russia was inhabited by spirits, not all of them benign. There were Dvorovoi (Yard Things), Domovoi (Cellar Things), even Vodyanoi (River Things). Most dangerous of all were the Rusalkas, the spirits of murdered girls. Rusalkas sustain their ghostly existence by absorbing the life forces of other creatures. Pyter and Sasha are two carefree boys living in the forest with the wizard Uulamets. Events at Uulamets's cottage seem innocent enough until the Yard Thing and Cellar Thing begin acting hostile toward Pyter. In fact, the River Thing tries to kill Pyter! The situation takes an even more dangerous turn when Pyter meets the Rusalka, the murdered ghost of Uulamets's daughter, whom the wizard is trying to bring back to life. Soon Pyter realizes that he's falling in love with the Rusalka and that she reciprocates those feelings. But no mortal man can long survive around the Rusalka's life-draining powers. Sequels: *Chernevog, Yvgenie.*

Other Recommended Titles

A Fine and Private Space by Peter S. Beagle

Homebody by Orson Scott Card

Knight of the Black Rose by James Lowder

Something's Alive on Titanic by Robert Serling

DEREK'S PICK

Shade of the Tree by Piers Anthony

BEST PICK FOR THE RELUCTANT READER

Treasure Box by Orson Scott Card

26

Demons Loose in the City

Urban Fantasy

Urban fantasy takes place on Earth in a contemporary period. For this reason it is often called "contemporary fantasy" by many customers, librarians, and fans of fantasy. I hesitate to use that term here because "contemporary" can be misinterpreted to mean all fantasy written after a certain date. In this book that would be all books published since 1980. Urban fantasy usually takes place in an indeterminable "present" and in cities like London or New York, but it can also take place in the suburbs. Sometimes magic has always existed and been used by humankind; other times magic is a recent addition to the world. The important point is that the magic exists in the here and now of our world, not in the historical past, an alternate world, or another universe.

***Running with the Demon* by Terry Brooks** Fourteen-year-old Nest Freemark has a big responsibility for one so young: guard Sinnissippi Park and prevent the evil it holds from being released upon the world. Nest is the park's protector because of the powers she inherited from the park's previous guardians: her mother and grandmother. Helping Nest in her duties is a six-inch-tall Sylvan named Pick and a spirit wolf named Wraith. On one hot Fourth of July weekend two men arrive in Nest's town. One is a demon, ancient champion of the Void and harbinger of darkness. The other is John Ross, Knight of the Word and champion of all things good. John is drawn to the town because of his nightmarish dreams of a future in which he fails in his duties. The demon is drawn to the town because of the evil that resides in Nest's park. Nest, who has never known the identity of her father, will discover his identity this weekend, and her talents will be challenged to their limits. If John should defeat the demon, he can anticipate a journey to a different place—another battle with the Void. If John should fail, however, humanity is doomed. Sequels: *A Knight of the Word, Angel Fire East.*

***Homebody* by Orson Scott Card**   Don Lark was a successful contractor before he lost the business and all his money in a protracted custody battle for his daughter. Then Don lost his will to live when his ex-wife killed his daughter in a drunk-driving accident. Now he spends his days looking for dilapidated houses to buy, renovate, and sell for a profit. The work is rewarding as well as therapeutic for the distraught contractor until he purchases his latest project in Greensboro, North Carolina. As the renovation progresses, Don uncovers some of the house's mysteries, including a tunnel in the basement connected to the Underground Railroad and an attractive squatter upstairs. But as he investigates these mysteries he uncovers a darker mystery that will lead to a showdown between good and evil.

***Into the Out Of* by Alan Dean Foster**   Through a rift in space-time come the Shetani, tiny creatures of evil and darkness whose goal is to destroy all humankind. Only three people dare stand before the darkness coming from the Shetani's shadowy realm of the Out Of. They are FBI agent Joshua Oak, bored retailer Merry Shadow, and Olkeloki, an elder of the Maasai tribe of Africa. Joshua and Merry are chosen because they have the innate ability to see the Shetani in any of the disguises the creatures use. Only Olkeloki can meld his abilities with those of Joshua and Merry to drive the Shetani back through the rift and seal it forever. I guarantee if you read this book you will never look at roadside debris the same way again.

***The Falling Woman* by Pat Murphy**   Archaeologist Liz Butler has achieved a great reputation in her field for her ability to find and excavate

Mayan sites. What Liz doesn't tell people is that she has been led to the sites by visions of people from the past. Although Liz's professional life is successful, her personal life is in shambles. She has divorced her husband and run from the responsibilities of motherhood. One day while she is on a dig, two shocking things happen to Liz: her estranged daughter arrives after the death of her father, and one of Liz's visions of the past begins speaking to her. The person in the vision is a Mayan princess who warns Liz that a cycle of pain is approaching and that the gods demand a sacrifice from Liz or a greater disaster will occur. *The Falling Woman* won the 1987 Nebula Award.

***Lord Demon* by Roger Zelazny and Jane Lindskold**   Thousands of years ago, the gods and demons fought a war over control of the fabled land of Origin, and the demons were exiled forever to Earth. Demon Kai Wren has spent the time since the exile mastering the art of glass blowing, and he creates bottles containing miniaturized universes that can be inhabited by demons. Kai's tranquility is shattered when his human assistant, Oliver, is murdered by lesser "scrub" demons. Incensed, Kai sets out to discover who assassinated his assistant and why. What Kai discovers threatens to upset the delicate balance between the gods and the demons and lead to another war.

Other Recommended Titles

Shade of the Tree by Piers Anthony

Eye of the Daemon by Camille Bacon-Smith

The Face of Time by Camille Bacon-Smith

Strands of Starlight Series by Gael Baudino

Ghostlight by Marion Zimmer Bradley

War for the Oaks by Emma Bull

Treasure Box by Orson Scott Card

The Forever King by Molly Cochran and Warren Murphy

World without End by Molly Cochran and Warren Murphy

Dreams Underfoot by Charles de Lint

Forests of the Heart by Charles de Lint

Greenmantle by Charles de Lint

Memory and Dream by Charles de Lint

Moonheart by Charles de Lint

Trader by Charles de Lint

The Art of Arrow Cutting by Stephen Dedman

Faerie Tale by Raymond E. Feist

American Gods by Neil Gaiman

Neverwhere by Neil Gaiman

Dark Cities Underground by Lisa Goldstein

Walking the Labyrinth by Lisa Goldstein

The Anita Blake Series by Laurell K. Hamilton

Brown Girl in the Ring by Nalo Hopkinson

Blood Price by Tanya Huff

Bedlam's Bard by Mercedes Lackey and Ellen Guon

Novels of the Serrated Edge by Mercedes Lackey et al.

Cold Iron by Melisa Michaels

Practical Demonkeeping by Christopher Moore

Mythology 101 by Jody Lynn Nye

Fool on the Hill by Matt Ruff

Son of Darkness by Josepha Sherman

The Flight of Michael McBride by Midori Snyder

DEREK'S PICK

Running with the Demon by Terry Brooks

BEST PICK FOR THE RELUCTANT READER

Lord Demon by Roger Zelazny and Jane Lindskold

27

Crossing Over
to the Other Side

Before 1937 most of the fantasy written was crossover fantasy. Crossover fantasy is fairly easy to understand. It involves a character who is magically transported from our world, Earth, to a world where magic exists. The mechanism of travel isn't very important. It can be as elaborate as an enchanted wardrobe or a liberal administration of pixie dust, or as simple as following a white rabbit down its hole. But the publication of J. R. R. Tolkien's *The Hobbit* changed all that by creating a fantasy world complete in itself. Before 1937, writers believed that readers would not relate to characters from another, magical world. For that reason they took people from our world where magic doesn't exist and inserted them into another world in which magic does exist. But *The Hobbit* proved that readers would relate to and enjoy characters from another world, and the world of fantasy literature has never been the same.

The Last Rune Series by Mark Anthony   In the first book in the series, *Beyond the Pale,* Travis Wilder is a barkeep in Castle City, Colorado, when he is summoned by his friend, the enigmatic Jack Graystone, for an important quest. When Travis arrives at his friend's house, Jack gives him a mysterious iron box and then pushes him out the back door moments before the house is attacked by mysterious beings. Outside,

Travis senses that these dark beings are pursuing him. By a fluke Travis escapes capture by falling through a portal into the world of Eldh. Meanwhile, emergency room doctor Grace Beckett has just finished an unsuccessful attempt to repair a gunshot victim's wounds when the body suddenly reanimates—Grace has discovered that its heart is made of iron. Soon afterward Grace too crosses over into Eldh and is almost immediately pressed into service as a spy by a local king. While Grace is adjusting to Eldh, Travis has learned why they were called over. The Pale King, a being of great evil and rapacious appetite, has been imprisoned for years behind the Rune Gate. But the gate is weakening and it is up to Grace and Travis to restore the runes on the Pale King's prison to prevent his release upon Eldh and eventually upon Earth. Titles in the series: *The Keep of Fire, The Dark Remains*.

Landover Series by Terry Brooks   In the first book in the series, *Magic Kingdom for Sale—Sold!*, Ben Holiday hasn't been the same since his wife and unborn child died. He has a great job and is a successful lawyer, but he finds himself moving from task to task searching for any sign of a higher meaning. Then he finds an ad in a catalog addressed to his deceased wife that simply states: "Magic Kingdom for Sale." The ad promises that the land, Landover, is an "island of enchantment and adventure" in which all his fantasies will become real. Needing a change in his dreary life, Ben does the unthinkable and purchases the kingdom for a million dollars. Once in Landover Ben learns that the advertisement wasn't misleading—it is a genuine magic kingdom. The ad has, however, taken some liberties in promising that his dreams will come true. Landover is a kingdom in trouble. Her barons refuse to believe that Ben is the new king, a dragon is ravaging the countryside, and an evil witch has set her sights on Ben's throne. Ben must set out with his few supporters to prove his right to rule through a series of tasks that seem all but impossible. Then Ben learns that the demon lord Iron Mask has issued a challenge to any who dare sit on the throne of Landover: meet the demon lord in a duel to the death, a duel that no mortal can hope to win. Ben's only hope of salvation rests with a mythical knight called the Paladin who has sworn to defend the kings of Landover but who has not been seen in decades. Luckily Ben is a stubborn man. Other titles in the series: *The Black Unicorn, Wizard at Large, The Tangle Box, Witches' Brew*.

Chronicles of Thomas Covenant by Stephen R. Donaldson   In the first book of the series, *Lord Foul's Bane,* Thomas Covenant has everything: a beautiful wife, an infant son, and a best-selling novel. Everything is going his way until his wife notices that a small wound on Thomas's hand is gangrenous. Covenant is in the beginning stages of leprosy. The wound eventually costs him two of the fingers on his left hand. The leprosy drives away his wife and son and makes him an outcast in his own town. Bitter and tortured by the blow that fate has dealt him, Covenant is infuriated when he finds that the townsfolk have been paying for his utilities and groceries to prevent him from coming to town. He immediately sets off to rectify the situation but he is struck by a car. When Covenant regains consciousness he finds himself in a world of unsurpassed beauty and magic called The Land. The people who inhabit The Land believe that Covenant is the reincarnation of their greatest hero: Berek Half-Hand. Both are missing fingers on one hand and both wear a ring of white gold, a talisman of great power in The Land. Covenant believes that he is suffering from a delusion, a dangerous thing for a leper to do, and he thinks he is lying in a coma in a hospital in the real world. This belief is strengthened when he discovers that his leprosy has been magically healed by The Land. This cure comes with a heavy price: The Land and its peoples want Covenant to confront an evil being named Lord Foul who is threatening to destroy The Land. Covenant is certain that if he gives in and begins believing in the delusion of this world then he is doomed to die, because a leper who believes in the impossible usually dies from lack of vigilance. Other titles in the series: *The Illearth War, The Power That Preserves.* Second Chronicles of Thomas Covenant the Unbeliever: *The Wounded Land, The One Tree, White Gold Wielder.*

***Dark Lord of Derkholm* by Diana Wynne Jones**   Would you want to visit a world that really has magic? Most people would say yes. This is what Mr. Chesney, a businessman from our world, is counting on when he creates Pilgrim Parties, a tour company that transports people to a magical realm via a portal. To ensure the best experience for his clients, Mr. Chesney, with the help of his pet demon, forces the wizards of that world to put together a show for the parties. Each year a dark lord must be chosen from among the wizards and this dark lord must be slain by each party. None of the wizards wants to be chosen as dark lord—not only is it a lot of hard work, but the pay is terrible and the lands surrounding the chosen one's home get torn apart by the rampaging armies of good and evil. This year's dark lord is the wizard Derk, whose only interest is in breeding unorthodox animals, such as flying pigs and horses, invisible cats, and griffins. Derk wants to do a good job, however, so he calls on his family to help set up the Dark Lord's manse, locate a dragon to act as a guardian, and coordinate the Pilgrim Parties. Everything is going well until Derk's daughter falls in love with an expendable. An expendable is a member of the Pilgrim Party who Mr. Chesney has been paid to make sure does not come back to Earth. Now Derk must find a way to save his daughter's love, save the countryside from the Pilgrim Parties, and stop Mr. Chesney and his pet demon. To make matters worse, the dwarves who were supposed to be making regular payments of gold to Derk to pay for the tours have been taking the shipments to the being who is the true dark lord: Mr. Chesney. Sequel: *Year of the Griffin.*

A Wizard in Rhyme Series by Christopher Stasheff   In first book in the series, *Her Majesty's Wizard,* Matthew Matrell is a graduate student in literature when he discovers a scrap of paper with strange writing on it. Soon he becomes obsessed with translating the words on the paper, but when he does so, he is transported to another world in which magic exists and spells are created through poetry verses. Matthew, with his background in literature, is perfectly suited to create spells through verse, making him one of the greatest wizards the world has ever seen. Soon he is captured by an evil sorcerer who hopes to harness the young man's potential. However, the sorcerer hasn't counted on a wizard capable of summonging dragons and rescuing damsels in distress. Other titles in the series: *The Oathbound Wizard, The Witch Doctor, The Secular Wizard, My Son, the Wizard, The Haunted Wizard, The Crusading Wizard, The Feline Wizard.*

Other Recommended Titles

The Gutbucket Quest by Piers Anthony and Ron Leming

No Earthly Sunne by Margaret Ball

Peter Pan by J. M. Barrie

Dragonsword by Gael Baudino

Strands of Starlight Series by Gael Baudino

Oz Series by L. Frank Baum

The Unicorn Sonata by Peter S. Beagle

Ravenloft Adventures by Marian Zimmer Bradley

Finder: A Novel of the Borderlands by Emma Bull

War for the Oaks by Emma Bull

Dreams Underfoot by Charles de Lint

Moonheart by Charles de Lint

Dragon Knight Series by Gordon R. Dickson

Yesterday We Saw Mermaids by Esther Friesner

Typewriter in the Sky by L. Ron Hubbard

Song of Albion by Stephen R. Lawhead

The Chronicles of Narnia by C. S. Lewis

Minerva Wakes by Holly Lisle

The Shadow of Albion by Andre Norton and Rosemary Edghill

Chronicles of Ynis Aielle by R. A. Salvatore

The Spearwielder's Tale by R. A. Salvatore

A Well-Timed Enchantment by Vivian Vande Velde

DEREK'S PICK

Chronicles of Thomas Covenant by Stephen R. Donaldson

BEST PICK FOR THE RELUCTANT READER

Dark Lord of Derkholm by Diana Wynne Jones

28

Sword and Sorcery

Sword and sorcery is the blood and guts of fantasy literature. Literally. You think I'm kidding? Just open any of the books in this chapter and you'll see more blood and guts than you ever thought you could see in your lifetime! The heroes in this chapter have a tendency to be direct and to the point, usually using the point of a sword to "ram" their point home—often into the gut of whoever is daring to disagree with them. These are heroes who rely on strength of arms and superior swordplay to carry the day, disdaining to use sorcery and often arrayed against those who do use it. Often these heroes carry swords of arcane power that augment their skills at swordplay, but just as often they are superior warriors who, to paraphrase a line from Mel Brooks's movie *Blazing Saddles*, "don't need no stinkin' magic swords" to defeat whatever force of evil is confronting them. The archetype of sword and sorcery fantasy is the character Conan the Barbarian created by Robert E. Howard in 1932. Conan was a man of imposing height and enormous power who was extraordinarily skilled in the use of a sword as well as an ax. Conan frequently used these swords and axes to defeat forces of evil, namely, wizards, priests of dark gods, witches, and necromancers.

The King's Blades Series by Dave Duncan   The first book in the series is *The Gilded Chain*. In the land of Chivial, which is loosely based on sixteenth-century Tudor England, the King's Blades are the protectors of the king of Chivial. The Blades are trained from boyhood at Ironhall to be the greatest swordsmen the world has ever seen. Upon their graduation from Ironhall, the men are bound by a thrust from a magical sword into their heart to forever protect their charges or die in the trying. The greatest of the King's Blades is Sir Durendal, but his dreams of great glory are shattered when King Ambrose binds him to a foppish courtier. Durendal's expectation of a mind-numbingly boring life with the courtier is overturned when he realizes that he is magically bound to protect a man who is plotting against King Ambrose. Sequels: *Lord of the Fire Lands, Sky of Swords*. Each of the books in the series is designed to be a stand-alone novel.

The Sword of Truth Series by Terry Goodkind   In the first book in the series, *Wizard's First Rule,* the boundaries between worlds are beginning to thin and the evil wizard Darken Rahl has set into motion a plot that, if successful, will allow the dead to walk upon the land. The only person who can stop Rahl is the Seeker of Truth, who wields the Sword of Truth: Richard Cypher, accompanied by the mysterious Kahlan Amnell and the sage Zedd, must find the last of the mystical boxes Rahl needs or die a horrible death. Other titles in the series: *Stone of Tears, Blood of the Fold, Temple of the Winds, Soul of the Fire, Faith of the Fallen, Pillars of Creation*.

The Tales of Fafhrd and the Gray Mouser by Fritz Leiber   Much like Robert E. Howard's Conan stories, the Tales of Fafhrd and the Gray Mouser were primarily short stories in the beginning and only later collected into novels. As a result, the two heroes' adventures seem rather episodic, but they are still fine examples of the sword and sorcery subgenre. Fafhrd is a barbarian of immense size who longs for the adventures that civilization offers. The Gray Mouser is a former magician's apprentice with a shadowy past. Both heroes are swordsmen without peer and are frequently advised by mysterious users of magic. Many of their adventures take place around the great city of Lankhmar and have a humorous feel to them. The Tales of Fafhrd and the Gray Mouser have been collected into the following titles: *Swords and Deviltry, Swords against Death, Swords in the Mist, Swords against Wizardry, The Swords of Lankhmar, Swords and Ice Magic, The Knight and Knave of Swords*. These books should be read in the order given here.

Elric Saga by Michael Moorcock   In the first book in the series, *Elric of Melnibone,* Elric is the albino emperor of the dying land of Melnibone. Physically frail, Elric is forced to rely on potions and his own sorceries for strength. Convinced that Elric is too weak to rule the cruel society of Melnibone, his cousin Yakoon sets into motion plot after plot to remove Elric from the throne. Each time Elric only barely manages to defeat Yakoon's intrigues with the help of his demonic sword Stormbringer, which steals the souls from its victims. But even as Elric must battle Yakoon and Yakoon's sword Mournblade for control of his throne, Elric must also battle Stormbringer for control of his very soul. Other titles in the series: *The Sailor on the Seas of Fate, The Weird of the White Wolf, The Vanishing Tower, The Bane of the Black Sword, Stormbringer.* The Elric saga is part of the Eternal Champions series, but the series that make up Eternal Champions do not have to be read in any specific order.

The Books of Swords by Fred Saberhagen   Years ago the gods called upon one of their own to forge twelve swords of incredible power. The forger, Vulcan the Master Smith, forged the swords on a lonely mountaintop, his tools the fires of Earth and metal from the sky. Vulcan infused the swords with special powers: one sword can heal any wound but cannot bring back the deceased. Another can cause entire armies to drop their weapons in despair. Yet another cannot be defeated by any other weapon, mortal or immortal. The gods' plan was to release the swords into the care of humans and then watch with amusement as people turned on one another for possession of the mighty blades. But the gods did not consider Vulcan's capriciousness—in forging the swords he has made them into weapons capable of defeating even the gods. His only witness is a human smith named Jord who gave his right arm, literally, for the opportunity to watch the Master Smith at his forge. In return Jord is given one of the swords, which he holds in his family for years. Jord's son Mark has no idea that his father's sword is anything but a weapon of incomparable beauty and perfection. When his home is attacked by men seeking the sword for Duke Fratkin, Jord successfully fends off the thieves but in doing so is slain by the sword's magic. With the Duke's men eager to exact vengeance, Mark has no choice but to take the sword and depart for safer lands. But Mark won't find those lands because mighty forces are massing to take possession of the sword. Titles in the series: *First Book of Swords, Second Book of Swords, Third Book of Swords.* These three books were collected into *First Swords* and *The Complete Sword.* The Lost Swords series: *Woundhealer's Story, Sightblinder's Story, Stonecutter's Story* (collected into *The Book of Lost Swords First Triad*); *Farslayer's Story, Coinspinner's Story, Mindsword's Story* (collected into *The Book of Lost Swords Triad*); *Wayfinder's Story, Shieldbreaker's Story* (collected into *The Book of Lost Swords End Game*).

Other Recommended Titles

Dragonsword by Gael Baudino

The Seer King by Chris Bunch

Barrenlands by Doranna Durgin

Dun Lady's Jess by Doranna Durgin

Seer's Blood by Doranna Durgin

Touched by Magic by Doranna Durgin

Wolverine's Daughter by Doranna Durgin

Band of Four Novels by Ed Greenwood

The Conan Chronicles by Robert E. Howard

Heroing by Dafydd ab Hugh

By the Sword by Mercedes Lackey

The Oathbound Series by Mercedes Lackey

The Rune Blade Trilogy by Ann Marston

Sword in Exile Trilogy by Ann Marston

Swords Trilogy by Michael Moorcock

Sword-Dancer Saga by Jennifer Roberson

The Crimson Shadow Trilogy by R. A. Salvatore

The Icewind Dale Trilogy by R. A. Salvatore

The Cage by S. M. Stirling and Shirley Meier

Touched by the Gods by Lawrence Watt-Evans

The Darksword Trilogy by Margaret Weis and Tracy Hickman

DEREK'S PICK

Elric Saga by Michael Moorcock

BEST PICK FOR THE RELUCTANT READER

The Sword of Truth Series by Terry Goodkind

29

The Magic of Music

Music has long held a position of importance for humanity. Most of us have heard a song or piece of music so beautiful that it speaks to us, practically transporting us to another world. Indeed, in his play *The Mourning Bride,* William Congreve wrote that "music hath charms to soothe the savage breast, to soften rocks, or bend a knotted oak." In Greek mythology the Sirens used seductive music to lure sailors to their doom. With a history that long it should come as no surprise that fantasy authors would use music as a means to make magic. The titles in this chapter feature characters that are either musicians, such as bards, or are able to make magic through music.

Spellsinger Series by Alan Dean Foster A great evil is confronting the wizard Clothahump's world, so he begins casting about for help from another world, for a person known as an "engineer." What he gets is stoned graduate student Jonathan Thomas Meriweather, aspiring rock guitarist and part-time sanitation "engineer." When Jon first awakens in Clothahump's world he is immediately confronted by Mudge, a five-foot-tall walking and talking otter. In fact, all the animals in Clothahump's world walk upright like humans and speak English. Clothahump himself is a turtle whose shell holds drawers of magical ingredients that fuel his spells. But all is not lost in bringing Jon in place of the engineer Clothahump was seeking, for Jon-Tom (as he is known to the denizens of this world) is a musician and is able to create magic as the Spellsinger. Forced into Clothahump's cause, Jon-Tom and his newly acquired friends Mudge, the human Talea, and Pug the bat must seek out the danger confronting the world and defeat them together. Other titles in the series: *The Hour of the Gate, The Day of the Dissonance, The Moment of the Magician, The Paths of the Preambulator, The Time of the Transference, Son of Spellsinger, Chorus Skating.*

Rhapsody Series by Elizabeth Haydon   In the first book in the series, *Rhapsody: A Child of the Blood,* Rhapsody is a singer of extraordinary talent. So powerful is her talent that she can name things, changing the fundamental nature of whatever she names to what she needs. This is what happens when Rhapsody runs into the half-breeds known as the Brother and Grunthor while running from an ex-suitor. The Brother is an assassin of deadly skill, and Grunthor is a gigantic warrior of ferocious nature and cannibalistic appetite. But by renaming the Brother to Achmed the Snake, Rhapsody breaks a diabolic bond between the Brother and a powerful demonic creature called a F'dor. Angered by this defection, the F'dor sends his minions to collect Achmed for punishment and rebinding. The companions only narrowly escape by journeying down the great roots of the World Tree—a tree whose roots travel through the very center of the world. When they emerge on the far side of the world after passing through the cleansing fires of the world's center, they find themselves fundamentally changed, and the world they knew no longer exists. Other titles in the series: *Rhapsody: A Child of the Earth, Destiny: Child of the Sky.*

Sing the Four Quarters **by Tanya Huff**   Bards in the land of Skodar perform several important tasks for their society. Their primary responsibility is to tour the land spreading the news and acting as witnesses, judges, and mediators. The bards call these tours Walks, and the bard Annice, a princess of Skodar, is returning from a Walk when she suddenly gets sick. The problem is that Annice is pregnant, and thus has committed treason against Skodar by meddling with the chain of succession for the throne and endangering her brother's right to rule. But

Annice is no ordinary bard, for she is able to sing the four quarters, a feat few bards can accomplish. The quarters are the songs that the bards sing to the elements, or kigh. Most bards can only sing to one or two kigh, and Annice's abilities make her a rarity among the druids. But the baby's father has been captured and is being held in the prison of the king of Skodar, and Annice refuses to allow an innocent man to die. Other titles in the series: *Fifth Quarter, No Quarter, The Quartered Sea.*

Bardic Voices Series by Mercedes Lackey   Rune's life is filled with frustrating drudgery as the daughter of a tavern wench. Rune wants to be a bard, and she's certain that she could be the greatest bard the world has ever seen. The problem is that she doesn't have any formal training. She has received some training from passing minstrels, a gypsy named Nightingale, even a bard of great renown. But one evening Rune makes the worst mistake of her life when she responds hotly to questions about her ability to fiddle by claiming that she can fiddle well enough for the Skull Hill Ghost. The Skull Hill Ghost was responsible for the disappearance of a great many people foolish enough to venture up the hill after dark. But when the ghost appears before Rune, he offers her a deal: play well enough to keep his attention until sunrise and he'll spare her life, but if his attention should wander even for a moment, he'll take her life before she has a chance to react. Now is the time to take up her bow and fiddle to see if she can earn her freedom or a spot in eternal torment. Other titles in the series: *The Robin and the Kestrel, The Eagle and the Nightingales, Four and Twenty Blackbirds, A Cast of Corbies* (with Josepha Sherman).

The Spellsong Cycle by L. E. Modesitt Jr.   In the first book in the series, *The Soprano Sorceress,* Anna Marshall is a middle-aged singer turned music professor whose world has been rocked by the recent death of her eldest daughter. When Anna makes the mistake of wishing she were anywhere but her home of Ames, Iowa, she finds herself in the enchanting land of Defalk. Defalk is under siege from its neighbors from Ebran when Anna appears and is immediately pressed into service for the Defalks. In the world of Defalk and Ebran, music is magic, and the better the singer the more powerful the sorceror. For professional soprano Anna this means she could be the most powerful sorceress the world has ever seen. Now if she can only learn how to harness those powers.

Other titles in the series: *The Spellsong War, Darksong Rising, The Shadow Sorceress, Shadowsinger.*

Other Recommended Titles

The Gutbucket Quest by Piers Anthony and Ron Leming

No Earthly Sunne by Margaret Ball

Gossamer Axe by Gael Baudino

Shroud of Shadow by Gael Baudino

The Unicorn Sonata by Peter S. Beagle

War for the Oaks by Emma Bull

The Einstein Intersection by Samuel R. Delany (winner of the 1967 Nebula Award)

Bard's Tale Series by Mercedes Lackey

Bedlam's Bard by Mercedes Lackey and Ellen Guon

Crystal Singer by Anne McCaffrey

Song for the Basilisk by Patricia A. McKillip

Cold Iron by Melisa Michaels

Songsmith by Andre Norton

The Memory of Whiteness by Kim Stanley Robinson

DEREK'S PICK

Rhapsody Series by Elizabeth Haydon

BEST PICK FOR THE RELUCTANT READER

Spellsinger Series by Alan Dean Foster

30

Talking Cats, Dragons, Elves, and Other Mythological Beasties

Have you ever wondered what an animal is thinking? As the proud pet of two cats, I have often wondered what they are thinking about as they lie in pools of sunlight on the carpet. Could it be as T. S. Eliot theorized in *Old Possum's Book of Practical Cats* that they are "engaged in a rapt contemplation . . . of the thought of [their] name"? Or are they planning more tricks to be played on their human pets along the lines of "tomorrow morning I think I shall wake them up thirty minutes before the alarm clock"? When I was younger a friend of mine named Brian had a yellow Labrador retriever named Bob. My friends and I theorized that Bob had to have a short, easy-to-remember name because he wasn't capable of remembering anything longer. We also guessed that if we could listen in on Bob's thoughts, we would hear something on the order of: "My name is Bob. Be-oh-be—Bob. Bob is my name. Be-oh-be . . . " in a never-ending stream. I can imagine that if Brian could have figured out a shorter name for Bob he probably would have, except that the only alternative to "Bob" was "Bo," and Bob just didn't look like a "Bo." The thoughts and activities of animals must have also fascinated authors of fantasy literature, because they have created works of fiction on that very subject. The books in this chapter have as their main characters or supporting characters animals who can either talk or think in a humanlike manner.

CATS AND OTHER BEASTS

Animist by Eve Forward   Young Alex has a large problem on his hands. He has just graduated from the College of Animism and must now journey out into the world to locate the animal with which he will form a lifelong link. Not only does he have to do so fairly quickly, but he also wants to find a "good" animal that will enable him to raise a large amount of money quickly. Alex is in desperate need of money because he is the slave of the college, and he'll remain so until he can raise enough money to buy his freedom. Alex is also impatient because an animist without an animal partner quickly becomes a target for the world's magicians, who believe that the only good animist is a dead animist because a bonded animist can use his or her powers to not only resist magic but also to break spells. The sooner that Alex can get bonded to an animal the better, but he doesn't count on getting stuck between opposing forces in a battle for the fate of the world.

Journeys of the Catechist Series by Alan Dean Foster   In the first book in the series, *Carnivores of Light and Darkness,* Etjole Ehomba is a cowherd with the ability to talk to any animal he meets. He also has a sense of honor and duty that would make most champions of good weep with envy. It is this sense of honor that prompts Etjole to accept the quest given to him by a dying warrior. The warrior charges Etjole to find and rescue the visioness Themaryl, who has been captured by the evil wizard Hymneth the Possessed and taken to a faraway land. Etjole immediately sets off to rescue the visioness, but the journey ahead of him is a long one—he must walk the entire breadth of his land to reach the place where she is hidden. Along the way Etjole must make use not only of all his skills in speaking the languages of the animals, but also of his wits and skills at negotiation to survive the myriad dangers that lie in his path. He also makes friends with a treasure hunter named Simna Ibn Sind and a large black cat who help him in his journeys. Other titles in the series: *Into the Thinking Kingdoms, A Triumph of Souls.*

Spellsinger Series by Alan Dean Foster—see p. 171.

Tailchaser's Song by Tad Williams   Tailchaser is a young tomcat from the Meeting Wall clan whose girlfriend Hushpad hasn't been seen lately. In fact, as Tailchaser learns at a clan meeting, a great many of the local cats have gone missing. The clan decides to send Tailchaser with a delegation of cats to the High Cat Queen in Firsthome, located deep in the great forest. But Tailchaser is impatient to find his lost love and sets off on the journey right away. He is greeted at the feline court with disinterest on the part of the Cat Queen, forcing Tailchaser and his friends Pouncequick and Roofshadow to continue the quest on their own. They find a place of evil in the woods called the Vastnir Mound and the home of an ancient evil from the cat Pantheon who won't stop at just a few missing cats. . . .

***A Night in the Lonesome October* by Roger Zelazny** In the late nineteenth century, a group of players have arrived in London to play the Great Game. Some of the players are Openers, who wish to see the return of the Old Ones and their destructive ways. Opposing the Openers are the Closers, who are fighting for the continued existence of society. Then there are the Wild Cards, people drawn to the game because of the participants. The Wild Cards can swing the balance at a crucial moment. But no one is certain who is on which side in this conflict and who can be trusted. Assisting the participants in the game are animals or familiars who communicate among themselves to aid their masters' quest and do their masters' bidding. Who will stand victorious when the game comes to an end on October 31? Will it be the mysterious Jack who wields an arcane knife with singular skill and only does his work at night? Will it be the Mad Monk? Or possibly the Good Doctor, who spends an inordinate amount of time digging in graveyards? Or could it be the Count, who is never seen in daylight but is a force to be reckoned with after sundown? The only certain thing is that in the Great Game, nothing is certain until it unfolds, and then anything can happen on All Hallow's Eve.

Other Recommended Titles

The Plague Dogs by Richard Adams

Watership Down by Richard Adams

The Unicorn Sonata by Peter S. Beagle

The Book of Night with Moon by Diane Duane (cats)

The Cat Who Walks through Walls by Robert A. Heinlein

Redwall Series by Brian Jacques

The Wild Road by Gabriel King (cats)

Animal Farm by George Orwell

The Legacy of Lehr by Katherine Kurtz (cats)

DEREK'S PICK

Animist by Eve Forward

BEST PICK FOR THE RELUCTANT READER

A Night in the Lonesome October by Roger Zelazny

HEROES: THE BREAKFAST OF CHAMPION DRAGONS

Dragons don't toss and turn in their sleep.
They're not built that way.

—Alan Dean Foster

The hero creeps down the hallway that leads to the great beast's lair. Trepidation shakes his large frame as he contemplates the task ahead of him. Too soon he is at the doorway and looking in at the great beast lying on its bed of ill-gotten booty. Slowly the hero sets the visor on his helm over his eyes and adjusts his sweaty grip on his spear. As he looks in on the beast he is overtaken with apprehension at the great bulk in front of him. Over twenty feet long, attired in impenetrable red scales, and possessing claws longer than a man is tall, with teeth like broadswords, the beast presents an insurmountable challenge. But this isn't the limit of the beast's deadly arsenal—with a single fiery breath, it can melt the hero's armor and vaporize his bones in an instant. That's right, I'm talking about mothers-in-law. I mean dragons. Dragons were possibly the first monsters to strike fear deep into the hearts of humankind. Given their vast size and deadly weapons designed to eliminate any resistance, to slay a dragon is a feat worthy of the ages. The books in this chapter feature dragons either as the main character or as the focus of the plot. This isn't to say that every fantasy book in which a character or a party of adventurers slays a dragon belongs in the dragon subgenre. In these books the dragon is just a plot device and doesn't really have much impact. In true dragon fiction, the emphasis has to be on the dragon. It is either a major or supporting character, or a human character has made the dragon her or his life focus, like the dragonriders in Anne McCaffrey's Dragonriders of Pern series.

***Dragonsword* by Gael Baudino**   Solomon Braithwaite is a professor in Arthurian studies at UCLA where he spends his old age teaching his classes, conducting research on Arthurian Britain, and longing for the day that the call will come once again. The call is from the dragon Silbakor, who periodically calls upon Braithwaite to come to the magical land of Gryylth, to once again take up the arcane sword Dragonmaster, and to be transformed into Dythragor Dragonmaster, Guardian of Gryylth, a mighty warrior in the prime of life. The professor is surprised one day when the call does come from Silbakor, but the call isn't for him alone but for his research assistant Suzanne Helling as well. Suzanne, however, is a pacifist, leading her to wonder what her role will be in Gryylth until the dragon presents her with her own Dragonmaster sword. When Suzanne accepts the sword she too is transformed into a warrior of legend, Alouzon Dragonmaster, and in a matter of moments she finds herself wielding the sword against forces that seek to destroy her and Dythragor. Suzanne must reconcile her own feelings about war with the grim realities of war-torn Gryylth and her new duties as the land's guardian. Sequels: *Duel of Dragons, Dragon Death*.

***The Last Dragonlord* by Joanne Bertin**   The Dragonlords are a race of dragons that can assume human shape and live extraordinarily long lives. Linden Rathan is the youngest of the Dragonlords and has always been told that he is the last of his kind, leading him to believe that he'll never find his soul twin, another Dragonlord who is analogous to being a soul mate, a female who will complete and share his life with him. Because of their long lives and great wisdom, the Dragonlords are often called upon to mediate or judge the merits of disputes. It is for this very reason that the people of the kingdom of Cassori call upon Dragonlords to mediate a dispute in their country. It seems that the kingdom is without a leader. The heir to the throne has been stricken by a strange malady and is unable to ascend to the throne, which leads the boy's two uncles to fight over the regency of the country. But not all humans hold the Dragonlords in such high regard; a group called the Fellowship sees this as the perfect time to remove the Dragonlords from the scene . . . permanently. Sequel: *Dragon and Phoenix*.

Dragon Knight Series by Gordon R. Dickson   In the first book in the series, *The Dragon and the George,* Jim Eckert and his girlfriend Angie's lives are a living hell. This is not to say that they aren't in love or happy together, for nothing could be farther from the truth. Jim and Angie's lives are hell because they both have low-level academic jobs with all the attendant frustrations: long hours, pitiful pay, and departmental politics. Their lives are about to get a bit more hellish because of the bungling of Angie's boss Grottwold. Grottwold is experimenting with astral projection and inadvertently transports the young lady to another world. Enraged, Jim demands that Grottwold send him after her but using a lower voltage this time. When Jim comes to in that other world he understandably feels very strange—his consciousness has been transported into the body of a dragon! Just as Jim is coming to terms with his new form he discovers that Angie, who is still a human (or "george," as the dragons call humans), is being held by an evil dragon in a place called the Loathly Tower. While learning his body's new powers, Jim must travel across a strange land to rescue Angie before all is lost. Other titles in the series: *The Dragon Knight; The Dragon on the Border; The Dragon at War; The Dragon, the Earl, and the Troll; The Dragon and the Djinn; The Dragon and the Gnarly King; The Dragon in Lyonese; The Dragon and the Fair Maid of Kent.*

***Song in the Silence: The Tale of Lanen Kaelar* by Elizabeth Kerner**   Long ago the dragons lived among humankind until a human mage waged war upon the dragons, killing and taking the soul gems from some dragons. The dragons in turn slew the mage and recovered the gems before leaving for a self-imposed exile on Dragon Isle. Years later, Lanen Kaelar, who has always dreamed of meeting the legendary dragons of Dragon Isle, has been told by everyone that it isn't possible. The death of her father, however, removes the last obstacle and Lanen seizes the opportunity to travel to the fabled isle. There she meets the great dragon Khordeshkhistriankhor (Akhor) and learns of the centuries-old attack upon the dragons. As time passes Lanen and Akhor begin to feel the stirrings of love, but their happiness is threatened by another human who wishes to steal some dragon gems for himself. Sequel: *Lesser Kindred*.

The Dragonriders of Pern Series by Anne McCaffrey   The colonizers of Pern might have saved later generations a great deal of trouble if they had undertaken some research before beginning to colonize the planet. Every two hundred years the Red Star's orbit around Pern swings it close enough to the planet to cause the Thread to drop. Thread are mindless organisms that burn their way through anything they come in contact with: vegetation, animals, people—everything. The residents of Pern respond by developing the dragons, sentient beings who can teleport, fly, and destroy the dangerous Thread in the upper atmosphere with a single blast of fiery breath. But after four hundred years the Thread haven't dropped, and the leaders of Pern begin to see the dragons and their Weyrs as costly burdens. The lords decide to cut the number of Weyrs from seven to one. But F'lar, dragonrider of the last Weyr, knows that the Thread will come again and that the Weyr is ill prepared to combat the drop. So he sets out to find a new leader for the Weyr and for the new queen dragon egg laid at the Weyr. F'lar thinks he's found that leader in Lessa, but can the two prepare the Weyr and Pern for war before the Thread fall? Or will political intrigue damn them all? Titles in the series: *Dragonquest, The White Dragon, Dragonsong, Dragonsinger, Dragondrums, Moreta: Dragonlady of Pern, Dragonsdawn, The Chronicles of Pern: First Fall, Dragonseye, The Girl Who Heard Dragons, The Renegades of Pern, The Masterharper of Pern, The Weyrs of Pern, The Dolphins of Pern, The Skies of Pern*.

Other Recommended Titles

The Dragonlord by David Drake

The Dragon Circle Series by
　Craig Shaw Gardner

Death of a Dragon by Ed
　Greenwood and Troy Denning

Dragonsbane by Barbara Hambly

The Elvenbane by Andre Norton
　and Mercedes Lackey

The Glass Dragon by Irene
　Radford

Bazil Broketail Series by
　Christopher Rowley

Dark Heart by Margaret Weis and David Baldwin

Dragonlance Chronicles by Margaret Weis and Tracy Hickman

Dragons of a Fallen Sun by Margaret Weis and Tracy Hickman

Dragons of Summer Flame by Margaret Weis and Tracy Hickman

DEREK'S PICK

Dragon Knight Series by Gordon R. Dickson

BEST PICK FOR THE RELUCTANT READER

The Dragonriders of Pern Series by Anne McCaffrey

ARE YOU CALLING ME A FAIRY? I'M AN ELF!

If you were to ask people on the street, "What is an Elf?" they would probably describe someone who is short, is good with his or her hands, and prefers to live in very cold climates with a jolly fat man. What they'd be describing is Santa's helpers and they wouldn't be wrong. But that isn't the only definition. For hundreds of years elves were small creatures with capricious natures who delighted in playing tricks on human beings. But then J. R. R. Tolkien published The Lord of the Rings series and his elves were as tall as human beings, with pointed ears and slightly tilted eyes. Tolkien's elves were creatures of honor and wisdom who lived extraordinarily long lives. This is the model that most fantasy writers use today to develop their own elven characters. The qualities of being short and mischievous are today generally attributed by fantasy writers to fairies. Fairies can have tiny wings that enable them to fly like Tinkerbell, but just as often they are wingless. Most of the books in this section have elves that are based on the Tolkien model, and many of the books either take place in the mythical land of Faerie or involve humans who travel through the veil of magic to Faerie. Elves are also frequently referred to by their Celtic names Sidhe or Tuatha De Dannan, the legendary residents of Faerie.

***Finder: A Novel of the Borderlands* by Emma Bull** The Borderlands is the place between our world and the world of Faerie. Technology is somewhat unreliable, and nowhere is that more apparent than in Bordertown, where the humans of our world mingle freely with the elves of Faerie. Anything goes in Bordertown, and the police turn a blind eye to much of the activity in the town. But a new drug that turns humans into parodies of elves is causing the police to rethink this policy. Several humans have died from ingesting the drug. When a drug runner is killed, the police contact Orient for help in tracking not only the murderer but also the drug's manufacturer. The police ask Orient for help because he has a talent for finding lost things. But a powerful group wants to keep Orient from finding the drug's source and will do anything to make sure he doesn't succeed. Unfortunately, murder is very high on the group's list of options for dealing with Orient.

The Last Hot Time by **John M. Ford**   The lands of Faerie have returned to Earth after an absence of several centuries. To be precise, the lands have returned to Earth right outside Chicago. Nineteen-year-old Danny Holman is a paramedic in Chicago when he witnesses a drive-by shooting perpetrated by elves. Danny stops to help the victim of the shooting and in doing so earns a new name and a job from Mr. Patrise. The name Danny earns is Doc Hallownight and the job is to be a medic for Mr. Patrise's organization. Mr. Patrise's organization comprises both humans and elves, and they are concerned about a series of disappearances that hint at the return of an ancient evil to Earth. The organization is determined to do anything to keep this from happening. In the coming conflict, Doc will be called upon to muster all the courage he possesses to do what is necessary to stop the evil. Courage Doc has in great supply, but he may be called upon to make a much larger sacrifice to end the evil.

Stardust by **Neil Gaiman**   Outside the village of Wall in England is an enchanted meadow that no one is allowed to enter except on one night every nine years when a fair is held for the people of Wall by the people of Faerie. It was on one fair night almost eighteen years ago that Tristan Thorn was conceived upon a lady of Faerie by Dunstan Thorn. Nine months later the baby Tristan was delivered to his father Dunstan to be raised in the mortal realm. Seventeen years later Tristan is walking with a young lady he loves when he sees a shooting star. Hoping to prove his love for his lady, Tristan foolishly promises to retrieve the star, which has fallen in the Faerie meadow. By passing beyond the wall, however, Tristan has entered into the land of Faerie and started a quest that could cost him everything, including his life.

***Cold Iron* by Melisa Michaels**   The holidays are rapidly approaching, forcing San Francisco private investigator Rosie Levine into a foul mood. So dark is her mood that she jumps at any case that will not only get her out of town but also get her mind off Christmas. She takes an assignment to investigate some threats against the elven rock band Cold Iron. But the client doesn't want Rosie to reveal her identity to the band, so she takes on the role of a band groupie. Plunged into a hedonistic lifestyle of casual sex, drugs, and rock 'n' roll, Rosie finds herself struggling to keep her sense of identity even as she tries to investigate a series of deaths of people involved with the band. To make matters worse, she's also starting to fall for the band's charismatic lead singer. . . .

***The Flight of Michael McBride* by Midori Snyder**   Since his birth in the 1850s, Michael McBride has been raised on his mother's tales of Ireland and of the elvish folk called the Tuatha Da Danann. But now his mother is dead, leaving Michael with a father who is both cold and distant. This angers Michael greatly, but before he has a chance to confront his father, he begins seeing strange things around the house. Then Michael encounters an evil man named Red Cap who intends to kill him. Michael just manages to escape from New York and from Red Cap to Red Wing, Texas. In Red Wing, Michael takes a job as a cowhand on a cattle drive but is forced to flee into the desert when someone or something begins killing the cowboys on the drive. In the darkness of the desert Michael will learn the truth of his heritage and face more than one evil from the Old World.

Other Recommended Titles

Jerlayne by Lynn Abbey

No Earthly Sunne by Margaret Ball

Strands of Starlight Series by Gael Baudino

Songs of Earth and Power (series) by Greg Bear

The Sword, the Ring, and the Chalice Trilogy by Deborah Chester

Evermeet by Elaine Cunningham

Strange Devices of the Sun and Moon by Lisa Goldstein

Bedlam's Bard by Mercedes Lackey and Ellen Guon

Novels of the Serrated Edge by Mercedes Lackey et al.

The Elvenbane by Andre Norton and Mercedes Lackey

Mythology 101 by Jody Lynn Nye

The Shattered Oath by Josepha Sherman

Son of Darkness by Josepha Sherman

The Hand and the Falcon Trilogy by Judith Tarr

DEREK'S PICK

The Last Hot Time by John M. Ford

BEST PICK FOR THE RELUCTANT READER

Stardust by Neil Gaiman

31

Humorous Fantasy

Humor really is the best stress reliever, in my opinion. There is just something about coming home from a hard day of work, reading a chapter in a book, and having a good laugh. I know most people turn on the television to a rerun of *Seinfeld, Friends,* or *Home Improvement* for a good laugh, but after a long day of being surrounded by technology there is something about picking up a book and reading for relaxation. There are times in people's lives when they don't want to be challenged by their reading, but just want to read for the sheer joy of reading. The books in this chapter fit into that last category because they're filled with humor, puns, and zany plot twists. But be warned—you might still find your beliefs and mind challenged because some of the authors listed here are able to cleverly slip in a different belief system or theology into all the fun and games.

Myth Series by Robert Aspirin   In the first book in the series, *Another Fine Myth,* Skeeve is a magician's apprentice with grand plans for his future occupation as a . . . thief. Instead of practicing levitation on objects like feathers the way his master wishes, Skeeve focuses on objects like keys and coins. But then Skeeve's master is killed by an assassin sent by the mysterious Isstvan, and Skeeve is left with a problem—a very large, purple-tongued, green-scaled demon, or dimensional traveler, named Aahz. Aahz is not very happy about being summoned by Skeeve's master, stripped of his powers, and stranded far from his home dimension of Perv, all for a practical joke on an apprentice. With no other option open to him, Aahz offers a deal to Skeeve: in exchange for completion of his magical training Skeeve will help Aahz get his powers back. In the meantime they have to deal with the mad wizard Isstvan's plans for taking over the universe. Other titles in the series: *Myth Conceptions, Myth Directions, Hit or Myth, Myth-ing Persons, Little Myth Marker, M.Y.T.H. Inc. Link, Myth-nomers and Im-Pervections, M.Y.T.H. Inc in Action, Sweet Myth-tery of Life.*

Sir Apropos of Nothing by **Peter David**   The product of a brutal rape, Apropos isn't exactly "hero" material. For one thing he is lame and must walk with the help of a staff. For another, his only goals are to look out for number one and to find and punish the knight who raped his mother. When his beloved mother is murdered, Apropos sets out to the court of King Runcible to claim revenge. However, he becomes apprenticed to the oldest and most inept knight at the court: Sir Umbrage of the Flaming Nether Regions. The two are given a rather routine mission that turns out to be anything but: fetch the Princess Entipy from the Holy Retreat of the Faith Women Nunnery. And that is precisely when everything that can go wrong does go wrong for Sir Apropos.

Good Omens by **Neil Gaiman and Terry Pratchett**   The end of the world is nigh! The Four Motorcyclists (hey, they had to get with the times) of the Apocalypse have begun their ride, and the forces of good and evil have descended upon the English town of Tadfield, home of the Anti-Christ. The only problem is that the Anti-Christ has been misplaced by the forces of evil and in the intervening years has grown into a rather nice young boy. Things are proceeding rather well for the end of the world until two of the participants, the demon Crowley and the angel Aziraphale, have decided that they *like* Earth just the way it is and want to stop the Apocalypse. But to do that they'll have to locate the Anti-Christ and kill him. What they don't know is that the Anti-Christ doesn't want the world to end either.

The Princess Bride by William Goldman   William Goldman loved the stories his father read him when he was young. One story in particular, *The Princess Bride* by S. Morgenstern, was his favorite. As a grown man Goldman sought out his own copy of the classic but was surprised that his copy didn't match what his father had read. Goldman's copy was boring. Really boring. It seems William's father had carefully left out the boring bits, telling only of the excitement and high adventure. This led William to prepare his own version of Morgenstern's tale, calling it the "Good Bits Version." *The Princess Bride* is about the love that farm boy Wesley and Princess Buttercup shared, a love that would prove to be legendary. The problem is that Buttercup, the most beautiful woman in the world, is engaged to be married to the despicable Prince Humperdink because Wesley has been killed by the Dread Pirate Roberts. Or so Buttercup thinks. The reality is that Wesley has taken on the role of the Dread Pirate Roberts because nobody would be afraid of the Dread Pirate Wesley, and Prince Humperdink is planning to start a war by murdering Princess Buttercup. But never fear, good reader, Wesley is coming to the rescue. . . .

Practical Demonkeeping by Christopher Moore   To the sleepy town of Pine Cove comes Travis O'Hearn, driving a car with a hellacious hood ornament. The ornament truly is hellacious: it is the demon known as Catch, and Travis has been bonded to it for the better part of seventy years. When Travis was in seminary, he inadvertently summoned Catch and was permanently bonded to him. In the intervening years Travis has not aged a day and Catch has indulged his appetite for human flesh, to Travis's chagrin. Travis hopes to find in Pine Cove the one woman who can help him be free of Catch. Catch hopes to find in Pine Cove a human buffet table. But Catch also sees in one resident of Pine Cove the means to achieve his plans for world domination. The only people standing in his way are Travis and his new friends, who must battle Catch in a humorous struggle between good and evil.

Other Recommended Titles

Alchemy Unlimited by Douglas Clark

The Garrett Files (series) by Glen Cook

Demon Blues by Esther Friesner

Here Be Demons by Esther Friesner

Hooray for Hellywood by Esther Friesner

Majyk Series by Esther Friesner

Dark Lord of Derkholm by Diana Wynne Jones

The Tough Guide to Fantasy Land by Diana Wynne Jones

Bloodsucking Fiends by Christopher Moore

Coyote Blue by Christopher Moore

Island of the Sequined Love Nun by Christopher Moore

The Lust Lizard of Melancholy Cove by Christopher Moore

Discworld Series by Terry Pratchett

One Foot in the Grave by William Mark Simmons

Split Heirs by Lawrence Watt-Evans and Esther Friesner

Bring Me the Head of Prince Charming by Roger Zelazny and Robert Sheckly

DEREK'S PICK

Myth Series by Robert Aspirin

BEST PICK FOR THE RELUCTANT READER

Good Omens by Neil Gaiman and Terry Pratchett

32

You Can't Keep an Elven Sherlock Holmes Down

Fantasy Mysteries

Fantasy mysteries are mysteries that take place in a fantasy setting. Sometimes the magic involved is wielded by the detective investigating the murder, but more often the magic is in the background of the story and the murder investigation is at the forefront. Vampires and other undead tend to figure very prominently in fantasy mysteries, either as clients of the detective or as suspects. Fantasy mysteries also, with rare exceptions, tend to take place in the contemporary world and are frequently set in major cities like Chicago or New York.

The Dresden Files by Jim Butcher   The first book in the series is *Storm Front*. If you look up "Wizard" in the Yellow Pages of an alternate-world Chicago where magic exists, you'll find only one listing: Harry Blackstone Copperfield Dresden. Despite the fact that magic exists in this world, most people turn a blind eye to the supernatural, preferring to believe that it doesn't exist. Naturally business is a bit slow for a "practicing professional wizard." When the police approach him about two murders they suspect were committed by a magic user, Harry takes the job without a second thought. Right away Harry can tell two things about the case: one, the murderer is a very powerful user of the dark arts, and two, by investigating the case Harry could get into very deep trouble with the White Council that supervises magic users. It then becomes apparent that Harry has revealed his identity to the murderer, and Harry must act quickly to preserve his life and solve the case. Sequels: *Fool Moon, Grave Peril, Summer Knight* (tentative title, forthcoming).

The Garrett Files by Glen Cook In the first book in the series, *Sweet Silver Blues,* Garrett, like most men his age, has done his turn of service in the unending wars in the Cantard. Unlike most men his age, Garrett survived his mandatory military service and has returned to his home city of TunFaire. Garrett's experience as a marine makes his career as a private investigator a bit easier. When necessary he can break heads and track down missing persons. One morning Garrett is awakened from a drink-inspired sleep by the family of one of his service friends. It seems that Garrett's friend Denny has died, and the family is trying to track down the woman he named as his heir. The problem is that the woman was last seen in the Cantard and no one in his right mind goes into the Cantard. Soon Garrett finds himself and his friend Marley Dotes, a dark elf bone-breaker, journeying into the Cantard in search of a woman who doesn't want to be found. What Garrett and company find in the Cantard raises the stakes beyond a simple track-and-bring-back job. Other titles in the series: *Bitter Gold Hearts, Cold Copper Tears, Old Tin Sorrows, Dread Brass Shadows, Red Iron Nights, Deadly Quicksilver Lies, Petty Pewter Gods, Faded Steel Heat.*

The Victory Nelson Series by Tanya Huff In the first book in the series, *Blood Price,* Vicki "Victory" Nelson was one of Toronto's finest homicide detectives before her failing eyesight forced her to retire. Now she is a private detective, and a series of grisly murders, in which the victims' throats are ripped out and the blood is drained from their bodies, is spreading across the city. Vicki finds herself present at one of the murders where she discovers another witness: a romance writer named Henry Fitzroy. But Henry is more than he seems thanks to centuries of experience with the occult. That's right, *centuries:* Henry is a vampire and the bastard son of Henry VIII. Henry is convinced that the murders are not the work of a vampire but of a demon summoned by dark magic. If Henry and Vicki can't locate the magic user in time, an even greater evil could be released upon the world. Other titles in the series: *Blood Trail, Blood Lines, Blood Pact, Blood Debt.*

***Sacred Ground* by Mercedes Lackey** Jennifer Talldeer is a Native American of the Osage and Cherokee tribes who works part-time as a private investigator. She is particularly adept at finding lost Native American artifacts because of her training as a shaman, a Native American magic user. Then Jennifer takes a job from an insurance company that believes their client Rod Calligan has submitted a false claim. As Jennifer investigates, she finds that relics sacred to the local Native American tribes were discovered at a construction site owned by Calligan. Then a bulldozer explodes, killing several Native American workers on the site and leading many to think the culprit is a local Native American activist group led by Jennifer's ex-boyfriend. But shaman-turned-P.I. Jennifer believes that culprits of an entirely different world, the spirit world, may be involved, and she'll do whatever is necessary to get to the bottom of the mystery.

***Dark Heart* by Margaret Weis and David Baldwin** Chicago homicide detective Sandra McCormick has been assigned two related cases that seem impossible to solve. They involve a police officer and another man who were found at separate scenes with their hearts ripped out of their chests. Disfiguring the body after death isn't uncommon among serial killers, but both men were still alive when their hearts were ripped from their bodies. What Sandra doesn't know is that the two men were murdered by Justinian, a man who has been kept alive for centuries so that he can perform this kind of murder for his master, a being known as Dragon. As Sandra gets closer and closer to solving the murders, she and Justinian find themselves doing the unthinkable: falling in love. And love is the one emotion that Dragon has no use for. This book is labeled as the first in the Dragon's Disciple Series, but no further titles have been released.

Other Recommended Titles

Eye of the Daemon by Camille
   Bacon-Smith

The Face of Time by Camille
   Bacon-Smith

Finder: A Novel of the Borderlands by Emma Bull

The Vampire Files (series) by P. N. Elrod

The List of 7 by Mark Frost

Walking the Labyrinth by Lisa Goldstein

Icefalcon's Quest by Barbara Hambly (thriller)

Those Who Hunt the Night by Barbara Hambly

The Anita Blake Series by Laurell K. Hamilton

Knights of the Blood by Scott MacMillian

Cold Iron by Melisa Michaels

The Holmes-Dracula Files (series) by Fred Saberhagen

Blood Secrets by Karen Taylor

Murder in Cormyr by Chet Williamson

Mairelon the Magician by Patricia Wrede

Plague of Sorcerors by Mary Zambreno

DEREK'S PICK

The Garrett Files by Glen Cook

BEST PICK FOR THE RELUCTANT READER

Victory Nelson Series by Tanya Huff

33

Fantasy Romance

What is the difference between a fantasy romance and a romantic fantasy? Actually a lot, but the difference is subtle. In a romantic fantasy, the romance is the main focus in a fantasy setting, such as in Susan Krinard's Werewolves series. But in fantasy romances, the fantasy is the main focus while the romance forms a subplot. If you remove the fantasy from a romantic fantasy, chances are you could still tell the story. If you remove the romance from a fantasy romance, again, you can still tell the story. Remove the romance from a romantic fantasy or the fantasy from a fantasy romance and the story will fall apart.

Outlander Series by Diana Gabaldon   Their marriage interrupted by World War II, Claire and Frank Randall are on their second honeymoon in Scotland when Claire vanishes after touching a stone at an ancient stone circle. Claire finds herself in 1743 and is immediately set upon by a man who greatly resembles her husband (he is in fact an ancestor of Frank's) and who attempts to rape her. Claire is rescued by a local Scottish clan called the MacKenzies, who offer her refuge in this strange world. Claire uses her nursing skills to help clan MacKenzie while she bides her time until she can return to the stones and, she hopes, her own time. Before she can make her escape, she is forced into a marriage with the handsome James Frazer. Soon Claire finds herself torn between honoring her wedding vows with Frank and pursuing the love she has for James. The Outlander series is comprised of: *Outlander, Dragonfly in Amber, Voyager, Drums of Autumn, Fiery Cross.*

A Kiss of Shadows **by Laurell K. Hamilton** Meredith Gentry is a private investigator with a firm that specializes in supernatural cases. Her colleagues don't know that Merry is the missing princess of the Faerie court, Meredith NicEssus. Merry's birth was intended to heal the rift between the two courts of Faerie, the Seelie and the Unseelie. Instead Merry became a target for cruel members of both courts, and after one particularly vicious encounter, she leaves the courts and hides in the real world as Merry Gentry. Merry is able to hide herself from the queen of Faerie, her Aunt Andais, for three years until her firm takes on a case that blows Merry's cover and exposes her to the queen's attention. Summoned to Faerie once again, Merry is shocked when she learns what her aunt has wanted all these years: for Merry to compete against her cousin, Queen Adais's son, for the throne of Faerie. The first one to conceive an heir to the throne and ensure the bloodline wins. Merry must choose from among dozens of suitors the one she will take into her bed to conceive an heir. Merry doesn't reckon with falling in love with the least likely suspect. Warning: This falls into the category of a "racy" romance. The sexual situations are very steamy. Sequel: *A Caress of Twilight.*

Once upon a Winter's Night **by Dennis L. McKiernan** Camille and her family live in a hovel on a tiny farm where they manage to eke out a meager existence. Camille is content with her life, however, spending her days working in the fields and singing and playing games with her brother. The family has very little hope that Camille and her sisters will marry, since there is no money or land to be given as a dowry. But in one night all of that is changed when there is a knock at their door. When they open the door the family finds a large polar bear with a marriage proposal from the prince of Summerwood, Alain. Alain has heard Camille singing in the fields and has fallen in love with her from afar. In return for Camille's hand in marriage, Alain offers a dowry that will keep her family in modest luxury for the rest of their lives. At first

Camille is reluctant, but eventually she accepts the proposal and climbs onto the great bear's back. Camille journeys on the bear's back through the fairy lands of Springwood, Winterwood, and Autumnwood to Summerwood, where she discovers a castle of surpassing beauty and dark secrets. Eventually Camille begins to reciprocate Prince Alain's affections despite his odd behavior. During the day Alain is nowhere to be found inside the castle. He appears only after dark wearing a mask. Soon Camille learns that Alain has been cursed by an evil troll. Determined to free Alain from the curse, Camille embarks on a journey to not only free her husband but unknowingly, an entire kingdom. *Once upon a Winter's Night* is a retelling of "Beauty and the Beast."

***The Shadow of Albion* by Andre Norton and Rosemary Edghill**　　The year is 1805 and young Baltimore resident Sarah Cunningham has just been orphaned by the death of her father. She reluctantly agrees to travel to London in the hope of creating a new life with a distant relative. Meanwhile, in another universe, the marchioness Sarah "Conyngham" Roxbury is on her deathbed. Lady Roxbury, who has sworn to protect her land and its peoples, decides to magically transport her counterpart in our world, Sarah Cunningham, to her world to assume the role of Lady Roxbury. In Lady Roxbury's world, the American Revolution never occurred, the colonies are governed by Thomas Jefferson, and the Stuarts are still in possession of the throne of England. Sarah, with the help of the sorceress, is given the knowledge and skill she'll need to survive the myriad plots of King Henry IX's court, but will it be enough for Sarah to survive in this dangerous new world?

***Fool on the Hill* by Matt Ruff**　　In the quiet college town of Ithaca, New York, resides a great evil, guarded from release by the creatures that imprisoned it: sprites. In this unassuming town great events are already occurring, set into motion by a Greek god calling himself Mr. Sunshine. Mr. Sunshine is a storyteller by trade, and he's mastered the art of writing without paper by influencing the people and events around him and then watching the changes unfold. But there is another storyteller at Cornell, writer-in-residence Stephen Titus George, who only desires to find true love and a great story to tell. Enter Calliope, destined to love S. T. George and to break his heart while pitting him against a dragon. Aiding S. T. George will be some modern-day knights-errant known as

197

FANTASY ROMANCE

the Bohemians, and an unlikely hero—the black knight known as Ragnarok.

Other Recommended Titles

A Fine and Private Space by Peter S. Beagle

The Innkeeper's Song by Peter S. Beagle

The Unicorn Sonata by Peter S. Beagle

The Last Dragonlord by Joanne Bertin

Finder: A Novel of the Borderlands by Emma Bull

Homebody by Orson Scott Card

Treasure Box by Orson Scott Card

Spellfire by Ed Greenwood

Bloodsucking Fiends by Christopher Moore

The Master of All Desires by Judith Merkle Riley

Summers at Castle Auburn by Sharon Shinn

DEREK'S PICK
The Shadow of Albion by Andre Norton and Rosemary Edghill

BEST PICK FOR THE RELUCTANT READER
Outlander Series by Diana Gabaldon

APPENDIX

HUGO AWARD WINNERS

The Hugo Award is bestowed on writers by the World Science Fiction Society. The following have received the Hugo Award for best novel.

2001   *Harry Potter and the Goblet of Fire* by J. K. Rowling

2000   *A Deepness in the Sky* by Vernor Vinge

1999   *To Say Nothing of the Dog* by Connie Willis

1998   *Forever Peace* by Joe Haldeman

1997   *Blue Mars* by Kim Stanley Robinson

1996   *The Diamond Age* by Neal Stephenson

1995   *Mirror Dance* by Lois McMaster Bujold

1994   *Green Mars* by Kim Stanley Robinson

1993   *A Fire upon the Deep* by Vernor Vinge and *Doomsday Book* by Connie Willis

1992   *Barravar* by Lois McMaster Bujold

1991   *The Vor Game* by Lois McMaster Bujold

1990   *Hyperion* by Dan Simmons

1989   *Cyteen* by C. J. Cherryh

1988   *The Uplift War* by David Brin

1987   *Speaker for the Dead* by Orson Scott Card

1986   *Ender's Game* by Orson Scott Card

1985   *Neuromancer* by William Gibson

1984   *Startide Rising* by David Brin

1983 *Foundation's Edge* by Isaac Asimov

1982 *Downbelow Station* by C. J. Cherryh

1981 *The Snow Queen* by Joan D. Vinge

1980 *The Fountains of Paradise* by Arthur C. Clarke

1979 *Dreamsnake* by Vonda McIntyre

1978 *Gateway* by Frederick Pohl

1977 *Where Late the Sweet Birds Sang* by Kate Wilhelm

1976 *The Forever War* by Joe Haldeman

1975 *The Dispossessed: An Ambiguous Utopia* by
Ursula K. Le Guin

1974 *Rendezvous with Rama* by Arthur C. Clarke

1973 *The Gods Themselves* by Isaac Asimov

1972 *To Your Scattered Bodies Go* by Philip Jose Farmer

1971 *Ringworld* by Larry Niven

1970 *The Left Hand of Darkness* by Ursula K. Le Guin

1969 *Stand on Zanzibar* by John Brunner

1968 *Lord of Light* by Roger Zelazny

1967 *The Moon Is a Harsh Mistress* by Robert A. Heinlein

1966 *And Call Me Conrad* by Roger Zelazny and *Dune* by
Frank Herbert

1965 *The Wanderer* by Fritz Leiber

1964 *Way Station* by Clifford D. Simak

1963 *The Man in the High Castle* by Philip K. Dick

1962 *Stranger in a Strange Land* by Robert A. Heinlein

1961 *A Canticle for Liebowitz* by Walter M. Miller Jr.

1960 *Starship Troopers* by Robert A. Heinlein

1959 *A Case of Conscience* by James Blish

1958 *The Big Time* by Fritz Leiber

1957 No award for best novel given

1956 *Double Star* by Robert A. Heinlein

1955 *They'd Rather Be Right* by Mark Clifton and Frank Riley

1954 No awards given

1953 *The Demolished Man* by Alfred Bester

1946 (awarded in 1996) *The Mule* by Isaac Asimov

NEBULA AWARD WINNERS

The Nebula Awards are given by the Science Fiction and Fantasy Writers of America.

2001 *The Quantum Rose* by Catherine Asaro

2000 *Darwin's Radio* by Greg Bear

1999 *Parable of the Talents* by Octavia Butler

1998 *Forever Peace* by Joe Haldeman

1997 *The Moon and the Sun* by Vonda McIntyre

1996 *Slow River* by Nicola Griffith

1995 *The Terminal Experiment* by Robert J. Sawyer

1994 *Moving Mars* by Greg Bear

1993 *Red Mars* by Kim Stanley Robinson

1992 *Doomsday Book* by Connie Willis

1991 *Stations of the Tide* by Michael Stanwick

1990 *Tehanu: The Last Book of Earthsea* by Ursula K. Le Guin

1989 *The Healer's War* by Elizabeth Ann Scarborough

1988 *Falling Free* by Lois McMaster Bujold

1987 *The Falling Woman* by Pat Murphy

1986 *Speaker for the Dead* by Orson Scott Card

1985 *Ender's Game* by Orson Scott Card

1984 *Neuromancer* by William Gibson

1983 *Startide Rising* by David Brin

1982 *No Enemy but Time* by Michael Bishop

1981 *The Claw of the Conciliator* by Gene Wolf

1980 *Timescape* by Gregory Benford

1979 *The Fountains of Paradise* by Arthur C. Clarke

1978 *Dreamsnake* by Vonda McIntyre

1977 *Gateway* by Frederick Pohl

1976 *Man Plus* by Frederick Pohl

1975 *The Forever War* by Joe Haldeman

1974 *The Dispossessed: An Ambiguous Utopia* by
Ursula K. Le Guin

1973 *Rendezvous with Rama* by Arthur C. Clarke

1972 *The Gods Themselves* by Isaac Asimov

1971 *A Time of Changes* by Robert Silverberg

1970 *Ringworld* by Larry Niven

1969 *The Left Hand of Darkness* by Ursula K. Le Guin

1968 *Rite of Passage* by Alexei Panshin

1967 *The Einstein Intersection* by Samuel R. Delany

1966 *Babel-17* by Samuel R. Delany and *Flowers for Algernon* by
Daniel Keyes

1965 *Dune* by Frank Herbert

MYTHOPOEIC AWARD WINNERS

The Mythopoeic Award is given by members of the Mythopoeic Society
for best fantasy novel. Books from a series are not considered unless
they are stand-alone novels or the last volume in a series.

2001 *The Innamorati* by Midori Snyder

2000 *Tamsin* by Peter S. Beagle

1999 *Stardust* by Neil Gaiman

1998 *The Djinn in the Nightingale's Eye* by A. S. Byatt

1997 *The Wood Wife* by Terri Windling

1996 *Waking the Moon* by Elizabeth Hand

1995 *Something Rich and Strange* by Patricia A. McKillip

1994 *The Porcelain Dove* by Delia Sherman

1993 *Briar Rose* by Jane Yolen

1992   *A Woman of the Iron People* by Eleanor Arnason

1991   *Thomas the Rhymer* by Ellen Kushner

1990   *The Stress of Her Regard* by Tim Powers

1989   *Unicorn Mountain* by Michael Bishop

1988   *Seventh Son* by Orson Scott Card

1987   *The Folk of the Air* by Peter S. Beagle

1986   *Bridge of Birds* by Barry Hughart

1985   *Cards of Grief* by Jane Yolen

1984   *When Voiha Wakes* by Joy Chant

1983   *The Firelings* by Carol Kendall

1982   *Little, Big* by James Crowley

1981   *Unfinished Tales* by J. R. R. Tolkien

1980–1976   No awards given

1975   *A Midsummer Tempest* by Poul Anderson

1974   *The Hollow Hills* by Mary Stewart

1973   *The Song of Rrhiannon* by Evangeline Walton

1972   *Red Moon and Black Mountain* by Joy Chant

1971   *The Crystal Cave* by Mary Stewart

WORLD FANTASY AWARD WINNERS

The World Fantasy Award is given annually at the World Fantasy Convention.

2001   *Declare* by Tim Powers

2000   *Thraxas* by Martin Scott

1999   *The Antelope Wife* by Louise Erdrich

1998   *The Physiognomy* by Jeffrey Ford

1997   *Godmother Night* by Rachel Pollack

1996   *The Prestige* by Christopher Priest

1995   *Towing Jehovah* by James Morrow

1994   *Glimpses* by Lewis Shiner

1993 *Last Call* by Tim Powers
1992 *Boy's Life* by Robert R. McCammon
1991 *Only Begotten Daughter* by James Morrow
1990 *Layonesse: Madouc* by Jack Vance
1989 *Koko* by Peter Straub
1988 *Replay* by Ken Grimwood
1987 *Perfume* by Patricia Suskind
1986 *Song of Kali* by Dan Simmons
1985 *Mythago Wood* by Robert Holdstock
1984 *The Dragon Waiting* by John M. Ford
1983 *Nifft the Lean* by Michael Shea
1982 *Little, Big* by John Crowley
1981 *The Shadow of the Torturer* by Gene Wolf
1980 *Watchtower* by Elizabeth A. Lynn
1979 *Gloriana* by Michael Moorcock
1978 *Our Lady of Darkness* by Fritz Leiber
1977 *Doctor Rat* by William Kotzwinkle
1976 *Bid Time Return* by Richard Matheson
1975 *The Forgotten Beasts of Eld* by Patricia A. McKillip

INDEX

Authors, book and series titles, and subjects are interfiled in this index. Author names appear in roman type, book titles in italic, series titles in quotation marks, and subjects in boldface.

A

Abbey, Lynn, 128, 184

Abductors: Conspiracy (Frakes), 73

Accidental Creatures (Harris), 67

Acts of God (Seigneur), 92

Adams, Douglas, 78–79

Adams, Richard, 177

Adiamante (Modesitt), 23, 35

"Admiral Thrawn Series" (Zahn), 99

Adventures of Lando Calrissian (Smith), 99

After the Blue (Like), 80

Aftermath (Sheffield), 48

"Age of Unreason Series" (Keyes), 50

Alchemy Unlimited (Clark), 188

Aldiss, Brian, 27, 57

Alexander, Roger, 45, 48, 90–91

Alice's Adventures in Wonderland (Carroll), 114

Alien Heat (Moorcock), 57

Alien invasion, 21–24

All Tomorrow's Parties (Gibson), 42

Allaby, Michael, 27

Allelulia Files (Shinn), 92

Allen, Roger MacBride, 34, 54, 70, 99

Alternate history, 49–51

Alvin Journeyman (Card), 142

American God (Gaiman), 134–35, 161

Ancient Shores (McDevitt), 73

And the Devil Will Drag You Under (Chalker), 83

Anderson, C. Dean, 151

Anderson, Dennis Lee, 57

Anderson, Kevin J., 26, 34, 66, 98–100

Anderson, Poul, 15, 19, 154

Androids/robots/cyborgs, 32–36

Andromeda Strain (Crichton), 74, 76

Angel Fire East (Brooks), 159

Animal Farm (Orwell), 178

Animist (Forward), 126, 176, 178

"Anita Blake Series" (Hamilton), 150–52, 161, 193

Anno Dracula (Newman), 151

Another Fine Myth (Aspirin), 186–87

Anthony, Kim, 34

Anthony, Mark, 128, 148, 162–63

Anthony, Patricia, 23, 70, 73

Anthony, Piers, 27, 45, 48, 51, 66, 73, 79, 82–87, 90, 92–94, 118, 124, 126, 155, 157, 160, 165, 174

Anti-Ice (Baxter), 15

Antieau, Kim, 48

Antrax: The Voyage of Jerle Shannara (Brooks), 125

Apacheria (Page), 51

Apocalypse Troll (Weber), 24

"Apprentice Adept Series" (Anthony), 83

Arachne (Mason), 42

"Arcana Series" (Llywelyn and Scott), 137

Archangel (Conner), 69, 71

Archangel (Shinn), 84, 92

Archer, Nathan, 61, 107

Ariadne's Web (Saberhagen), 136

Armageddon the Musical (Rankin), 80

Armed Memory (Young), 67
Arms of Hercules (Saberhagen), 136
Art of Arrow Cutting (Dedman), 161
Arthur (Lawhead), 138
Arthur, King (Anderson), 57
Arthurian legend, 57, 137–40
"Arthurian Saga" (Stewart), 114,
    139–40
Article 23 (Forstchen), 27
Asaro, Catherine, 54, 66, 87–90
Ascendant Sun (Asaro), 89
Ashes of Victory (Weber), 95
Asimov, Isaac, 9–10, 33, 35, 70
Asimov, Janet, 70
Aspirin, Robert, 54, 79, 186–87, 189
"Asteroid Wars" (Bova), 31
Atlantis Found (Roberts), 55
Attanasio, A. A., 27, 35
Atwater-Rhodes, Amelia, 150, 152

B
Back to the Moon (Hickam), 29, 73
Bacon-Smith, Camille, 160, 192
Baird, Wilhelmina, 87
Baker, Kage, 34, 53
Baldwin, David, 182, 192
Ball, Margaret, 165, 174, 184
Balshazzar's Serpent (Chalker), 92
"Band of Four Novels" (Greenwood), 170
Bane of the Black Sword (Moorcock),
    169
"Banned and the Banished Series"
    (Clemens), 146
"Bardic Voices Series" (Lackey), 173
"Bard's Tale Series" (Lackey), 174
Barnes, John, 15
Barnes, Steven, 16, 23, 70, 73
Barrenlands (Durgin), 170
Barrie, J. M., 165
Barron, Thomas A., 140
Batman: A Death in the Family (Starlin),
    63
Batman: A Lonely Place of Dying
    (Wolfman), 63
Batman: Knightfall (O'Neil), 60–61
Batman: Knightfall Who Rules the Night
    (Dixon), 62

Batman: No Man's Land (Rucka), 61
Batman: Prodigal (Dixon), 62
Batman: The Dark Knight Returns
    (Miller), 62
Batman: The Killing Joke (Moore), 62
Batman: The Long Halloween (Loeb),
    62
Batman: Thrillkiller (Chaykin), 62
Batman: Year One (Miller), 62
Battle Lines (Galanter and Brodeur),
    107
Battlefield Earth (Hubbard), 12, 23
Battlestations! (Carey), 102
Baudino, Gael, 160, 165, 170, 174, 179,
    184
Baum, L. Frank, 112–13, 166
Baxter, Stephen, 15, 23, 27–30, 48, 51,
    54–55, 67
"Bazil Broketail Series" (Rowley), 181
Beagle, Peter S., 156, 174, 177, 197
Bear, Greg, 26, 51, 55, 75, 98, 100, 184
Beauty (Tepper), 57, 130–31
Bedlam's Bard (Lackey and Guon), 161,
    174, 185
Beggars and Choosers (Kress), 66
Beggars in Spain (Kress), 66–67
Beggars Ride (Kress), 66
"Beggars Trilogy" (Kress), 65–66
Beholder's Eye (Czerneda), 73
"Belgariad Series" (Eddings), 119
Benford, Gregory, 19, 27, 51, 55, 71
Beowulf's Children (Niven, Pournelle,
    and Barnes), 16, 23
Berman, Rick, 100
Berserker! (Saberhagen), 38
Berserker Base (Saberhagen), 38
Berserker Blue Death! (Saberhagen), 38
Berserker Fury (Saberhagen), 38
Berserker Kill (Saberhagen), 38
Berserker Lies (Saberhagen), 38
Berserker Man (Saberhagen), 38
Berserker Planet (Saberhagen), 38
Berserker Throne (Saberhagen), 38
Berserker Wars (Saberhagen), 38
"Berserkers!" (Saberhagen), 13, 37–38
Berserkers: The Beginning (Saberhagen),
    38

Bertin, Joanne, 179–80, 197
Besher, Alexander, 44
Bester, Alfred, 12, 38, 55, 70, 79, 86–87
Betancourt, John, 105
Better Man (Weinstein), 102
Beyond the Pale (Anthony), 162–63
"Bill the Galactic Hero Series"
   (Harrison), 80
Bimbos of the Death Sun (McCrumb),
   70–71
"Bio of a Space Tyrant" (Anthony),
   93–94
Biotech thrillers, 74–76
Birth of an Age (Seigneur), 92
Bishop, Michael, 55
Bisson, Terry, 27, 45, 73
Bitter Gold Hearts (Cook), 191
"Bitterbynde Series" (Dart-Thorton),
   125, 127
Black Chalice (Jakober), 144
Black Company (Cook), 146
Black Horses for the King (McCaffrey),
   140
Black Trillium (Bradley, May, and
   Norton), 126
Black Unicorn (Brooks), 163
Blackgod (Keyes), 136
Blade Runner (movie), 34
Bleak Seasons (Cook), 146
Bless the Beasts (Haber), 108
Blind Waves (Gould), 47, 73, 89
Blish, James, 12, 101
Blood: A Southern Fantasy (Moorcock),
   84
Blood and Chocolate (Klause), 153–55
Blood Debt (Huff), 192
Blood Lines (Huff), 192
Blood of the Fold (Goodkind), 168
Blood Pact (Huff), 192
Blood Price (Huff), 161, 191–92
Blood Secrets (Taylor), 152, 193
Blood Trail (Huff), 192
Bloodsucking Fiends (Moore), 152, 189,
   197
*Bloodties: Featuring the Avengers,
   Avengers West Coast, and the X-
   Men* (Idelson), 62

Bloody Bones (Hamilton), 151
Bloom (McCarthy), 48
Blue Mars (Robinson), 27
Blue Moon (Hamilton), 151
Bodyguard (Dietz), 73
Bone Forest (Holdstock), 135
Book of Lost Swords End Game
   (Saberhagen), 170
Book of Lost Swords First Triad
   (Saberhagen), 170
Book of Lost Swords Triad
   (Saberhagen), 170
Book of Night with Moon (Duane), 177
Book of the Cauldron (Paxson), 143
Book of the Spear (Paxson), 143
Book of the Stone (Paxson), 143
Book of the Sword (Paxson), 143
"Books of Ash Series" (Gentle), 144
Books of Merlin (Tolstoy), 140
"Books of Swords" (Saberhagen),
   169–70
"Books of the Damned" (Foster), 23
"Books of the Gods Series"
   (Saberhagen), 136
"Books of the North" (Cook), 146
"Books of the South" (Cook), 146
Borchardt, Alice, 144, 153
"Bounty Hunter Wars Series" (Jeter),
   98–99
Bova, Ben, 15, 27, 29–31, 44–45, 55,
   67, 73, 79
Boy and His Tank (Frankowski), 38
Bradbury, Ray, 11–13, 26–27, 148
Bradley, Marion Zimmer, 126, 138, 140,
   156, 160, 166
Braga, Brannon, 100, 108
Brain Plague (Slonczewski), 75
Brazen Rule (Burgauer), 75
Brian Boru: Emperor of the Irish
   (Llywelyn), 137, 144
Bridge (Young), 20, 76
Briggs, Patricia, 148
Brightness Reef (Brin), 21
Brin, David, 15, 21, 24, 48, 67
Bring Me the Head of Prince Charming
   (Zelazny and Checkly), 189
Brodeur, Greg, 107

Brooks, Terry, 99, 124–25, 148, 158–59, 161, 163

Brother Assassin (Saberhagen), 38

Brother Termite (Anthony), 23, 51

Brother to Shadows (Norton), 16

Brown, Mary, 126

Brown Girl in the Ring (Hopkinson), 161

Brust, Steven, 79

Brute Orbits (Zebrowski), 31

Buddy Holly Is Alive and Well on Ganymede (Denton), 80

Budrys, Algis, 29

Bujold, Lois McMaster, 65, 89, 95–96

Bull, Emma, 160, 166, 174, 182–83, 193, 197

Bunch, Chris, 95, 170

Burgauer, Steven, 75

Burning Stone (Elliott), 142

Burnt Offerings (Hamilton), 151

Burroughs, Edgar Rice, 26

Burton, Levar, 48

Busiek, Kurt, 61–62

Butcher, Jim, 190–91

Butler, Octavia, 22, 46, 48

By Honor Betrayed (Doyle), 95

By the Sword (Lackey), 170

Byers, Richard Lee, 61

C

Cadigan, Pat, 70

Cage (Stirling and Meier), 170

Calculus of Angels (Keyes), 50

Calder, Richard, 42

"Callahan Chronicles" (Robinson), 80

Camelot 30K (Forward), 20

Candle in the Wind (White), 140

Canticle for Liebowitz (Miller), 13, 47–48

Card, Orson Scott, 22, 24, 48, 54, 57, 67, 114–15, 117, 130, 133, 141–42, 144, 156–57, 159–60, 197

Caress of Twilight (Hamilton), 195

Caretaker (Graf), 108

Carey, Diane, 101–3, 105–7

Carmody, Isobele, 87

Carnivores of Light and Darkness (Foster), 176

Carr, Caleb, 48, 67

Carroll, Jerry Jay, 80

Carter, Raphael, 45

Carter, Tonya, 128

Cary, Devin, 116

Case of Conscience (Blish), 12

Cast of Corbies (Lackey and Sherman), 173

Cat Who Walks through Walls (Heinlein), 177

Catch the Lightning (Asaro), 54, 87, 89

Cats, 175–78

Catspaw (Vinge), 42

"Catspaw Series" (Vinge), 87

Cavern of Black Ice (Jones), 126

Caverns of Socrates (McKiernan), 38, 44–45

Caves of Steel (Asimov), 9

Celestial Matters (Garfinkle), 51

Chalker, Jack L., 42, 44, 55, 80, 83, 95

Chamberlin, Ann, 144

Champetieur, Joel, 15

Changeling Prince (Velde), 154

Changer of Worlds (Weber), 95

Changewinds (Chalker), 83

Chaos Come Again (Baird), 87

Chapterhouse: Dune (Herbert), 12

Chaykin, Howard, 62

Chernevog (Cherryh), 157

Cherryh, C. J., 15, 19, 23, 31, 67, 95, 126, 157

Chester, Deborah, 126, 184

Child of Flame (Elliott), 142

Child of the Eagle (Friesner), 137, 144

Childhood's End (Clarke), 10, 23

Children of Dune (Herbert), 12

"Children of the Changeling Series" (Keyes), 135–36

Chimera (Shetterly), 66–67, 71

Chorus Skating (Foster), 172

"Christ Clone Trilogy" (Seigneur), 92–93

Christian, Deborah, 126

"Chronicles of Narnia" (Lewis), 113–15, 166

Chronicles of Pern: First Fall (McCaffrey), 181
"Chronicles of the Black Company" (Cook), 146
"Chronicles of Thomas Covenant" (Donaldson), 114, 148, 164, 166
"Chronicles of Ynis Aielle" (Salvatore), 166
Chrysalis (Wilson), 108
Chung Kuo (Wingrove), 96
Ciencin, Scott, 128, 148
Circle of One (Fullilove), 70
Circuit of Heaven (Danvers), 45, 89
Circus of the Damned (Hamilton), 151
"Cities in Flight Series" (Blish), 12
Citizen of the Galaxy (Heinlein), 13
Clark, Douglas, 188
Clarke, Arthur C., 10, 14–15, 23, 37, 39, 47, 92
Classic science fiction, 8–14
Clemens, James, 146
Clement, Hal, 30–31
Climbing Olympus (Anderson), 26, 28, 66
Clough, Brenda M., 82, 87
Clute, John, 8
Cochran, Molly, 140, 160
Code of Conduct (Smith), 73
Code of the Lifemaker (Hogan), 31, 34, 91
Codename: Wolverine (Golden), 61
Codger Space (Foster), 80
Coe, David B., 84
Cohen, Jack, 24, 48
Coinspinner's Story (Saberhagen), 170
Cold as Ice (Sheffield), 67
Cold Copper Tears (Cook), 191
Cold Iron (Michaels), 161, 174, 184, 193
Cole, Allan, 95
Coleman, Loren L., 128
Collins, Nancy, 154
Colonization, 26–31
Companions of the Night (Velde), 152
Company of Stars (Hogan), 80
Compleat McAndrew (Sheffield), 73
Complete Paratime (Piper), 55

Complete Robot (Asimov), 9
Complete Sword (Saberhagen), 170
Computer Connection (Bester), 38, 79
Computer intelligence, 36–39
Conan Chronicles (Howard), 170
Conan the Barbarian, 167
Confessions of an Ugly Stepsister (Maguire), 132
Confluence (McAuley), 67
Conner, Michael, 69, 71
Conqueror's Pride (Zahn), 24
Conscience of the Beagle (Anthony), 34, 73, 87
Cook, Glen, 146, 188, 191, 193
Cool, Tom, 38
Cordelia's Honor (Bujold), 89
Cornwell, Bernard, 140
"Correllian Trilogy" (Allen), 99
Corrupting Dr. Nice (Kessel), 55, 80
Cosm (Benford), 71
Count Zero (Gibson), 41
Courage of Falcons (Lisle), 154
Covey, Michael Greatex, 140
Cowboy Feng's Space Bar and Grill (Brust), 79
Cox, Greg, 61, 105
Coyote Blue (Moore), 136–37, 189
Cragg, Dan, 96
Crazy Jack (Napoli), 132
Crichton, Michael, 54–55, 71–74, 76
"Crimson Shadow Trilogy" (Salvatore), 170
Crisis on Infinite Earths (Wolfman), 63
Crispin, A. C., 99, 102
Crompton, Anne Eliot, 140
"Cross-Time Engineer Series" (Frankowski), 55
Crossover (Friedman), 102
Crossover fantasy, 162–66
Crown of Stars (Elliott), 142
"Crown of Stars Series" (Elliott), 142
Crusading Wizard (Stasheff), 165
Crystal Cave (Stewart), 139
Crystal Singer (McCaffrey), 174
Cunningham, Elaine, 128, 185
Cyber Way (Foster), 69
Cyberbooks (Bova), 79

Cyberpunk, 40–42
Cyberstorm (Skurzynski), 45
Cyberweb (Mason), 38
Cyborgs. *See* **Androids/robots/cyborgs**
"Cycle of Count Ragoczy Saint-Germain" (Yarbro), 152
Cyteen (Cherryh), 67
Czerneda, Julie, 23, 73, 86

D
Dahl, Roald, 112
Daley, Brian, 99
Dance of the Dead (Golden), 148
Dancers at the End of Time (Moorcock), 56–57
Dancing on Air (Kress), 70
Daniell, Tina, 128
Danvers, Dennis, 45, 89, 90
Daredevil: Born Again (Miller), 62
Dark Cities under Ground (Goldstein), 147, 161
Dark fantasy, 145–48
Dark Heart (Weis and Baldwin), 182, 192
Dark Light (Yarbro), 126, 152
Dark Lord of Derkholm (Jones), 164–66, 189
Dark Mirror (Duane), 103, 105
Dark Remains (Anthony), 163
Darksaber (Anderson), 99
Darksong Rising (Modesitt), 174
"Darksword Trilogy" (Weis and Hickman), 170
Dart-Thorton, Cecilia, 125, 127
Darwinia (Wilson), 51
Darwin's Radio (Bear), 75
Datlow, Ellen, 132, 148
Daughter of the Forest (Marillier), 132
Daughters of Bast (Isidore), 137
David, Peter, 62, 103, 106, 187
Dawn (Butler), 22
Day of the Dissonance (Foster), 172
Days of Cain (Dunn), 55
DC versus Marvel (Marz, David, and Kahan), 62
De Camp, L. Sprague, 56, 57
De Lancie, John, 104

de Lint, Charles, 42, 82–83, 160, 166
Dead Girls (Calder), 42
Deadly Quicksilver Lies (Cook), 191
Death and Life of Superman (Stern), 60
Death Dream (Bova), 44–45, 73
Death of a Dragon (Greenwood and Denning), 181
Death of a Neutron Star (Kotani and Smith), 108
Death of Princes (Peel), 105
Death of Sleep (McCaffrey), 96
Deathday (Dietz), 23
Decision at Doona (McCaffrey), 20
Dedman, Stephen, 55, 72, 161
Deep Domain (Weinstein), 102
Deepness in the Sky (Vinge), 16
Defalco, Tom, 61
Defender (Cherryh), 19
Deighton, Len, 51
Delacorte, Peter, 55
Delany, Samuel R., 13, 174
Demolished Man (Bester), 12, 70, 86–87
Demon Blues (Friesner), 189
Demon in My View (Atwater-Rhodes), 150
Demon Sword (Hood), 144
Denning, Troy, 128, 181
Denton, Bradley, 80
Depths of Time (Allen), 54
Design for a Great Day (Foster), 87, 95
Destiny: Child of the Sky (Haydon), 172
Destroying Angel (Russo), 70
Deus Machine (Ouellette), 37, 39
Deus X (Spinard), 92
Devil's World (Eklund), 102
Di Filippo, Paul, 42, 51
"Diaries of the Family Dracul" (Kalogridis), 144, 152
Diaspora (Egan), 35
Dick, Philip K., 13, 27, 33–34, 87
Dickson, Gordon R., 27, 80, 166, 180, 182
Dietz, William C., 23, 34, 73
Digital Effect (Perry), 70
Dillard, J. M., 100, 102
Dinosaur Summer (Bear), 51

Dirk Gently's Holistic Detective Agency (Adams), 79
"Discworld Series" (Pratchett), 189
Dixon, Chuck, 62
Do Androids Dream of Electric Sheep? (Dick), 13, 33–34
Dolphins of Pern (McCaffrey), 181
Donaldson, Stephen R., 94, 96, 148, 164, 166
Donnerjack (Zelazny and Lindskold), 45
Doohan, James, 95
Doomsday Book (Willis), 54–55
Door into Summer (Heinlein), 55
Door Number Three (O'Leary), 55, 80
Dorothy and the Wizard in Oz (Baum), 113
Double Star (Heinlein), 28
Douglas, Ian, 27
Downbelow Station (Cherryh), 95
Downtiming the Night Side (Chalker), 55
Doyle, Debra, 94–95
Dracula Unbound (Aldiss), 57
Dragon and Phoenix (Bertin), 180
Dragon and the Djinn (Dickson), 180
Dragon and the Fair Maid of Kent (Dickson), 180
Dragon and the George (Dickson), 180
Dragon and the Gnarly King (Dickson), 180
Dragon at War (Dickson), 180
"Dragon Circle Series" (Gardner), 181
Dragon Death (Baudino), 179
Dragon in Lyonese (Dickson), 180
Dragon Knight (Dickson), 180
"Dragon Knight Series" (Dickson), 166, 180, 182
Dragon Lord (Drake), 140
Dragon on the Border (Dickson), 180
Dragon, the Earl, and the Troll (Dickson), 180
Dragondrums (McCaffrey), 181
Dragonfly in Amber (Gabaldon), 195
"Dragonlance Chronicles," 128
"Dragonlance Chronicles" (Weis and Hickman), 182
Dragonlord (Drake), 181

Dragonquest (McCaffrey), 181
Dragonriders of Pern (McCaffrey), 84
"Dragonriders of Pern Series" (McCaffrey), 181–82
Dragons, 178–82
Dragon's Eye (Champetieur), 15
Dragon's Honor (Johnson and Cox), 105
Dragonsdawn (McCaffrey), 181
Dragonseye (McCaffrey), 181
Dragonsinger (McCaffrey), 181
Dragonsong (McCaffrey), 181
Dragonstone (McKiernan), 126
Dragonsword (Baudino), 165, 170, 179
"Draka Series" (Stirling), 51
Drake, David, 51, 140, 181
Dread Brass Shadows (Cook), 191
Dreadnought (Carey), 101, 103
"Dream Park Series" (Niven and Barnes), 70
Dreamcatcher (King), 23
Dreams of Steel (Cook), 146
Dreams Underfoot (de Lint), 160, 166
Dreamships (Scott), 38, 42
Dreamsnake (McIntyre), 47
"Dresden Files" (Butcher), 190–91
Dreyfuss, Richard, 51, 73
Druid of Shannara (Brooks), 125
Druids (Llywelyn), 144
Drums of Autumn (Gabaldon), 195
Duane, Diane, 59, 61, 103–5, 177
Duel of Dragons (Baudino), 179
Dun Lady's Jess (Durgin), 170
Duncan, Dave, 167–68
Dune (Herbert), 12, 96
Dune: House Atreides (Herbert), 12
Dune: House Harkonnen (Herbert), 12
Dune Messiah (Herbert), 12
Dungeons and dragons, 127–28
Dunn, J. R., 55
Durgin, Doranna, 170
Dyson Sphere (Zebrowski), 104

E
Eagle and the Nightingale (Lackey), 173
Earth (Brin), 15

Earth the Final Conflict: Requiem for Boone (Doyle and MacDonald), 95

Earth X (Ross), 63

"Earthsea Tetralogy" (Le Guin), 113

Echoes (Smith), 108

Echoes in Time (Norton and Smith), 23, 55

Echoes of Honor (Weber), 95

Ecklar, Julie, 101

Eddings, David, 119

"Eden Trilogy" (Harrison), 51

Edghill, Rosemary, 144, 166, 196–97

Effinger, George Alec, 70

Egan, Greg, 35, 38

Einstein Intersection (Delany), 13, 174

Eklund, Gordon, 102

Elementals (Llywelyn), 144

Elfqueen of Shannara (Brooks), 125

Elfstones of Shannara (Brooks), 125

Ella Enchanted (Levine), 132

Elliott, Kate, 142

Elric of Melnibone (Moorcock), 169

"Elric Saga" (Moorcock), 114, 148, 169–70

Elrod, P. N., 151, 193

Elvenbane (Norton and Lackey), 181, 185

Emerald City of Oz (Baum), 113

Emery, Clayton, 128

Empire of Fear (Stableford), 50

Empire of Unreason (Keyes), 50

Enchantment (Card), 57, 130, 133

Encyclopedia of Fantasy (Clute), 8

End of All Songs (Moorcock), 57

End of an Era (Sawyer), 55

Ender's Game (Card), 22, 24

Endymion (Simmons), 15

Enemy Within (Golden), 148

Engines of God (McDevitt), 73

Entoverse (Hogan), 38

Eon (Bear), 55

Epic fantasy, 118–22

Escape from Kathmandu (Robinson), 80

Escape Velocity (Stasheff), 87

"Eschaton Sequence" (Pohl), 23

Et Tu Babe (Leyner), 80

"Eternal Champions" (Moorcock), 169

Eternity Road (McDevitt), 48

"Ethan Hamilton Cyber-Thriller Series" (Scott), 91

Etruscans (Llywelyn), 144

Evans, Linda, 54–55

Evermeet (Cunningham), 185

Executive (Anthony), 94

Expendable (Gardner), 20

Exploration, 26–31

Eye of the Daemon (Bacon-Smith), 160, 192

Eye of the Hunter (McKiernan), 126

Eyes of the Dragon (King), 116–17

F

Face of Apollo (Saberhagen), 136

Face of Time (Bacon-Smith), 160, 192

Faded Steel Heat (Cook), 191

Faerie Tale (Feist), 130, 161

Faery in Shadow (Cherryh), 137

Fahrenheit 451 (Bradbury), 11

Fairies, 182–85

Fairy tales, 129–33

Fairyland (McAuley), 67

Faith of the Fallen (Goodkind), 168

Fall of Atlantis (Bradley), 137

Fall of Hyperion (Simmons), 15

Falling Free (Bujold), 65

Falling Woman (Murphy), 159–60

Family Tree (Tepper), 57

Fang the Gnome (Covey), 140

Fantasy
    Arthurian legend, 137–40
    awards, 201–4
    blended with science fiction, 81–84
    cats, 175–78
    classic, 111–15
    crossover, 162–66
    dark side of, 145–48
    dragons, 178–82
    dungeons and dragons, 127–28
    epic, 118–22
    fairies, 182–85
    fairy tales, 129–33
    general, 115–17
    ghosts/undead, 155–57
    historical, 141–44

humorous, 186–89
music and, 171–74
mysteries of, 190–93
quest, 123–27
romance in, 194–97
sword and sorcery, 167–70
urban legends, 158–61
vampires, 149–52
werewolves, 152–55
Far Call (Dickson), 27
Far Edge of Darkness (Evans), 55
Farmer, Philip Jose, 13, 27
Farslayer's Story (Saberhagen), 170
Farthest Shore (Le Guin), 113
Fatherland (Harris), 49, 51
Fearful Summons (Flinn), 102
Federation (Reeves-Stevens and Reeves-Stevens), 102
Feintuch, David, 14
Feist, Raymond E., 130, 161
Feline Wizard (Stasheff), 165
Fellowship of the Ring (Tolkien), 114, 123
Ferguson, Brad, 104
Field of Dishonor (Weber), 95
Fiery Cross (Gabaldon), 195
Fifth Quarter (Huff), 173
Finder: A Novel of the Borderlands (Bull), 166, 182–83, 193, 197
Fine and Private Space (Beagle), 157, 197
Finn MacCool (Llywelyn), 137, 144
Finney, Jack, 12, 23, 55, 90
Fire in the Mist (Lisle), 117
Fire Rose (Lackey), 153–55
Fire upon the Deep (Vinge), 96
Firebird (Lackey), 132
Firebird (Tyers), 92, 96
Firelord (Godwin), 140
Firelord (Miller), 117
Firestar (Flynn), 15
First Book of Swords (Saberhagen), 170
First contact novels, 18–21
First King of Shannara (Brooks), 125
First Swords (Saberhagen), 170
Fitzhugh, Bill, 80
Flag in Exile (Weber), 95

Flash: Race against Time! (Waid), 63
Flashback (Braga), 108
Flesh and Gold (Gotlieb), 70
"Flight Engineer Series" (Doohan and Stirling), 95
Flight of Michael McBride (Snyder), 161, 184
Flinn, Denny Martin, 102
Flint, Eric, 80
Flint, James, 15
Flowers for Algernon (Keyes), 13, 67
Flynn, Michael F., 15
Folk on the Fringe (Card), 48
Fool Moon (Butcher), 191
Fool on the Hill (Ruff), 161, 196–97
Fool's War (Zettel), 39
For Want of a Nail: If Burgoyne Had Won at Saratoga (Sobel), 51
Ford, John M., 101–2, 183, 185
Foreign Bodies (Dedman), 55, 72
Foreigner: A Novel of First Contact (Cherryh), 19
Forest House (Bradley), 138
Forests of the Heart (de Lint), 160
Forever King (Cochran and Murphy), 140, 160
Forever Peace (Haldeman), 34
Forever War (Haldeman), 13, 96
"Forgotten Realms," 128
Forgotten War (Forstchen), 104
Forstchen, William R., 27, 104
Forsyth, Kate, 126
Fortunate Fall (Carter), 34, 45
Forward, Eve, 125–27, 176, 178
Forward, Robert L., 20
Foster, Alan Dean, 23, 69, 78, 80, 87, 95, 126, 159, 171–72, 174, 176
Foundation (Asimov), 10
Foundation and Empire (Asimov), 10
"Foundation Series" (Asimov), 9–10
Foundation's Edge (Asimov), 10
Foundations of Paradise (Clarke), 14
Four and Twenty Blackbirds (Lackey), 173
Fourth World (Danvers), 90
Foy, George, 70
Frakes, Jonathan, 73

Frankenstein Unbound (Aldiss), 57
Frankowski, Leo, 38, 55
"Freedom Series" (McCaffrey), 23
Freer, Dave, 80, 96
Fresco (Tepper), 24, 73
Frezza, Robert, 80
Friday (Heinlein), 65, 67
Friedman, Michael Jan, 61, 102, 104–7
Friesner, Esther, 45, 80, 144, 166, 189
Frontera (Shiner), 28
Fullilove, Eric James, 70
Fury Scorned (Sargent), 105

G
Gabaldon, Diana, 57, 194–95, 197
Gaia Websters (Antieau), 48
Gaia's Toys (Ore), 42
Gaiman, Neil, 134–35, 146–47, 161, 183–85, 187, 189
Galanter, Dave, 107
Galveston (Stewart), 84
Gamma Quest (Cox), 61
"Gap Series" (Donaldson), 94, 96
Garden of Rama (Clarke), 10
Garden of Stone (Strauss), 117
Gardner, Craig Shaw, 59, 181
Gardner, James Alan, 20, 67, 73
Garfinkle, Richard, 51
Garland, Mark, 96, 107–8
"Garrett Files" (Cook), 188, 191, 193
Gates of Horn (Holdstock), 135
Gates of Ivory (Holdstock), 135
"Gates of Time Series" (Parkinson), 55
Gateway (Pohl), 13
Gathering Flame (Doyle), 95
Gawain and Lady Green (Crompton), 140
Gemmel, David, 117, 144
Gene Roddenberry's Earth the Final Conflict: The Arrival (Saberhagen), 24
General science fiction, 14–16
Genetic engineering, 63–67
Gentle, Mary, 144
Gerrold, David, 16, 23
Ghost of a Chance (Garland and McGraw), 96, 107–8

Ghostlight (Bradley), 156, 160
Ghosts/undead, 155–57
Gibson, William, 40–41, 42, 48, 73
Gilded Chain (Duncan), 167–68
Girl Who Heard Dragons (McCaffrey), 181
Glass Dragon (Radford), 181
Glass Harmonica (Marley), 84
Glimpses (Alexander), 45, 48, 90–91
Glinda of Oz (Baum), 113
Glory Lane (Foster), 78, 80
Glory Season (Brin), 15, 67
Glut, Donald, 99
Goblin Mirror (Cherryh), 126
God Emperor of Dune (Herbert), 12
God of the Golden Fleece (Saberhagen), 136
God's Fires (Anthony), 23, 92
Gods of Fire and Thunder (Saberhagen), 136
Gods Themselves (Asimov), 10
Godwin, Parke, 78–79, 140
Golden, Christie, 108, 148
Golden, Christopher, 61, 151–52
Golden Fleece (Sawyer), 70
Golden Globe (Varley), 31
Goldman, William, 188
Goldstein, Lisa, 140, 144, 147, 161, 185, 193
Good Omens (Gaiman and Pratchett), 187, 189
Goodkind, Terry, 168, 170
Gossamer Axe (Baudino), 174
Gotlieb, Phyllis, 70
Gould, Steven, 47, 73, 87, 89
Graf, L. A., 108
Graphic novels, 61–63
Grave Peril (Butcher), 191
Gravelight (Bradley), 156
Graveyard Game (Baker), 53
Gravity Dreams (Modesitt), 67
"Great War Series" (Turtledove), 51
Green, Roland, 20, 96
Green Lantern: Aliens (Marz), 62
Green Lantern: New Journey, Old Path (Winick), 63
Green Mars (Robinson), 27

Greenberger, Robert, 104
Greening of Mars (Allaby), 27
Greenland, Colin, 38
Greenmantle (de Lint), 160
Greenwood, Ed, 128, 170, 181, 197
Griffith, Nicola, 42
Grub, Jeff, 128
Guardian of the Balance (Radford), 139
Guardian of the Trust (Radford), 139
Guardian of the Vision (Radford), 139
Guilty Pleasures (Hamilton), 150–51
Gunn, James, 102
Guns of the South (Turtledove), 50–51
Guon, Ellen, 161, 174, 185
Gust Front (Ringo), 96
Gutbucket Quest (Anthony and
    Leming), 165, 174

H
Haber, Karen, 108
Habitus (Flint), 15
Hacker and the Ants (Rucker), 38, 41
Hainish Cycle (Le Guin), 13
Haldeman, Joe, 13, 34, 96
Half-Life (Clement), 30–31
"Hallowed Isle Series" (Paxson), 140,
    143
Halo (Maddox), 38
Hambly, Barbara, 99, 126, 150, 193
Hamilton, Laurell K., 150–52, 161, 193,
    195
Hamilton, Peter F., 69, 73, 87
"Hammer and the Cross Series"
    (Harrison), 137, 142–43
Hammer of God (Clarke), 47, 92
"Han Solo Adventures" (Daley), 99
"Han Solo Trilogy" (Crispin), 99
Hand, Elizabeth, 55
"Hand and the Falcon Trilogy" (Tarr),
    144, 185
Happy Policeman (Anthony), 70
Hard Merchandise (Jeter), 98
Hard Sell (Anthony), 27, 79
Harris, Anne, 67
Harris, Robert, 49, 51
Harrison, Harry, 35, 38, 49–51, 79, 80,
    142–43

Hart's Hope (Card), 115–17
Harvest of Stars (Anderson), 15
Haunted Wizard (Stasheff), 165
Hautman, Pete, 57
Have Spacesuit Will Travel (Heinlein),
    13
Hawke, Simon, 104
Haydon, Elizabeth, 172, 174
Hearlight (Bradley), 156
Heart of a Warrior (Betancourt), 105
Heart of Gold (Shinn), 16
Heart of Midnight (King), 148, 154
Heart of the Sun (Sargent), 102
Heartfire (Card), 142
Heaven's Reach (Brin), 21
Heavy Time (Cherryh), 31
Heavy Weather (Stirling), 42
Heinlein, Robert A., 11, 22–23, 26–27,
    28, 29–30, 55, 65, 67, 80, 90, 92,
    96, 177
Hemry, John G., 96
Henderson, Jason, 61
Her Majesty's Wizard (Stasheff), 165
Herbert, Frank, 12, 96
Here Be Demons (Friesner), 189
Heroing (Hugh), 170
Hickam, Homer, 29, 73
Hickman, Tracy, 23, 84, 128, 182
High House (Stoddard), 147–48
Higher Education (Sheffield and
    Pournelle), 15, 16
Hinz, Christopher, 48, 67
Historical fantasy, 141–44
History, alternate, 49–51
Hit or Myth (Aspirin), 187
"Hitch Hiker's Guide to the Galaxy
    Trilogy" (Adams), 78, 80
Hitler Victorious (Benford), 51
Hobbit (Tolkien), 114, 162
Hobb's Bargain (Briggs), 148
Hogan, James P., 16, 31, 34, 38, 80,
    91–92
Holder, Nancy, 152
Holdstock, Robert, 135, 137, 140
Hollow Hills (Stewart), 139
Hollow Lands (Moorcock), 57
Hollow Man (Simmons), 86–87

Hollowing (Holdstock), 135
"Holmes-Dracula Files" (Saberhagen), 193
Holocaust fiction, 46–48
Holy Fire (Stirling), 76
Homebody (Card), 157, 197
Honor among Enemies (Weber), 95
"Honor Harrington Series" (Weber), 95
Honor of the Queen (Weber), 95
Hood, Ken, 144
Hooray for Hellywood (Friesner), 189
Hopkinson, Nalo, 83, 161
Horse and His Boy (Lewis), 114
Horse Goddess (Llywelyn), 144
Hour of the Gate (Foster), 172
How Like a God (Clough), 82, 87
How Much for Just the Planet? (Ford), 101–2
How to Mutate and Take Over the World (Sirrius and St. Jude), 80
Howard, Robert E., 167, 170
Hubbard, L. Ron, 12–13, 23, 55, 166
Huff, Tanya, 148, 152, 161, 172–73, 191–93
Hugh, Dafydd ab, 106, 170
Hugo Award, 199–201
Hulk: Transformations (Lee), 62
Humor (science fiction), 77–80
Humorous fantasy, 186–89
Hunted (Gardner), 67
Hyperion (Simmons), 15, 16

I

I, Q. (De Lancie), 104
I, Strahd (Elrod), 151
I Am Dracula (Anderson), 151
I Am Mordred (Springer), 140
Icarus Hunt (Zahn), 72–74
Icefalcon's Quest (Hambly), 126, 193
Icehenge (Robinson), 28, 73
"Icewind Dale Trilogy" (Salvatore), 170
Idelson, Matt, 62
Idle, Eric, 80
Idoru (Gibson), 73
If the Stars Are Gods (Benford), 19
Ill-Made Knight (White), 140
Illearth War (Donaldson), 164

Illegal Alien (Sawyer), 20, 71
Illustrated Man (Bradbury), 12
Ilse Witch: The Voyage of Jerle Shannara (Brooks), 125
Immortal (Golden and Holder), 152
Immortality Option (Hogan), 34
Imperium Game (Wentworth), 39
In Death Ground (Weber), 24, 96
In Enemy Hands (Weber), 95
In His Image (Seigneur), 92
In Legend Born (Resnick), 117
In the Company of Others (Czerneda), 23
In the Cube (Smith), 73
In the Forests of the Night (Atwater-Rhodes), 150, 152
In the Garden of Iden (Baker), 53
"Incarnations of Immortality Series" (Anthony), 82, 84
Incredible Hulk: Future Imperfect (David), 62
Incredible Shrinking Man (Matheson), 13
Independence Day (ID4) (McNeff et al.), 23
Independence Day: Silent Zone (Molstad), 20
Infecress (Cool), 38
Infinity Beach (McDevitt), 73
Infinity Gauntlet (Starlin), 63
Infinity's Shore (Brin), 21
Inherit the Earth (Stableford), 75–76
Inheritor (Cherryh), 19
Inhuman Beings (Carroll), 80
Inhumans (Jenkins), 62
Innkeeper's Song (Beagle), 197
Insurrection (Weber), 96
Intellivore (Duane), 104
Into the Out Of (Foster), 159
Into the Thinking Kingdoms (Foster), 176
Invader (Cherryh), 19
Invasion of the Body Snatchers (Finney), 12, 23
Invisible Man (Wells), 13
Iron Bridge (Morse), 48, 55
Iron Man: The Armor Trap (Cox), 61

Isaac Asimov's Caliban (Allen), 34, 70
"Isaac Asimov's Robots in Time Series"
   (Wu), 55
Island of Doctor Moreau (Wells), 13, 66
Island of the Sequined Love Nun
   (Moore), 189

J
Jabkklokov, Alexander, 70
Jacques, Brian, 177
Jaivin, Linda, 80
Jakober, Marie, 144
Jed the Dead (Foster), 80
"Jedi Academy Series" (Anderson), 98,
   100
Jehovah's Angel (Shinn), 92
Jemas, Bill, 62
Jenkins, Paul, 62
Jensen, Jan Lars, 84
Jericho Iteration (Steele), 38, 73
Jerlayne (Abbey), 184
Jesus on Mars (Farmer), 27
Jeter, K. W., 70, 98–99, 106
JLA: Earth Two (Morrison and Quietly),
   63
JLA: Tower of Babel (Waid), 63
JLA: World War III (Morrison), 63
Job: A Comedy of Justice (Heinlein), 80,
   90, 92
Johnson, Kij, 105
Jones, Diana Wynne, 164–66, 189
Jones, Gwyneth, 20, 87
Jones, J. V., 126
Jones, Terry, 80
"Journeys of the Catechist Series"
   (Foster), 126, 176
Joy Machine (Gunn and Sturgeon), 102
Jumper (Gould), 87
Jumping off the Planet (Gerrold), 16
Jupiter (Bova), 31
Jurassic Park (Crichton), 7, 71–72, 74

K
Kahan, Bob, 62
Kahless (Friedman), 104–5
Kalogridis, Jeanne, 144, 152
Kanaly, Michael, 23, 74

Keep of Fire (Anthony), 163
Kelly, James P., 35
Kenyon, Kay, 55
Kerner, Elizabeth, 180–81
Kerr, Katherine, 70
Kessel, John, 55, 80
Key out of Time (Norton), 55
Keyes, Daniel, 13, 67
Keyes, J. Gregory, 50, 135–36
Khan, James, 99
Killing Dance (Hamilton), 151
Killing Time: A Novel of the Future
   (Carr), 48, 67
Killobyte (Anthony), 45
Kindred (Butler), 53
King, Gabriel, 178
King, J. Robert, 128, 148, 154
King, Stephen, 23, 116–17
King and Emperor (Harrison), 143
King Kobold Revived (Stasheff), 83
King of Infinite Space (Steele), 35, 38
Kingdom Come (Maggin), 59–61
Kingdome Come (Waid), 63
"King's Blades Series" (Duncan), 167–68
King's Dragon (Elliott), 142
Kirchoff, Mary, 128
Kiss of Shadows (Hamilton), 195
Klause, Annette Curtis, 152, 153, 155
Knight and Knave of Swords (Leiber),
   168
Knight of the Black Rose (Lowder), 148,
   157
Knight of the Word (Brooks), 159
Knights of the Black Earth (Weis and
   Perrin), 35
Knights of the Blood (Kurtz and
   MacMillan), 152, 193
Kobayashi Maru (Ecklar), 101
Kornwise, Robert, 126
Kotani, Eric, 108
Kress, Nancy, 19–21, 65–66, 67, 73, 75
Kurtz, Katherine, 70, 152, 178, 193

L
Labyrinth of Night (Steele), 28
Lackey, Mercedes, 132, 144, 153–55,
   161, 170, 173–74, 185, 192

Lady El (Starlin), 38
Lady of Avalon (Bradley), 138
Ladylord (Miller), 125–26
Laertian Gamble (Sheckley), 106
Land of Oz (Baum), 113
"Landover Series" (Brooks), 163
Last Avengers Story (David), 62
Last Battle (Lewis), 114
Last Dragonlord (Bertin), 179–80, 197
Last Enchantment (Stewart), 139
Last Hawk (Asaro), 89–90
Last Hot Time (Ford), 183, 185
"Last Legion Series" (Bunch), 95
"Last Rune Series" (Anthony), 148, 162–63
Last Stand (Ferguson), 104
Last Unicorn (Beagle), 113
Laughing Corpse (Hamilton), 151
Lauria, Frank, 20, 73
Lavondyss (Holdstock), 135
Lawhead, Stephen R., 138, 166
Le Guin, Ursula K., 13, 113
Lebaron, Francis, 128
Lee, Stan, 62
Legacy of Lehr (Kurtz), 70, 178
Legends and myths, 134–37
Legion of the Damned (Dietz), 34
Leiber, Fritz, 168
Leming, Ron, 165, 174
Leonard Nimoy's Primortals: Target Earth (Perry), 23
Lesser Kindred (Kerner), 181
Lest Darkness Falls (De Camp), 56, 57
Lethe (Sullivan), 48
Levine, Gail Carson, 132
Lewis, C. S., 13, 28, 92, 112–15, 166
Lewitt, Shariann, 67
Leyner, Mark, 80
Librarians
    reference interview and, xi–xv
    and staying current, xv
Life, the Universe, and Everything (Adams), 78
Light of Other Days (Clarke), 15
Like, Russel, 80
Lindskold, Jane, 45, 160–61

Lion, the Witch, and the Wardrobe (Lewis), 113
Lion of Ireland (Llywelyn), 137, 144
Lion of Macedon (Gemmell), 137, 144
Lisle, Holly, 117, 126, 154
List of 7 (Frost), 193
Little Myth Marker (Aspirin), 187
Llywelyn, Morgan, 137, 144
Loeb, Jeph, 62
Long Hunt (Doyle), 95
Long Night (Smith), 106
"LonTobyn Chronicle" (Coe), 84
Lord Demon (Zelazny and Lindskold), 160–61
Lord Foul's Bane (Donaldson), 164
Lord of the Fire Lands (Duncan), 168
"Lord of the Rings Tetralogy" (Tolkien), 112, 114–15, 118, 123
"Loregiver Series" (Christian), 126
Lost Millennium (Moscoe), 55
Lost Princess of Oz (Baum), 113
"Lost Swords" (Saberhagen), 170
Lowder, James, 148
Lunatic Café (Hamilton), 151
Lust Lizard of Melancholy Cove (Moore), 189

M
MacDonald, John D., 95
Mackay, Scott, 55
MacMillan, Scott, 152, 193
Mad Amos (Foster), 80
Maddox, Tom, 38
"Mag Force 7 Series" (Weis and Perrin), 96
"Mageworlds Series" (Doyle), 94–95
Maggin, Elliot S., 59–61
Magic Circle (Napoli), 132
Magic Kingdom for Sale—Sold! (Brooks), 163
Magic of Oz (Baum), 113
"Magic of Xanth" (Anthony), 118, 121, 124
"Magic: The Gathering," 128
Magician's Nephew (Lewis), 114
Magnificent Wilf (Dickson), 80
Maguire, Gregory, 132

Mairelon the Magician (Wrede), 193
"Majyk Series" (Friesner), 189
Malory, Thomas, 138–39
Man O' War (Shatner), 28, 96
Man Plus (Pohl), 28, 34
Mandalorian Armor (Jeter), 98
Manifold: Time (Baxter), 48, 67
Manjinn Moon (Vitola), 71
Mantle of Kendis Dai (Weis and
    Hickman), 84
Mariller, Juliet, 132
Marley, Louise, 84
Marooned (Galanter), 108
Marrow (Reed), 73
Mars, 26–28
Mars (Bova), 27
Mars Attacks! (movie), 21
Mars Crossing (Landis), 28
Mars Plus (Pohl), 34, 38
Mars Prime (Dietz), 27, 73
Marston, Ann, 170
Martian Chronicles (Bradbury), 13, 27
Martian Race (Benford), 27
Martian Time Slip (Dick), 13, 27
Martian Viking (Sullivan), 28
Marvel Super-Heroes: Secret Wars
    (Shooter), 63
Marvels (Busiek and Ross), 62
Marz, Ron, 62
Mason, Lisa, 38, 42, 55
Master of All Desires (Riley), 144, 197
Masterharper of Pern (McCaffrey),
    181
Matheson, Richard, 13
Matz, Marc, 42, 72
Maximum Light (Kress), 67, 73
May, Julian, 55, 96, 126
"Mayflower Trilogy" (Card), 67
McAuley, Paul J., 28, 45, 67, 75
McCaffrey, Anne, 20, 23, 35, 84, 86–87,
    96, 140, 174, 181–82
McCarthy, Wil, 48, 69–70
McCrumb, Sharyn, 70–71
McDevitt, Jack, 29, 48, 73
McGraw, Charles, 96, 107–8
McHugh, Maureen, 16
McIntyre, Vonda, 35, 47, 100, 143–44

McKiernan, Dennis L., 38, 44–45, 126,
    132, 195–96
McKillip, Patricia A., 126, 174
McKinley, Robin, 130–31, 132
McMullen, Sean, 48
McNeff, Dionne, 23
Meier, Shirley, 170
"Memory, Sorrow and Thorn Series"
    (Williams), 121, 122
Memory and Dream (de Lint), 160
Memory of Whiteness (Robinson), 73,
    174
Men in Black (Perry), 23, 80
Mendoza in Hollywood (Baker), 53
Mercenary (Anthony), 94
Merchanter's Luck (Cherryh), 15
Mercycle (Anthony), 48
Merlin (Lawhead), 138
Merlin Codex (Holdstock), 140
Merlin Effect (Barron), 140
Merlin of St. Giles Well (Chamberlain),
    144
Merlin's Bones (Saberhagen), 140
"Merlin's Descendants Series"
    (Radford), 139
Merlin's Wood (Holdstock), 135
Michaels, Melisa, 161, 174, 184, 193
Michelinie, David, 61
Midnight Robber (Hopkinson), 83
Midshipman's Hope (Feintuch), 14
Millar, Mark, 62
Miller, Frank, 62
Miller, Sarah, 117
Miller, Sasha, 125–26
Miller, Walter, Jr., 13, 47–48
Million Open Doors (Barnes), 15
Mind, Machines, and Evolution
    (Hogan), 16
Mind Meld (Vornholt), 102
Mindstar Rising (Hamilton), 69, 73, 87
Mindsword's Story (Saberhagen), 170
Minerva Wakes (Lisle), 166
Minsky, Marvin, 35, 38
Mirage (Wilson), 73, 76
*Mirage: An Isaac Asimov's Robots
    Mystery* (Tiedemann), 35, 71
Mission Child (McHugh), 16

Mists of Avalon (Bradley), 138, 140
"Mithgar Series" (McKiernan), 120
M'lady Witch (Stasheff), 83
Modesitt, L. E., Jr., 23, 35, 51, 67,
 173–74
Molstad, Stephen, 20
Moment of the Magician (Foster), 172
Mona Lisa Overdrive (Gibson), 41
Moon, 28–30
Moon and the Sun (McIntyre), 143–44
Moon Is a Harsh Mistress (Heinlein),
 11, 29–30
Moonfall (McDevitt), 29, 48
Moonheart (de Lint), 160, 166
Moonrise (Bova), 29–30
Moonseed (Baxter), 28–29
Moorcock, Michael, 56–57, 84, 148,
 169
Moore, Christopher, 136–37, 152, 161,
 188–89, 197
Moore, Vance, 128
Moorek, Alan, 62
More than Honor (Weber), 95
More than Human (Sturgeon), 87
Moreta: Dragonlady of Pern
 (McCaffrey), 181
Morningstar (Gemmel), 117
Morrison, Grant, 63
Morse, David E., 48, 55
Morte d'Arthur (Malory), 138–39
Mosaic (Taylor), 108
Moscoe, Mike, 55, 96
Mostly Harmless (Adams), 78
Moving Mars (Bear), 26
Mr. Was (Hautman), 57
Mudd in Your Eye (Oltion), 102
Murder at the Galactic Writers' Society
 (Asimov), 70
Murder in Cormyr (Williamson), 193
Murder in the Solid State (McCarthy),
 69–70
Murdered Sun (Golden), 108
Murphy, Pat, 14–15, 159–60
Murphy, Warren, 140, 160
Music, 171–74
Mute (Anthony), 73, 85–87
My Son, the Wizard (Stasheff), 165

Mysteries (fantasy), 190–93
Mysteries (science fiction), 68–71
Myth Conceptions (Aspirin), 187
Myth Directions (Aspirin), 187
M.Y.T.H. Inc. in Action (Aspirin), 187
M.Y.T.H. Inc. Link (Aspirin), 187
Myth-ing Persons (Aspirin), 187
Myth-nomers and ImPervections
 (Aspirin), 187
"Myth Series" (Aspirin), 186–87, 189
Mythago Wood (Holdstock), 135, 137
"Mythago Woods Series" (Holdstock),
 135, 137
Mythology 101 (Nye), 161, 185
Mythopoeic Award, 202–3
Mythopoeic Society, 202

N

Naked Sun (Asimov), 9
Nano Flower (Hamilton), 23, 69
Napoli, Donna Jo, 132
Narcissus in Chains (Hamilton), 151
Nebula Award, 201–2
Neuromancer (Gibson), 40–41, 42
Neverwhere (Gaiman), 146–47, 161
"New Earth Series" (Carey), 102
Newman, Kim, 151
Newton's Cannon (Keyes), 50
Night in the Lonesome October
 (Zelazny), 177–78
Night of the Wolf (Borchardt), 153
Night Parade (Ciencin), 148
Night Sky Mine (Scott), 42, 45
Niles, Douglas, 128
Nimbus (Jabkklokov), 70
Niven, Larry, 12, 16, 23, 70, 73
No Earthly Sunne (Ball), 165, 174, 184
No Enemy but Time (Bishop), 55
No Quarter (Huff), 173
Nocenti, Ann, 61
Nocturne for a Dangerous Man (Matz),
 42, 72
Noir (Jeter), 70
Nor Crystal Tears (Foster), 23
Norman, Lisanne, 87
Norton, Andre, 16, 23, 55, 126, 144,
 166, 185, 196–97

Novak, Kate, 128
"Novels of the Company" (Baker), 34,
    53
"Novels of the Serrated Edge" (Lackey
    et al.), 161, 185
Number of the Beast (Heinlein), 13, 23
Nye, Jody Lynn, 161, 185
Nylund, Eric S., 41, 45

O

O Pioneer (Pohl), 23
Oath of Swords (Weber), 137
"Oathbound Series" (Lackey), 170
Oathbound Wizard (Stasheff), 165
Oaths and Miracles (Kress), 75
Obernewtyn (Carmody), 87
Objective: Bajor (Peel), 106
Oblique Approach (Drake), 51
Obsidian Butterfly (Hamilton), 151
Oceanspace (Steele), 73
O'Donohoe, Nick, 70
Of Tangible Ghosts (Modesitt), 51
Old Tin Sorrows (Cook), 191
Ole Doc Methuselah (Hubbard), 13
O'Leary, Patrick, 55, 80
Oltion, Jerry, 102
On Basilisk Station (Weber), 95
"Once and Future King Series" (White),
    139–40
Once upon a Winter's Night
    (McKiernan), 132, 195–96
One Foot in the Grave (Simmons), 151,
    189
One King's Way (Harrison), 143
One Tree (Donaldson), 164
O'Neil, Dennis, 60–61
Operation Chaos (Anderson), 154
Ore, Rebecca, 42
Organ Grinders (Fitzhugh), 80
"Orion Series" (Bova), 55, 67
Ouellette, Pierre, 37
Out of the Silent Planet (Lewis), 13, 28,
    92
Outlander (Gabaldon), 195, 197
"Outlander Series" (Gabaldon), 57,
    194–95, 197
Outpost (Mackay), 55

Outposts (Resnick), 23
"Oz Series" (Baum), 112–13, 166
Ozma of Oz (Baum), 113

P

Page, Jake, 51
Parable of the Sower (Butler), 46
Parafaith War (Modesitt), 23
"Paratwa Saga" (Hinz), 48, 67
Parkinson, Dan, 55
Passion Play (Stewart), 71
Pastwatch: The Redemption of
    Christopher Columbus (Card), 54
Patchwork Girl of Oz (Baum), 113
Paths of the Preambulator (Foster), 172
Pathways (Taylor), 108
Paxson, Diana L., 140, 143
Peace on Earth (Kessel), 80
Peacekeepers (Bova), 15
Peel, John, 106
Pegasus in Flight (McCaffrey), 86
Pegasus in Space (McCaffrey), 86
"Pegasus Saga" (McCaffrey), 86
Pendragon (Lawhead), 138
"Pendragon Cycle" (Lawhead), 138
Permutation City (Egan), 38
Perriman, Cole, 73
Perrin, Don, 35, 96
Perry, Steve, 23, 70, 80, 99
Peter Pan (Barrie), 165
Petty Pewter Gods (Cook), 191
Phoenix Code (Asaro), 89
Phule's Company (Aspirin), 79
Piercy, Marge, 57
Pigs Don't Fly (Brown), 126
Pillars of Creation (Goodkind), 168
Piper, H. Beam, 55
Pitch Black (Lauria and Twohy), 20, 73
Plague Dogs (Adams), 177
Plague of Angels (Tepper), 84
Plague of Sorcerors (Zambreno), 193
Planet of Twilight (Hambly), 99
Platt, Charles, 37, 39, 42, 45
Playing God (Zettel), 75
Podkayne of Mars (Heinlein), 13, 28
Pohl, Frederick, 13, 23, 28, 34, 38, 73
Polar City Blues (Kerr), 70

Politician (Anthony), 94
Porath, Ellen, 128
Positronic Man (Asimov), 9
Pournelle, Jerry, 15–16, 23, 35
Power That Preserves (Donaldson), 164
Practical Demonkeeping (Moore), 161, 188
Pratchett, Terry, 187, 189
Precursor (Cherryh), 19
Prelude to Foundation (Asimov), 10
Prentice Alvin (Card), 142
Priam's Lens (Chalker), 95
Price of Peace (Moscoe), 96
Priestess of Avalon (Bradley), 138
Primary Inversion (Asaro), 66, 87–90
Prime Directive (Reeves-Stevens and Reeves-Stevens), 102–3
Prince Caspian (Lewis), 114
Prince of Dogs (Elliott), 142
Princess Bride (Goldman), 188
Princess of Mars (Burroughs), 26
Prisoner X (Nocenti), 61
Privateers (Bova), 15
Probability Moon (Kress), 19–21
Probability Sun (Kress), 20
Psychoshop (Bester and Zelazny), 55, 79
Puppet Masters (Heinlein), 13, 22

Q
Q-Squared (David)
Quantum Murder (Hamilton), 69
Quantum Rose (Asaro), 89
Quartered Sea (Huff), 173
Queen of Air and Darkness (White), 140
Quest fantasy, 123–27
Quest for Tomorrow (Shatner), 96
Quicksilver Knight (Stasheff), 83
Quiet Invasion (Zettel), 31
Quietly, Frank, 63
Quintara Marathon (Chalker), 83, 95
Quozl (Foster), 80

R
Radiant Seas (Asaro), 89–90
Ragnarok (Archer), 107
Rama II (Clarke), 10

Rama Revealed (Clarke), 10
"Rampart Worlds Series" (May), 96
Rankin, Robert, 80
Rats, Bats, and Vats (Freer and Flint), 80, 96
"Ravenloft Adventures" (Bradley), 166
Rebel Sutra (Lewitt), 67
"Rebels Trilogy" (Hugh), 106
Red Dust (McAuley), 28, 45
Red Iron Nights (Cook), 191
Red Mars (Robinson), 27–28
Red Planet (Heinlein), 13
Red Prophet (Card), 142
Red Tape Wars (Chalker), 80
"Redwall Series" (Jacques), 177
Reed, Robert, 73
Reeves-Stevens, Garfield, 102–3
Reeves-Stevens, Judith, 102–3
Reference interviews, xi–xv
Refugee (Anthony), 94
Religion (science fiction), 90–92
Rendezvous with Rama (Clarke), 10
Renegades of Pern (McCaffrey), 181
Republic (Friedman), 102
Requiem of Stars (Hickman), 23
Resnick, Laura, 117
Resnick, Michael D., 23, 70
Restaurant at the End of the Universe (Adams), 78
Resurrection, Inc. (Anderson), 34
Return of the King (Tolkien), 114
Reunion on Neverend (Stith), 71
Revolt in 2100 (Heinlein), 13
Rewolinski, Lea, 80
Rhapsody: A Child of the Blood (Haydon), 172
Rhapsody: A Child of the Earth (Haydon), 172
"Rhapsody Series" (Haydon), 172, 174
Richardson, David, 80
Rift (Williams), 48
"Riftwar Series" (Feist), 119, 122
Riley, Judith Merkle, 144, 197
RIM: A Novel (Besher), 44
Ringo, Jolin, 96
Ringworld (Niven), 12
Rinkitink in Oz (Baum), 113

Rise of Endymion (Simmons), 15
Road to Mars (Idle), 80
Road to Oz (Baum), 113
Roberson, Jennifer, 126, 170
Roberts, R. Garcia Y., 55
Robin and the Kestrel (Lackey), 173
Robinson, Kim Stanley, 26–28, 73, 80, 174
Robinson, Spider, 80
Robot Dreams (Asimov), 9
"Robot Series" (Asimov), 9, 14, 33, 35, 70
Robot Visions (Asimov), 9
Robots. *See* **Androids/robots/cyborgs**
Robots and Empire (Asimov), 9
Robots of Dawn (Asimov), 9
Rock 'n' Roll Babes from Outer Space (Jaivin), 80
Roddenberry, Gene, 100
Rogers, Mark E., 80
Rogue Moon (Budrys), 29
Rogue Planet (Bear), 98, 100
"Rogue Wizard Series" (Stasheff), 84
Romance (fantasy), 194–97
Romance (science fiction), 88–90
Romkey, Michael, 152
Romulan Prize (Hawke), 104
Romulan Stratagem (Greenberger), 104
Ronin (Miller), 62
Rose Daughter (McKinley), 132
Ross, Alex, 62–63
Rowley, Christopher, 181
Rucka, Greg, 61
Rucker, Rudy, 38, 41–42
Ruff, Matt, 16, 79, 161, 196–97
"Rune Blade Trilogy" (Marston), 170
Running with the Demon (Brooks), 148, 158–59, 161
Rusalka (Cherryh), 157
Rusch, Kristine, 61
Russo, Richard Paul, 70

S
Saberhagen, Fred, 13, 24, 38, 136, 140, 152, 169–70, 193
Sacred Ground (Lackey), 192
"Saga of the Pliocene Exile" (May), 55

"Saga of the Skolian Empire" (Asaro), 89
"Saga of the Well World Series" (Chalker), 23, 83
Sailor on the Seas of Fate (Moorcock), 169
Salvatore, R. A., 99, 128, 166
"Samurai Cat Series" (Rogers), 80
Saratoga (Friedman), 106–7
Sarek (Crispin), 102
Sargent, Pamela, 102
Saturn, 30–31
Saturn's Race (Niven and Barnes), 73
Sawyer, Robert J., 20, 55, 70, 71
Scarecrow of Oz (Baum), 113
Schisimatrix (Sterling), 35, 67
Schmitz, James, 13, 87
Scholar of Decay (Huff), 148
Schroeder, Karl, 38
Science fiction
  awards, 199–202
  blended with fantasy, 81–84
  classics, 8–14
  general, 14–16
  humorous, 77–80
  mysteries, 68–71
  religion in, 90–92
  romance in, 88–90
  thrillers, 71–74
Science Fiction and Fantasy Writers of America, 201
Scott, Jefferson, 45, 91
Scott, Melissa, 38, 41–42, 45, 92
Scott, Michael, 144
"Seas of Kilmoyn Series" (Green), 20
Second Book of Swords (Saberhagen), 170
"Second Chronicles of Thomas Covenant the Unbeliever" (Donaldson), 164
Second Foundation (Asimov), 10
Secret of Life (McAuley), 75
Secret of Spring (Anthony), 66, 79, 83, 90
"Secret Texts Series" (Lisle), 126, 154
Secular Wizard (Stasheff), 165
Seer King (Bunch), 170

Seer's Blood (Durgin), 170

Seigneur, James Beau, 91–92

Semper Mars (Douglas), 27

Serpent's Shadow (Lackey), 132, 144

Seventh Son (Card), 141–42

Sewer, Gas and Electric (Ruff), 16, 79

Shade of the Tree (Anthony), 155, 157, 160

Shadow and Claw (Wolfe), 84

Shadow Games (Cook), 146

Shadow of Albion (Norton and Edghill), 144, 166, 196–97

Shadow Sorceress (Modesitt), 174

Shadow's End (Tepper), 84

Shadows Linger (Cook), 146

Shadows of the Empire (Perry), 99

Shadowsinger (Modesitt), 174

Shaman (Stasheff), 117

"Shannara" (Brooks), 125

Shapes of Their Hearts (Scott), 38, 92

Shatner, William, 28, 73, 96

Shattered Oath (Sherman), 144, 185

She Is the Darkness (Cook), 146

Sheckley, Robert, 106, 132, 189

Sheffield, Charles, 15–16, 48, 67, 73

Sherlock Holmes in Orbit (Resnick), 70

Sherman, David, 96

Sherman, Josepha, 102, 161, 185

Sherwood Game (Friesner), 45, 80

Shetterly, Will, 66–67, 71

Shieldbreaker's Story (Saberhagen), 170

Shift (Foy), 70

Shiner, Lewis, 28

Shinn, Sharon, 16, 84, 90, 92

Ship Who Sang (McCaffrey), 35

Shiva 3000 (Jensen), 84

Shiva in Steel (Saberhagen), 38

"Sholan Alliance Series" (Norman), 87

Shooter, Jim, 63

Short Victorious War (Weber), 95

Shroud of Shadow (Baudino), 174

Sightblinder's Story (Saberhagen), 170

Signal to Noise (Nylund), 41, 45

Silicon Man (Platt), 37, 42, 45

Silver Chair (Lewis), 114

Silver Kiss (Klause), 152

Silver Wolf (Borchardt), 144, 153

Silverberg, Robert, 13, 55

Simmons, Dan, 15, 86–87

Simmons, William Mark, 151, 189

Simulacra (Dick), 13, 87

Sing the Four Quarters (Huff), 172–73

Singer from the Sea (Tepper), 84

Sir Apropos of Nothing (David), 187

Sirrius, R. U., 80

Six Moon Dance (Tepper), 16

Skies of Pern (McCaffrey), 181

Skurzynski, Gloria, 45, 67

Sky Coyote (Baker), 53

Sky of Swords (Duncan), 168

Slave Ship (Jeter), 98

Slonczewski, Joan, 75

Slow River (Griffith), 42

Smith, Dean Wesley, 31, 61, 73, 102, 106, 108

Smith, Kristine, 73

Smith, L. Neil, 99

Smith, Sherwood, 23, 55

Snake Oil Wars (Godwin), 79

Snow Crash (Stephenson), 42

Snow Queen (Vinge), 131–33

Snow White, Blood Red (Datlow and Windling), 132, 148

Snyder, Midori, 161, 184

So Long, and Thanks for All the Fish (Adams), 78

Sobel, Robert, 51

Software (Rucker), 42

Soldiers Live (Cook), 146

Solis (Attanasio), 27, 35

Something Wicked This Way Comes (Bradbury), 148

Something's Alive on the Titanic (Serling), 157

Son of Darkness (Sherman), 161, 185

Son of Spellsinger (Foster), 172

Song for the Basilisk (McKillip), 174

Song in the Silence: The Tale of Lanen Kaelar (Kerner), 180–81

Song of Albion (Lawhead), 137, 166

"Songs of Earth and Power" (Bear), 184

Songsmith (Norton), 174

Soprano Sorceress (Modesitt), 173–74

Soul of the Fire (Goodkind), 168

Souls in the Great Machine (McMullen), 48

Soulsaver (Steven-Arce), 92

Source of Magic (Anthony), 124

Space operas, 93–96

　Star Trek (*Deep Space Nine*), 105–7

　Star Trek (original series), 100–3

　Star Trek (*The Next Generation*), 103–5

　Star Trek (*Voyager*), 107–8

　Star Wars, 96–100

Spearwielder's Tale (Salvatore), 166

Spell for Chameleon (Anthony), 114

Spellbound Scholar (Stasheff), 83

Spellfire (Greenwood), 197

"Spellsinger Series" (Foster), 171–72, 174

"Spellsong Cycle (Modesitt), 173–74

Spellsong War (Modesitt), 174

Sphere (Crichton), 73

Spider Legs (Anthony), 66

Spider-Man: Carnage in New York (Michelinie and Smith), 61

Spider-Man: Emerald Mystery (Smith), 61

Spider-Man: Goblin Moon (Busiek and Archer), 61

Spider-Man: The Lizard Sanction (Duane), 61

Spider-Man: Venom Factor (Duane), 59

Spider-Man: Wanted Dead or Alive (Gardner), 59

Spiderman: Valley of the Lizard (Vornholt), 61

Spinard, Norman, 92

Spindle's End (McKinley), 130–31

Spinners (Napoli), 132

Split Heirs (Watt-Evans and Friesner), 189

Spock Must Die! (Blish), 101

S.S.-G.B. Nazi Occupied Great Britain 1941 (Deighton), 51

St. Jude, 80

Stableford, Brian, 50, 75–76

Stainless Steel Rat (Harrison), 79

"Stainless Steel Rat" (Harrison), 79

Stainless Steel Rat for President (Harrison), 79

Stainless Steel Rat Gets Drafted (Harrison), 79

Stainless Steel Rat Goes to Hell (Harrison), 79

Stainless Steel Rat Is Born (Harrison), 79

Stainless Steel Rat Joins the Circus (Harrison), 79

Stainless Steel Rat Saves the World (Harrison), 79

Stainless Steel Rat Sings the Blues (Harrison), 79

Stainless Steel Rat Wants You (Harrison), 79

Stainless Steel Rat's Revenge (Harrison), 79

Star Trek

　Deep Space Nine, 105–7

　The Next Generation, 103–5

　original series, 100–3

　Voyager, 107–8

Star Trek II: The Wrath of Khan (McIntyre), 100

Star Trek III: The Search for Spock (McIntyre), 100

Star Trek IV: The Voyage Home (McIntyre), 100

Star Trek V: The Final Frontier (Dillard), 100

Star Trek VI: The Undiscovered Country (Dillard), 100

Star Trek *Next Generation: First Contact* (Berman and Braga), 100

Star Trek *Next Generation: Generations* (Dillard), 100

Star Trek *Next Generation: Insurrection* (Vornholt), 100

Star Trek: The Lost Years (Dillard), 102

Star Trek: The Motion Picture (Roddenberry), 100

Star Wars, 32, 96–100

Star Wars Episode I: The Phantom Menace (Brooks), 99

Star Wars Episode I: The Phantom Menace (movie), 97

Star Wars: Return of the Jedi (Khan), 99
Star Wars: The Empire Strikes Back (Glut), 99
"Starcruiser Shenandoah Series" (Green), 96
Stardust (Gaiman), 183–85
"Stardwarves Trilogy" (Richardson), 80
Starfarers (Anderson), 19–20
Starfish (Watts), 67
"Starfist Series" (Sherman and Cragg), 96
Stark's War (Hemry), 96
Starlin, Jim, 38, 63
Starpilot's Grave (Doyle), 95
Starplex (Sawyer), 20
Stars and Stripes Forever (Harrison), 49–51
Stars Are Also Fire (Anderson), 15
Stars Asunder (Doyle), 95
"Stars of the Guardians Series" (Weis and Perrin), 96
Starship Titanic (Jones), 80
Starship Troopers (Heinlein), 11, 23, 96
Starship Troupers (Stasheff), 80
"Starstone Duology" (Stasheff), 117
Starswarm (Pournelle), 35
Startide Rising (Brin), 21
"Starwreck Series" (Rewolinski), 80
Stasheff, Christopher, 80, 83–84, 87, 117, 165
Statesman (Anthony), 94
Steampunk Trilogy (Di Filippo), 42, 51
Steel Beach (Varley), 29, 38
Steele, Allen M., 28, 35, 38, 73
Steelheart (Dietz), 23, 34
Stein, Kevin, 128
Sten (Cole and Bunch), 95
Stephenson, Neal, 42
Sterling, Bruce, 35, 67
Stevens-Arce, James, 92
Stewart, Jan, 24, 48
Stewart, Mary, 139–40
Stewart, Sean, 71, 84
Stirling, Bruce, 42
Stirling, S. M., 51, 95, 170
Stith, John E., 71
Stoddard, James, 147–48

Stone of Tears (Goodkind), 168
Stonecutter's Story (Saberhagen), 170
Storm Front (Butcher), 190–91
Stormbringer (Moorcock), 169
"Strands of Starlight Series" (Baudino), 160, 165, 184
Strange Devices of the Sun and Moon (Goldstein), 140, 144, 185
Strange New Worlds (Smith), 102
Stranger in a Strange Land (Heinlein), 11, 14, 27
Strauss, Victoria, 117
Sturgeon, Theodore, 87, 102
Sullivan, Tim, 28
Sullivan, Tricia, 48
Summer King, Winter Fool (Goldstein), 137
Summer Knight (Butcher), 191
Summer of Love (Mason), 55
Summer Queen (Vinge), 132
Summers at Castle Auburn (Shinn), 197
Sundiver (Brin), 21
Superheroes, 58–61
Superluminal (McIntyre), 35
Superman for All Seasons (Loeb), 62
Svaha (de Lint), 42, 82–83
Swamp Thing: The Curse (Moore), 62
Sweet Myth-tery of Life (Aspirin), 187
Sweet Silver Blues (Cook), 191
"Sword, the Ring, and the Chalice Trilogy" (Chester), 126, 184
Sword and sorcery, 167–70
"Sword-Dancer Saga" (Roberson), 122, 126, 170
"Sword in Exile Trilogy" (Marston), 170
Sword in the Stone (White), 139–40
Sword of Shannara (Brooks), 114, 124–25
"Sword of Truth Series" (Goodkind), 168, 170
Swords against Death (Leiber), 168
Swords against Wizardry (Leiber), 168
Swords and Deviltry (Leiber), 168
Swords and Ice Magic (Leiber), 168
Swords in the Mist (Leiber), 168
Swords of Lankhmar (Leiber), 168

T

Tailchaser's Song (Williams), 176–77

Take Back Plenty (Greenland), 38

Tales from Jabba's Palace (Anderson), 99

Tales from Mos Eisley Cantina (Anderson), 99

"Tales of Alvin Maker" (Card), 141–42

"Tales of Fafhrd and the Gray Mouser" (Leiber), 168

Tales of the Bounty Hunters (Anderson), 99

Taliesin (Lawhead), 138

Talismans of Shannara (Brooks), 125

Tamsin (Beagle), 156

Tangle Box (Brooks), 163

Tangled Up in Blue (Vinge), 132

Tarr, Judith, 144, 185

Taylor, Jeri, 108

Taylor, Karen, 152, 193

Tea from an Empty Cup (Cadigan), 70

Tehanu (Le Guin), 113

Tek War (Shatner), 73

Telepathic mutants/weirdos, 85–87

Telzey Amberdon (Schmitz), 13, 87

Tempest (Wright), 106

Temple of the Winds (Goodkind), 168

Tenth Planet (Smith), 31

Tepper, Sheri S., 16, 24, 57, 73, 84, 131

Terminal Experiment (Sawyer), 71

Terminal Games (Perriman), 73

Thebes of the Hundred Gates (Silverberg), 55

There and Back Again (Murphy), 14–15

Third Book of Swords (Saberhagen), 170

Thompson, Paul B., 128

Those Who Hunt the Night (Hambly), 150, 193

Thousand Words for Stranger (Czerneda), 86

Three Laws of Robotics (Asimov), 33

Thrillers (science fiction), 71–74

Through the Ice (Anthony and Kornwise), 126

Tiedemann, Mark W., 35, 71

Time and Again (Finney), 55, 90

Time Enough for Love (Heinlein), 13, 90

Time Machine (Wells), 13, 55

Time of Changes (Silverberg), 13

Time of the Transference (Foster), 172

Time on My Hands (Delacorte), 55

"Time Scout Series" (Aspirin and Evans), 54

Time Ships (Baxter), 54

Time travel
    fantasy, 56–57
    science fiction, 52–56

Timelike Infinity (Baxter), 23, 55

Timeline (Crichton), 54–55

"Time's Arrow Series" (Defalco and Henderson), 61

Timescape (Benford), 55

Tin Woodsman of Oz (Baum), 113

Titan (Baxter), 30

To Bring the Light (De Camp), 56

To Ride Pegasus (McCaffrey), 86

To Say Nothing of the Dog (Willis), 55, 89–90

To Your Scattered Bodies Go (Farmer), 13

Tolkien, J. R. R., 112, 114–15, 118, 123, 162

Tolstoy, Nikolai, 140

Tombs of Atuan (Le Guin), 113

Too, Too Solid Flesh (O'Donohoe), 70

Top Ten (Moore), 62

Total Recall (Anthony), 27, 87

Touched by Magic (Durgin), 170

Touched by the Gods (Watt-Evans), 170

Tough Guide to Fantasy Land (Jones), 189

"Tower and Hive Series" (McCaffrey), 87

Tower at Stony Wood (McKillip), 126

Trader (de Lint), 160

Treasure Box (Card), 156–57, 160, 197

Trials and Tribble-ations (Carey), 105–7

Triumph of Souls (Foster), 176

Trouble and Her Friends (Scott), 41–42, 45

TSR (of Wizards of the Coast), 127

Tunnel in the Sky (Heinlein), 13

Turing Option (Harrison and Minsky), 35, 38

Turtledove, Harry, 24, 50–51, 73

12 Monkeys (Hand), 55

Twilight's End (Oltion), 102

Two Georges (Dreyfuss and Turtledove), 51, 73

2001: A Space Odyssey (Clarke), 10, 37, 39

Two Towers (Tolkien), 114

Twohy, David, 20, 73

Tyers, Katherine, 92, 96

Typewriter in the Sky (Hubbard), 166

U

Ultimate Enemy (Saberhagen), 38

Ultimate Spider-Man: Power and Responsibility (Jemas), 62

Ultimate X-Men (Millar), 62

Uncharted Territory (Willis), 16

Unicorn Sonata (Beagle), 166, 174, 177, 197

Unlikely Ones (Brown), 126

"Uplift Series" (Brin), 21, 24

Uplift War (Brin), 21

Urban legends, 158–61

V

"Vampire Files" (Elrod), 151, 193

Vampire Hunter (Romkey), 152

Vampire of the Mists (Golden), 148, 151

"Vampire Series" (Saberhagen), 152

Vampires, 149–52

Vanishing Tower (Moorcock), 169

Varley, John, 29, 31, 38

Vector Prime (Salvatore), 99

Veiled Web (Asaro), 89

Velde, Vivian Vande, 132, 152

Vengeance of Dragons (Lisle), 154

Ventus (Schroeder), 38

Venus, 30–31

Venus (Bova), 30

"Venus Trilogy" (Sargent), 31

Very Strange Trip (Kenyon), 55

"Victory Nelson Series" (Huff), 152, 191–93

Vigilant (Gardner), 73

Villains by Necessity (Forward), 125, 127

Vinge, Joan, 16, 42, 87, 131–33

Vinge, Vernor, 96

Virgin and the Dinosaurs (Roberts), 55

Virtual Light (Gibson), 48

Virtual Punk (Gibson), 42

Virtual reality, 43–45

Virtual War (Skurzynski), 45, 67

Virtually Eliminated (Scott), 45

Virtuosity (Bisson), 45, 73

Virus Clans: A Story of Evolution (Kanaly), 23, 74–75

Vitola, Denise, 71

VMR Theory (Frezza), 80

"Vorkosigan Saga" (Bujold), 95

Vornholt, John, 61, 100, 102

Voyage (Baxter), 27, 51

Voyage of the Dawn Treader (Lewis), 114

Voyage to the Red Planet (Bisson), 27

Voyager (Gabaldon), 195

Vulcan's Forge (Sherman), 102

W

Waid, Mark, 63

Waiting for the Galactic Bus (Godwin), 78–79

Walking the Labyrinth (Goldstein), 161, 193

"War against the Chtorr Series" (Gerrold), 23

War for the Oaks (Bull), 160, 166, 174

War of the Worlds (Wells), 13, 21, 22–23

Warlock and Son (Stasheff), 83

Warlock Enraged (Stasheff), 83

Warlock Heretical (Stasheff), 83

Warlock in Spite of Himself (Stasheff), 83

Warlock Insane (Stasheff), 83

Warlock Is Missing (Stasheff), 83

Warlock Rock (Stasheff), 83

"Warlock Series" (Stasheff), 83–84

Warlock Unlocked (Stasheff), 83

Warlock Wandering (Stasheff), 83

Warlock's Companion (Stasheff), 83
"Warlock's Heirs" (Stasheff), 83
Warped (Jeter), 106
Watchmen (Moore), 62
Water Sleeps (Cook), 146
Watership Down (Adams), 177
Watt-Evans, Lawrence, 170, 189
Watts, Peter, 67
Wayfinder's Story (Saberhagen), 170
We Can Build You (Dick), 13, 34
Weber, David, 24, 95–96
Weinstein, Howard, 102
Weird of the White Wolf (Moorcock), 169
Weirdos, 85–87
Weis, Margaret, 35, 84, 96, 128, 182, 192
Well-Timed Enchantment (Velde), 166
Wells, H. G., 13, 21–23, 55, 66
Wentworth, K. D., 39
Werewolves, 152–55
Weyrs of Pern (McCaffrey), 181
What You Leave Behind (Carey), 106
"Wheel of Time Series" (Jordan), 120
Wheelers (Stewart and Cohen), 24, 48
When Gravity Fails (Effinger), 70
White, T. H., 139–40
White Abacus (Broderick), 34
White Dragon (McCaffrey), 181
White Gold Wielder (Donaldson), 164
White Mars; or, The Mind Set Free (Aldiss), 27
White Queen (Jones), 20, 87
White Rose (Cook), 146
Wicked Day (Stewart), 139
Wild Blood (Collins), 154
Wild Road (King), 178
Wildlife (Kelly), 35
Williams, Michael, 128
Williams, Tad, 176–77
Williams, Teri, 128
Williams, Walter, 48
Williamson, Chet, 193
Willing Spirit (Anthony), 137
Willis, Connie, 16, 54–55, 89–90
Wilson, David, 108
Wilson, F. Paul, 73, 76

Wilson, Robert Charles, 51
Windling, Terri, 132, 148
Wingrove, David, 96
Winick, Judd, 63
Winter, Steve, 128
Winter King (Cornwell), 140
Winter Queen (Cary), 116
Winter Warriors (Gemmel), 117
Wishsong of Shannara (Brooks), 125
Witch Doctor (Stasheff), 165
Wit'ch Fire (Clemens), 146
Wit'ch Gate (Clemens), 146
Witch in the Wood (White), 140
Wit'ch Storm (Clemens), 146
Wit'ch War (Clemens), 146
Witches' Brew (Brooks), 163
Witches of Eileanan (Forsyth), 126
Witchlight (Bradley), 156
Wizard at Large (Brooks), 163
Wizard in Absentia (Stasheff), 83
"Wizard in Rhyme Series" (Stasheff), 165
Wizard of Earthsea (Le Guin), 113
Wizard's First Rule (Goodkind), 168
Wizards of the Coast, 127
Wolf King (Borchardt), 153
Wolf King (Wood), 57
Wolfe, Gene, 84
Wolfman, Marv, 63
Wolverine's Daughter (Durgin), 170
Wolverton, Dave, 55
Woman on the Edge of Time (Piercy), 57
Wonderland Gambit (Chalker), 42, 44
Wood, Bridget, 57
World at the End of Time (Pohl), 73
World Fantasy Award, 203–4
World Science Fiction Society, 199
"World War Series" (Turtledove), 24, 51
World without End (Cochran and Murphy), 137, 160
Worlds of Honor (Weber), 95
Worm Ouroboros (Eddison), 114
Wounded Land (Donaldson), 164
Woundhealer's Story (Saberhagen), 170
Wrapt in Crystal (Shinn), 90
Wrath of the Prophets (David), 106
Wrede, Patricia, 193

Wright, Susan, 106
Wu, William F., 55

X
X-Men (Rusch), 61
X-Men: Empire's End (Duane), 61
X-Men: Shadows of the Past (Friedman),
    61
X-Men: Soul Killer (Byers), 61
X-Men: The Dark Phoenix Saga (Lee),
    62

Y
Yarbro, Chelsea Quinn, 126, 152
Yesterday We Saw Mermaids (Friesner),
    166
Young, Janine Ellen, 20, 76

Young, Jim, 67
"Young Jedi Knights Series" (Anderson),
    99
Yvgenie (Cherryh), 157

Z
Zahn, Timothy, 24, 72–74, 99
Zambreno, Mary, 193
Zebrowski, George, 31, 104
Zelazny, Roger, 45, 55, 79, 132,
    160–61, 177, 189
Zero-gravity biotech thrillers, 74–76
Zero-gravity mysteries, 68–71
Zero-gravity thrillers, 71–74
Zettel, Sarah, 31, 39, 75
Zombies of the Gene Pool (McCrumb),
    70

Derek M. Buker is the webmaster at the Frederick County Public Library in Maryland. He was previously a youth services specialist at the Charles E. Miller Branch of the Howard County Library System in Maryland. A lifelong reader of science fiction and fantasy and a writer in the genres since 1985, Buker is the Science Fiction and Fantasy Reader's Advisory Trainer for the Maryland Library Associate Training Institute.